# Parenting
# Without Borders

# Parenting Without Borders

SURPRISING LESSONS
PARENTS AROUND THE WORLD
CAN TEACH US

## CHRISTINE GROSS-LOH

AVERY

*A member of Penguin Group (USA) Inc.*

*New York*

30630 6052
R

Published by the Penguin Group
Penguin Group (USA) Inc., 375 Hudson Street,
New York, New York 10014, USA

USA · Canada · UK · Ireland · Australia
New Zealand · India · South Africa · China

Penguin Books Ltd, Registered Offices:
80 Strand, London WC2R 0RL, England
For more information about the Penguin Group visit penguin.com

Most Avery books are available at special quantity discounts for bulk purchase for
sales promotions, premiums, fund-raising, and educational needs. Special books or
book excerpts also can be created to fit specific needs. For details, write Penguin
Group (USA) Inc. Special Markets, 375 Hudson Street, New York, NY 10014.

Library of Congress Cataloging-in-Publication Data

Gross-Loh, Christine.
Parenting without borders: surprising lessons parents around the world can teach us /
Christine Gross-Loh.
p.      cm
Includes bibliographical references and index.
ISBN 978-1-58333-455-3 (alk. paper)
1. Parenting—Cross-cultural studies.   2. Parenting.   I. Title.
HQ755.8.G756      2013                    2013003704
649'.1—dc23

Printed in the United States of America
1   3   5   7   9   10   8   6   4   2

BOOK DESIGN BY AMANDA DEWEY

While the author has made every effort to provide accurate telephone numbers, Internet
addresses, and other contact information at the time of publication, neither the publisher
nor the author assumes any responsibility for errors, or for changes that occur after
publication. Further, the publisher does not have any control over and does not
assume any responsibility for author or third-party websites or their content.

Penguin is committed to publishing works of quality and integrity. In that spirit,
we are proud to offer this book to our readers; however, the story, the experiences,
and the words are the author's alone. Some names and identifying characteristics
have been changed to protect the privacy of the individuals involved.

For Benjamin, Daniel, Mia, and Annabel

# CONTENTS

# PART 3

## The Teaching of Children

# PART 4

## The Character of Children

# INTRODUCTION

We all want the best for our children, but what does that mean? Robert LeVine, an eminent Harvard anthropologist, determined that parents around the world universally share three goals in raising their children. The first goal is survival and health: Parents want their children to stay alive. For those who live in societies where they can be reasonably sure of being able to meet children's most basic survival needs past infancy, though, the second universal goal is to raise children who will have the basic skills they'll need to sustain themselves economically once they grow up. And finally, there's the goal of self-maximization—of raising a socially competent child who possesses the cultural values that are considered important, and who will succeed in that society: *a child who will thrive.*

I didn't know if I would ever have a child. Pregnancy didn't come easily to me, and my husband, David, and I experienced the heartache of infertility before conceiving our first baby. But I always loved children and longed for the day I might become a mother. When I finally became pregnant, survival was a question: I hemorrhaged so severely in my seventh month that doctors told us the pregnancy was in danger. It wasn't until tiny Benjamin was born and safely in my arms, when I looked at his face with his wide brown eyes, mop of black hair, and the puzzled expression that elicited such fierce protectiveness inside me, that I started to think about what kind of parent I would be and how I could best raise a child who would not only survive but also thrive.

My parents immigrated to the United States from South Korea shortly before I was born in 1968. Growing up in the 1970s in small-town Pennsylvania, I straddled two cultures every day of my childhood. In some ways my parents were very Korean in how they raised us: We used chopsticks at the dinner table; kimchi, seaweed, and rice were staples in our home; I was taught not to call adults by their first names and to behave respectfully toward older relatives. Education was highly valued in our house and we were expected to complete our homework on time and get good grades. Sometimes this felt like a lot of pressure. At the same time, my parents had a broad perspective and were enthusiastic and relaxed about the things my brothers and I wanted to do, whether it was make our own Halloween costumes, pretend to pan for gold in a creek, watch movies for hours with our friends, or eat or read whatever we wanted. When I look back on my childhood, I am actually astounded by how little my parents questioned the things we were doing with our time and where our lives were going, especially since our American small-town childhood was so different from their own.

They had their worries, as many immigrant families who strongly want their children to thrive in their new society often do. I remember hushed conversations between my mom and dad about whether we were really getting a good education, and get-togethers with other Korean immigrant families where parents exchanged questions about the schools their children were attending as they tried to navigate an alien school system. Sometimes our differences really compounded my self-consciousness about being one of the few Asian-American students in school. But like many American parents of my generation, I find myself looking back with amazement at a degree of freedom and acceptance that seems virtually lost today. Even though my parents always conveyed the value of holding high expectations, they gave us so much time and space to experiment, play, and just *be*. They were always trying to do their best for us. They believed in our potential to flourish. But they weren't always trying to mold and change us.

During my twenties I lived in Japan several times, first to study Japanese and then to do research for a doctorate in East Asian history. In a remote village nestled in the mountainous countryside, I met David, who, like me, was a student who had come to Japan to learn the language. When David and I returned to the United States and decided to get married, we also knew that we might eventually be going back to Japan one day and maybe even raising children there. No matter where our children would grow up, though, I knew I loved America. And I knew there were many things from my own Korean-American upbringing and my Jewish-American husband's that would shape our family's life.

Now that we have four children, it seems incredible to me that I once wondered whether I would ever have the chance to be a mother. But having children has also humbled me, opened my eyes to how many decisions there are for parents to make, to how hard parenting can sometimes be, and to how uncertain I sometimes feel about whether I'm making the right choices and doing right by my kids.

I was sure about so many things before my children were born: They would eat no junk food, watch no violent TV. If my children were raised peacefully, they would never show interest in weapons or war. I would be attentive to them and watchful of their feelings. I would be an accepting, protective parent to give them a secure base.

When Benjamin was five and his little brother, Daniel, was three, we moved to Tokyo. I'd been a mother for five years already; I was certain that the way I parented (or at least tried to)—the way I'd learned in America—was the best way, and continued to feel like I was doing things right as our family expanded (our two daughters, Mia and Anna, were born in Japan). I'd been taught it was important to put our kids' needs first, to give them lots of choices, to praise them to make them feel confident. Like me, the American parents I knew made sure to keep their kids safe from risks, and spent "quality time" playing with them (or else felt guilty about not playing with them). My American friends and I sought out the right classes, toys, and books to foster our young children's development, helped oversee their relationships and disagreements with other children, went to bat for them with their teachers and coaches, and guided what they did in their free time. We devoted ourselves to being the best parents we could be.

But as my own children attended local Japanese schools and we spent time with Japanese families, I saw children raised in a very different way who were clearly thriving, just as much—and sometimes more—than our own. Moms in Japan were surprised by how uptight I was about allowing sweets and were startled by how I monitored what my kids were allowed to watch on TV and the way I tried to stay on top of their behavior. My Japanese friends, unlike me, left their children on their own to figure out their relationships with other kids. They didn't closely watch over their behavior or worry they weren't giving their young kids the right opportunities. But despite how lax these Japanese moms seemed to me, I was constantly surprised by how mature and well-adjusted their children were, how capable, and how pleasant. These kids were being raised in ways that the American parents I knew might look at as simultaneously too permissive and too strict, yet they were clearly thriving.

It was during that time that I realized something that would change me completely: The parenting assumptions I'd held to be utterly and universally true were culturally based. Japanese parents had their own notions about good parenting, notions that were often startlingly different from my own. Sometimes even practically the opposite.

Even though I'd thought that the American way was the best, most progressive and enlightened way to raise all kids, it turned out this wasn't totally true. Our way was the best way from our point of view, because we were taught it was how to cultivate the things that happen to matter to many American parents (raising happy, high-achieving, creative, self-expressive, and unique kids) and the values we hold (egalitarianism, material success). Because of the history and the baggage that our generation has brought to parenting, much of child-rearing today is an understandable reaction to an era when children were to be seen, not heard, and their feelings and rights weren't considered equally important as those of adults.

Of course, all families are different, and it's really important to note that our considerable diversity means that class, region, and religious or ethnic background affect parenting styles too. There are many different childhoods in America. But I would argue that there is a distinctive American script about what constitutes "good parenting," especially for a typical middle-class or affluent family whose kids are college bound, and for the most part, that's the script I'll be talking about in this book.

This script isn't always visible to us unless we see it from the outside. That's what happened to me: The protectiveness, the degree and type of involvement and intensive cultivation that characterizes "good parenting" in our culture were pretty much invisible to me until I saw how startling my own behavior (which would have blended perfectly well in most American town and city playgrounds) appeared when we went to Japan. Parents wondered why I was following my children around the playground, why I talked to them so much about their feelings, gave them so many choices, tolerated so much negotiation, and why I was opposed to sending them to sleepaway camp in preschool.

When we returned to the United States, I was a different person and a different parent. I felt baffled by the dad I saw in a mall who told his toddler "good riding!" after a jaunt on the merry-go-round. To him, there was nothing distinctive about his behavior, and that's why he felt comfortable doing it. To me the excessive praise was jarring (though I understood where he was coming from and just a few years before wouldn't have given it a second thought). I was viewing him through a different cultural lens, one I acquired by parenting abroad.

I feel fortunate to be raising children in the United States. In the two years I've been researching this book and the ten years I've been thinking about these issues, I've come to appreciate the unique and positive aspects of American child-rearing today: our awareness of diversity, the way we strive to teach our kids tolerance and a passion for social justice (which seems to be successful in a way I haven't seen elsewhere), and the way we cultivate a can-do and innovative attitude in our kids. We know how important it is to make our children feel respected and valued for the unique individuals they are, and we cherish the warm and close relationships with our kids that our culture encourages us to have. We value creativity, independence, and individualism: all good things in raising children who we fervently hope will become capable architects of their own meaningful and successful adult lives.

At the same time, many of us are more insecure than ever before, unsure if we are doing right by our children, and trying to figure out how to do better. There are many external indications that American children are suffering: We have one of the highest child obesity rates in the world, one in four American children is on medication, and American kids are three times more likely than some European children to take psychotropic drugs. Our kids score lower on standardized tests than many of their international peers, and even their empathy and creativity have been falling. We are increasingly alarmed as our children lag behind their peers in other countries in various measures of well-being, as they flounder and find it hard to gain their footing as adults in a difficult economic climate. Our joy in parenting is clouded by a drumbeat of worry. According to a recent major study of the American family, one of the main challenges facing American parents is their perception of how vulnerable their children are: a perception that makes today's parents markedly more anxious than previous generations. Despite the considerable and unprecedented amounts of parental investment we commit to our kids, we worry we are simply not doing enough. Often overscheduled and stressed out, children seem to lack initiative and self-reliance, even at relatively mature ages. Parents suffer too: Our beliefs about the right way to parent have been correlated with increased depression and stress. In this context it's easy to idealize other countries (Pamela Druckerman's book *Bringing Up Bébé*, which portrays French parenting as flawlessly relaxed, is a good case in point) or look back nostalgically at how good things "used to be."

French parents are not flawless. Japanese childhood isn't perfect, nor is childhood anywhere. Not only that, cultures are complex, dynamic, and ever evolving. But living abroad had many unexpected benefits for our kids that they couldn't have gotten back home. Once I realized this I started asking myself: Are there practices that other cultures and countries might be getting "right" about childhood too? What do parents in other cultures believe helps them to raise children who will thrive? Is there a sweet spot between culture (what society expects) and biology (what children evolved to thrive on) that other countries have hit upon in ways that we could learn from too? Could the child-rearing practices of other cultures help us nurture positive and important aspects of childhood in America—the things we do so well?

This book is about my search for answers to those questions. As we prepared to leave Japan in 2010 with our four kids to return to our American lives after five years abroad, I started to actively seek the stories of parents in other countries. I wanted to know more about the wisdom of parents in other cultures to meld with our own. While I looked at parenting norms all around the world, I mostly focused on countries where children's well-being (as measured by internationally agreed-upon indicators, such as UNICEF's Convention on the Rights of the Child) is generally high, or where their child-rearing practices have some unique and important lessons to teach us.

Over the course of the year that followed, I traveled to Finland, China, South Korea, Germany, and Japan. I met with foreign parents from more than twelve different countries who were living in the United States, like Christa from Greece. She told me about her summers back home, where she could plunk her five-year-old twins down with family or friends with no advance notice or prescheduled playdates, where kids play freely by the sea or wield giant shears to prune grapes, where parents don't struggle to control everything, and a community raises kids in an enfolding, embracing way, ignoring (or even celebrating) their bumps and scrapes as part of an utterly ordinary, yet healthy, childhood.

I talked to and observed small children, school-age children, teens and college students and parents from around the world and interviewed our country's most innovative and forward-thinking teachers and researchers—psychologists, educators, anthropologists, and sociologists—to find out about what was working and what wasn't in American parenting. I was surprised by how greatly parents around the world could differ in their expectations of their kids: what they should wear, how and what they ought to eat, or what kind of manners they should have—and how these small and seemingly unrelated notions actually reflected a coherent overall vision about child-rearing. Babies and toddlers who never left an adult's side day or night grew up to be astonishingly self-reliant children. Children seemed to feel more belonging, happiness, and security from seeing themselves as part of a community of people, rather than as individuals with individual needs that urgently had to be met. Some children who had everything they could possibly want experienced feelings of isolation and other disorders, despite the material abundance surrounding them.

I found there are reasons why many Scandinavians say their young ones should nap outdoors (because they believe fresh air, and being outdoors as much as possible, is good for them), why French parents teach their toddlers to sit at the table and eat politely (because they want to cultivate an appreciation for food as early as possible), and why American pediatricians tell their patients that the best place for a baby to sleep is in a crib (because they believe it's not only safest, but crucial for a child's independence) and recommend that parents read aloud to their young children (to hone cognitive and verbal skills).

Some of the most interesting and revealing moments happened when I asked parents about things that were so far outside their experience or cultural norms that they couldn't at first understand the question. One German mother lamented the fact that her children barely got any time to play out of doors. It turned out that her children actually spent two hours playing outdoors daily, about seventeen times more than their American peers, but from her German perspective, it wasn't nearly enough. Once I asked a Turkish mother how long they might let babies cry in her country and she looked at me with confusion—because in her worldview, a baby should always be held and comforted. It took me time to recognize that when Japanese parents remarked on how friendly I was with my children, it wasn't always a compliment; to them it seemed to blur the line between being a friend (which isn't what the role of a good parent is in Japan) and a guide who had her child's best interests at heart.

Each encounter was like discovering another piece of a puzzle whose final shape I could not yet picture. But, as time went by, I found myself at last drawing closer to recognizing what it was that other countries had that we in the United States did not.

The more parents, teachers, and researchers I spoke with—all people who were intimately familiar with the mandate of raising children—the easier it became to connect the dots. Unlike in the United States, parents overseas were confident and certain where we Americans were beset by too many options, which tended to make us feel confused about our role. As I learned more about the history behind many of our contemporary parenting practices, I wondered if perhaps we Americans were paying a price for what we thought were enlightened and modern parenting ways, ways that give us choices, along with the mistaken (but oppressive) belief that as long as we choose wisely, we will be able to completely and perfectly control how our children's lives turn out.

Scholars from a variety of disciplines are discovering that the keys to raising resilient, compassionate, competent children can be found in the simplest practices. Often it means doing less, like giving kids time to play away from adult eyes, even if that means they will have disagreements with their friends that an adult won't help them solve. Sometimes it means doing more, like requiring them to do regular chores so they feel competent and needed.

Protecting our kids from discomfort isn't the same as doing what's best for them. Many parents in other countries strongly believe that cultivating children's character should be as much a parenting goal as cultivating their academic achievement. In countries such as Japan, Sweden, and France, parents told me that teaching children to care for one another, to be compassionate and present members of the family, and to think also about the needs in their communities were the most important jobs in raising them. In America, and in my own family, I realized, while we also care about these things, we too often encourage our children's self-expression, uniqueness, and individual achievement to the detriment of the community and to the detriment of their happiness.

For many of us, parenting has become an individualized experience, especially since we—not society, not other parents, friends, family, or teachers, but parents alone—feel so responsible for our children's entire lives. The kind of parent we are (or the way our child turns out) defines the kind of person we are. No wonder American parents are having such an identity crisis and feel inadequate and judged so much of the time.

I have come to understand that many parenting practices can be traced not just to culture, but also to where a culture lies on the continuum between promoting individualism and promoting community cohesiveness. The most successful parenting practices are consistent, reinforced by others, and have conviction behind them. Parenting is so much easier if raising children is not up to an individual parent or family, but is considered a community mandate that everyone shares.

There's no more revealing (if humbling) way to see what we're doing and why we are doing it than to look at ourselves through the eyes of another culture. This book examines parenting practices in America and throughout the world to look at why we parent the way we do, what parents in other countries do, and what our collective wisdom can teach all of us about raising capable and confident children who thrive.

PART 1

# The Care and Feeding of Children

ONE

# SLEEP TIME:
## Keep Our Babies Close
## or Give Them Space?

W hen Lisa, a mom from suburban Pennsylvania, first got pregnant, she did everything right. She took prenatal swimming, HypnoBirthing and Bradley classes, drank all the right herbal teas (red raspberry leaf, no sugar), and even became certified as a prenatal yoga instructor. Admittedly nervous about becoming a mother for the first time, she felt well prepared and confident.

But once Isabel arrived, Lisa felt blindsided by motherhood. Forget the cuddly image of a little baby curled up peacefully in a crib as her parents gaze lovingly from the doorway. Baby Isabel slept fitfully, as though she were on high alert. She napped for only twenty minutes at a time. When Lisa put Isabel in a bassinet by the bed, she would jolt awake every time the baby sighed. When she had her in a crib down the hall with a baby monitor, she anxiously tuned in to every sound.

When the baby was two months old, she began to wake less at night. Lisa was cautiously elated. "I couldn't wait to get a full night's sleep. I assumed it would be right around the corner!" she told me. But then Isabel started day care and went through a spate of illnesses. Once she started getting sick, she stopped sleeping. "I tried everything. Nothing worked," Lisa remembered. "She kept waking every two hours. Sometimes during the day I would nap with her. Those were the only times she would sleep really long and deep, but it terrified me." The research Lisa had done cautioned strongly against co-sleeping because of the risk of suffocation. Isabel's crib had no bumpers, because Lisa had read those were unsafe. She was careful not to use a blanket and to always put her baby to sleep on her back.

Lisa was exhausted. Sleep is linked with cognitive development. It consolidates memory in children and adults alike, and helps us learn. Sleep disturbances have been associated with everything from attention deficits to negative mood to obesity. A freelance writer working from home, Lisa was making careless mistakes like dialing into a conference call on the wrong day. Clients were visibly disappointed. She stopped going to her book club, which was one thing she'd loved in her pre-baby days, and fell out of touch with her friends. People called to see how she was doing, but she would be too tired to talk to them. She became snippy with her mother and mother-in-law whenever they gently suggested a different parenting strategy. Her marriage began to founder too—she and her husband stopped having sex and communicated only when they fought. The lack of sleep was casting a shadow over her entire life.

Lisa's friends, her pediatrician, and her lactation nurse urged her to let the baby cry it out—to put her in her crib and let her cry herself to sleep. The idea was that self-soothing would become Isabel's new normal, and soon she wouldn't need a human being's presence to fall or stay asleep. *She would be able to do it on her own.* And Lisa would be a good— and much saner—parent for teaching her baby to be more independent. So finally, when Isabel was eight months old and Lisa was at the end of her rope, she gave it a try. Lisa put baby Isabel in her crib at bedtime and left the room.

It was really hard to hear her cry. "The first night I sat outside her door and listened to her scream, shake the rails on her crib, and choke on her own mucus for almost two hours," Lisa remembered. "It was horrible. I sat outside her door the whole time with my heart pounding, my eyes glassy, and questioning myself, 'How could this possibly be the right thing to do?'"

But it worked. Within three nights Isabel was waking only once. She still has a lot of separation anxiety, though. Eight years old and in third grade, Isabel still asks to sleep in Lisa's bed and still wants her mom to sit next to her in the backseat of the car.

## THE AMERICAN WAY OF SLEEP

Could there have been another way for Lisa to get enough rest in those difficult early days of transitioning into motherhood? Could there be a gentler way for her baby to have learned to sleep?

Most American parents believe it's normal for babies to sleep alone. They consider a full night of solid, uninterrupted sleep to be ideal, even for a baby who is just a few weeks old. Our cultural belief about infant sleep is that it should be solitary, scheduled, independent, and fuss-free.

We're told solitary sleep is a skill and that we should teach our children how to do it. Sleep is highly valued in America and though studies show we exaggerate how little sleep we get, Americans are often convinced they are not getting enough. That's why there are thousands of articles on the Internet and in parenting magazines about babies and sleep, and dozens of books on the topic. Experts love to offer exhausted American parents salvation in the form of sleep-training methods, which change a baby's sleep associations. They urge mothers to avoid nursing or rocking their babies to sleep, keep to a regular nap and bedtime schedule, and aim for the graduated "extinction" of unhealthy sleep habits through crying it out and encouraging babies to self-soothe so they'll sleep through the night.

In America we believe solitary sleep is necessary to raising an autonomous and independent child. We think we're being good parents when we set up a baby nursery, buy a crib and baby monitors, and teach our baby to sleep separately from us. If we don't teach our babies to sleep on their own, the thinking goes, they will never leave our beds.

. . .

sk parents in other parts of the world where a baby should sleep, and you may just get a baffled look. In most cultures around the world, human babies do not sleep alone. Most of the world assumes babies weren't meant to sleep by themselves, so babies usually sleep with their mothers and children sleep with siblings or other family members. In a study of 136 societies, infants slept in bed with their mothers in two-thirds of the communities; in the other third, most babies slept with another combination of family members. Out of one hundred countries in another survey, only American parents had a separate sleeping space for their children.

What we consider normal shapes our expectations—and sets us up for disappointment when reality (in the form of an otherwise adorable twelve-pound "light sleeper") fails to match up. If Lisa had not expected her baby to sleep alone without waking, would she have been so upset? Her feelings of anxiety and guilt might have been less painful if she had understood that babies are not sound sleepers and don't have to be, that all around the world, they wake up at night, needing to be nursed or reassured. And then they go back to sleep (usually snuggled next to a parent).

Lisa instinctively noticed that Isabel slept best in her arms. What Lisa didn't know is that Isabel slept best that way because that's how human babies evolved to sleep. Research suggests that co-sleeping is more in sync with an infant's primal attachment needs, and that separation of the newborn and his mother can lead to the very sleep problems American parents fear. "Resisting the intense desire of young children for close proximity with caregivers at night may set the stage for bedtime protest and persistent night waking in the United States," says one study comparing children's sleep in Japan and the United States. Peter Gray, a professor of psychology at Boston College, argues solitary sleep is an "evolutionary mismatch," noting that parents in hunter-gatherer societies "know very well why young children protest against being left alone in the dark." Gray points out that for most of human history (and even today in some places) any child who was left alone at night was in danger of being eaten by predators. A human baby is hardwired to feel that lying alone in the dark without any adults nearby puts him in the ultimate danger. Furthermore, young infants do not understand object permanence—the concept that though something disappears from view it still exists. So how will he understand that come morning, his parents will be there for him again?

## Co-sleeping Is Safe

But many parents believe that having babies sleep alone is better for babies and better for us. Not only is solitary sleep our cultural ideal, we are told that bed sharing is potentially lethal. A 2011 advertisement from Milwaukee's health department shows a white infant wearing only a diaper sleeping in an adult's bed surrounded by fluffy bedding, so close to a butcher knife that one finger actually rests on the handle. Doctors and public health officials warn us that we run the risk of rolling onto our infants and smothering them to death, they can get tangled in the bedsheets, and they have a higher likelihood of dying from sudden infant death syndrome (SIDS). "Babies can die when sleeping in adult beds," the ad reads.

American parents are right to be concerned about SIDS. In a survey of fifteen countries, the United States ranked second highest in the world in SIDS incidences. But SIDS is notably low in countries like Japan, where co-sleeping is the norm. Although the American Academy of Pediatrics (AAP) argues against it (it endorses room sharing but warns against bed sharing) and chances are your pediatrician will advise you to train your baby to sleep alone, other scientists, researchers, and pediatricians have found that co-sleeping, when practiced safely, is actually safer for infants than sleeping alone.

Anthropologist James McKenna, director of the Mother-Baby Behavioral Sleep Lab at the University of Notre Dame, has been researching mother-baby pairs for more than thirty years. McKenna first became intrigued by the question of sleep when he and his wife, both trained anthropologists, became parents. They found themselves wondering why so much of the pediatric advice they were getting seemed at odds with all they had learned about human evolution and development. Observing mother-baby pairs in slumber, McKenna found that co-sleeping mothers' and babies' sleep cycles tended to be remarkably synchronized, which helped the mother get more restful sleep because she and the baby tended to enter lighter sleep at the same time. Tending to a baby who is right there next to her, when she's in a light stage of sleep anyway, isn't as disruptive to a mother's sleep as having to rouse herself out of a deep, groggy sleep, get out of bed, and walk to another room.

And while a co-sleeping infant wakes more frequently than an infant who sleeps alone, McKenna has found that these shorter cycles of sleep make it less likely an infant will have trouble rousing himself from deep sleep if his body is still too immature to deal with physiological crises (think of light sleep as nature's way of protecting a very young baby). Co-sleeping moms and babies tend to face each other during the night. Not only does her own breathing "cue" her baby to breathe, she is also right there to monitor her baby if he should run into trouble. In this way mother-child sleep may actually protect against sudden infant death syndrome. "Mothers and babies have been sleeping together for millions of years—we're here because of that," McKenna told me. "Anytime you have baby closer to the mother in a safe way, it reduces the chances of SIDS. That proximity provides a stream of interaction and a way to monitor baby. The presence of the mother is the primary inhibitor of SIDS."

When you look more closely at the studies that conclude co-sleeping is dangerous, you realize that the problem is the context in which these tragic incidents occurred. What the U.S. statistics and news stories don't show is that the overwhelming majority of accidental suffocations or overlays associated with co-sleeping occur in situations of urban poverty, where a number of risk factors tragically converge. Smoking, drug or alcohol use, co-sleeping on unsafe, non-bed surfaces (such as sofas or waterbeds), or falling asleep by accident with a baby in an unsafe environment all significantly increase the risk of SIDS. In one study, 99 percent of SIDS deaths had at least one of these risk factors. In an analytical report of infant deaths in Milwaukee that occurred between 2006 and 2008, on average, four risk factors were present. To blame an infant smothering by an intoxicated parent on co-sleeping is like blaming the act of driving for a drunk-driving accident: It's not that he was driving that caused the crash, it's that he was driving under the influence.

On the other hand, in a safe sleeping environment, proximity protects babies. "I have thoroughly researched this common concern and written two books on the subject," writes pediatrician William Sears, who has seen the advantages of co-sleeping in the thirty-five years he has been practicing. "I've come to the conclusion that co-sleeping, if practiced safely, can actually lower the risk of SIDS." When babies sleep in the same room with a parent, SIDS death rates are reduced by up to half. Cribs themselves aren't a guarantee of safety. (Most parents are surprised to learn that an average of twenty-six children are hurt by cribs, playpens, and bassinets each day in the United States.) But when babies die in cribs, no one takes this to mean we should stop using them.

## Brief Nighttime Wakings Are Normal

Even after infants start sleeping through the night, parents are more likely than not to find themselves revisiting sleep issues during childhood. Once babies become toddlers, they may start waking up at night. This toddler night-waking happens to most kids, peaking between one and a half and two years, when they get their two-year molars. There are other reasons for disrupted sleep at this age besides teething pain. They've come far in that first year, and they're now aware of how separate they are from their parents. Life isn't just an amorphous blur of sound and sensation. If they're sleeping separately, they wake up instinctively wanting to go in search of a parent.

Interestingly, studies show that co-sleeping children experience more frequent but shorter night-wakings than children who sleep alone. A child wakes up, quietly opens his eyes, but soon drifts right back to sleep, reassured by the presence of adults or siblings nearby. These wakings usually aren't disruptive. But if a child who sleeps alone wakes up repeatedly, sometimes frightened and crying, then gets out of bed to search for his parents and needs help calming down before returning to sleep, both the child and his parents get a lot less sleep.

Allison, a mom of four living in Wisconsin, tried a variety of sleep methods with each of her children. She made a halfhearted attempt to sleep train her first child ("My husband wondered why I was doing it as I sat in the living room crying"), put her second and third children to sleep in their own beds, but co-slept with her fourth child, Delena, through toddlerhood. She said, "I recall awakening as Delena's arm reached out for me. She would briefly touch me and then settle back to sleep. I don't know if she even fully woke up. I thought it was so sweet that she was so aware of my presence that it reassured her so quickly."

## THE HISTORY OF SOLITARY SLEEP

Americans didn't always sleep separately from their babies. The Western idea that mothers and babies should sleep separately originated in ecclesiastical laws to protect babies against "overlaying" (in some cases a covert method of infanticide) in the Middle Ages. Still, most Western babies continued to sleep together with an adult as they always had (cold houses made it unthinkable to put a newborn to sleep by herself), and our modern practice of solitary infant sleep would have seemed very odd to most parents. Communal sleep was so normal that it wasn't unusual for men to share a bed when lodging at an inn while traveling.

As living conditions changed in the wake of the Industrial Revolution, though, and more families had the space to provide separate sleeping spaces for their children, having a separate nursery for children became desirable, a tangible sign of "progress" and modernity that Western families aspired to.

These kinds of shifts are nothing new. Parents have ricocheted from one philosophy to another over the years as they try to make sense of the wordless little beings in their care. Mid-nineteenth-century English parents were exhorted to bathe their babies in cold water to strengthen their bodies and souls. This was in the days before modern plumbing; hot water for a bath was painstakingly difficult to come by. It became almost necessary to tout the moral good of cold water for little bodies and developing characters. As historian Christina Hardyment tells us in her book *Dream Babies: Childcare Advice from John Locke to Gina Ford*, when piped hot water developed several decades later, popular opinion changed.

Until the late nineteenth century, there wasn't a lot of attention paid to children's sleep. What advice there was focused on things like the sleep environment—how warm or cool the sleeping area should be, or what kind of mattress to use—rather than on sleep itself. People assumed that babies and children knew how to sleep, that they could regulate themselves, and, most surprisingly, that they didn't need a whole lot of nighttime sleep. But anxiety about children's well-being was gradually rising, and sleep became a part of this anxiety too. Professional advice and rules about infant and child sleep—how babies should sleep, how many hours they ought to sleep—increased as it became less common for families to have paid help, extended family under the same roof, or many siblings to share a bed. Experts began to warn mothers against rocking their babies to sleep, for fear of creating bad habits. Cradles were out; cribs, which couldn't be moved easily from room to room and didn't require an adult's presence, were in.

Once a mother, and no one else, was fully responsible for nighttime care, it became more important for a baby to be able to sleep long hours. The accompanying surge of expert advice on sleep gave parents a new concern to focus upon: how to get children to sleep for those long hours alone. But the new view of sleep as needing to be structured and regimented, ironically, may have contributed most to our poor and problematic sleep habits. Historian Peter Stearns and his colleagues write, "The goal was, of course, to train children so well for sleep that they would carry secure patterns through the rest of their lives. But surrounding sleep with rules and anxiety could be counterproductive." Once sleep became something to achieve, rather than something that just happened, adulthood sleep problems also started to become the norm.

## THE JAPANESE WAY OF SLEEP

In Japan, friends always asked me the same question: Is it *really* true that American parents put their babies to sleep in a separate room?

Masako, a mother of four living near Nagoya, couldn't imagine separate sleep. She laughed about the contortions her children get into spreading their futons out on the floor each night so that each child could have a little bit of contact with her at nighttime. With all those kids, she told me, this inevitably meant that one child ended up sleeping right up near her head. Masako, a homemaker, and her husband, who is a dentist, are affluent by Japanese standards, but space is at a premium in Japan and their family of six lives in a traditionally small home. (Still, there is room for Masako and her husband to sleep separately from their kids if they want to.) Masako told me almost every Japanese baby sleeps in the same room as his mother. She was surprised when I told her about the typical American way of solitary sleep. It was a hard concept for a Japanese mother to fathom. What if the baby needed comforting in the night? Wasn't everyone lonely?

After talking to Masako, I began to notice that the sleep of Japanese babies looked different. I saw babies and toddlers sleeping everywhere: in their mothers' arms, in slings, in strollers, on futons on the floor, in parent meetings at school, or at the grocery store. Little Hitoha-chan, a toddler with curly black hair, snugly rode on her mother's back for four hours one morning while a bunch of parents cooked lunch together at my daughter's preschool. Her mother didn't interrupt helping out at school to rush Hitoha-chan home for a nap.

Some families had cribs, kept in the middle of the living room or near the heart of family activity. No one I knew had a separate nursery in Japan, even in homes where there was space for one. Cribs were used for naps, not nighttime sleep. *There was just no concept that a baby needed her own space. To the contrary, Japanese mothers didn't want little babies to feel too alone.* Being a good parent meant anticipating a child's needs before the child even asked, with the idea that responding quickly to a baby would help her become a harmonious child. So what I saw was a flexible, relaxed attitude. Babies were brought along everywhere, sleeping whenever they felt sleepy, wherever they happened to be. Japanese parents didn't talk about putting their babies on a sleep schedule. Nor, in fact, did I hear parents talk about their own sleep deprivation. It was as though the concept didn't exist. (Insomnia and sleeplessness—common problems in our culture—aren't such identifiable disorders in Japan.)

At pediatrician visits or during casual conversations with other parents, everyone in Japan simply assumed that my baby was sleeping next to me at night. Children's books featured co-sleeping animals or children. I opened a baby goods catalog to see an advertisement for giant family-size futons, featuring two beaming children cozily tucked in between their parents. Our local elementary school showed parents of incoming students a movie with a scene of a mother lying down next to her grade-schooler as he drifted off to sleep. And of course, most of our kids' friends were also sharing sleep in their families. Sharing sleep seemed so normal to our kids that they actually were surprised to see babies sleeping alone in their own rooms when we visited the United States. They thought baby monitors were used to help babies hear their families, not the other way around.

## A PUSH TOWARD EARLY INDEPENDENCE

Why would it matter so much where and how a baby sleeps, anyway? Sleep, as important as it is, isn't just about sleep. Parents in cultures around the world believe that what happens during nighttime hours shapes children's behavior during waking hours, their confidence levels, and their sense of self.

In America, many of our parenting strategies even from infancy are geared toward the goal of raising children who will be able to develop a solid sense of themselves as separate, distinct individuals. Not only do babies sleep in private, quiet sleeping environments, we also embrace other practices that aim to foster a sense of independence from others. We seat a baby in her own car seat, push her in her own stroller, talk to her as an equal, face-to-face. We respond animatedly to her smiling or babbling—which psychologists call "positive cues"—to encourage the qualities we prize: interactive communication, self-expression, and self-awareness.

These are what we consider good parenting practices. Our job is to help our kids become independent. When a baby seems too attached to us, we worry about her future, wondering if she will ever feel comfortable out of our sight. If an American baby is crying at night, her mother of course knows the baby is distressed, but her reaction to this is shaped by the idea that good parents help their babies get used to separation, because this will give them confidence.

Parents in a lot of non-Western cultures, on the other hand, would be alarmed by this much focus on things such as stimulating a baby, keeping him separate, and not responding quickly to his cries. They believe that close physical touch and shared sleep are healthy because they enfold a child into an interwoven network of clearly defined social relationships. The idea is this: If you hone a baby's sense of affiliation to those around him, and respect his innate sense that he is one with others, he will feel security as he grows up and eventually become an independent contributing member of his community who can take responsibility for himself.

While we tend to think of solitary sleep as the first step to creating an independent, autonomous child, parents in non-Western cultures like Japan believe that by sleeping next to other people children feel more connected. They see that babies who have their nighttime needs met in turn grow into children who are able to intuit and respond sensitively to the needs of other people. The Japanese don't see the early attachment between a baby and mother as unhealthy dependence, but instead as one of the first steps to fostering important skills children need to thrive and succeed later on.

Parents in these interdependent cultures don't focus as much direct attention on babies or rearrange their houses to accommodate them. Instead, babies nap amidst the bustle and noise of ordinary daily living. If a baby is waking at night, Japanese parents believe responding, rather than becoming anxious that the baby isn't meeting a developmental goal such as sleeping through the night by twelve weeks, is the best way to raise a good sleeper. They can't put their whole lives on hold for a baby by adjusting their schedule so he can stay home for his nap. If a baby is waking at night, it's a sign of some underlying need to respond to.

## EARLY SHARED SLEEP FOSTERS LATER INDEPENDENCE

Meret Keller and Wendy Goldberg, psychology professors at the University of California at Irvine, found that it's true that solitary sleepers achieve some goals of independence earlier: They learned to fall asleep alone, sleep through the night, and wean slightly earlier than co-sleepers. But, their more surprising finding was that early co-sleepers—children whose parents had intentionally chosen to co-sleep with them from infancy—later became *more* independent and self-reliant. In one of their studies, mothers of preschoolers reported that co-sleepers were more socially independent—dressing themselves, working out problems with playmates by themselves—than either solitary sleepers or children whose parents had co-slept with them after age one.

Keller and Goldberg's research squarely contradicts the Western idea that sleeping *alone* will foster more independent children. In fact, if we broaden how we define independence, the opposite seems to be true. "Many people throw the word 'independence' around without thinking conceptually about what it actually means," Keller explained to me. "Do they mean ability to fall asleep alone, and ability to sleep through the night alone, without parent assistance? If so, then yes, co-sleepers are often less independent—within this specific sleep domain. What most people do not think about is the possibility of independence for many, many daytime behaviors, and in other domains such as cognitive, social, emotional, or daily living skills." Keller noted that independence can also include self-care, basic chores such as setting the table, relationships with peers, dressing oneself, and entertaining oneself alone with a book or toy. She and Goldberg are exploring in their research how attachment security formed between parents and children who sleep together at night might serve as a sort of springboard for independent behavior during the day.

My son's friend Tomo, a ten-year-old boy living in the neighborhood adjoining ours in Tokyo, was certainly independent. He started walking to school without an adult at age six. He rode his bike to the park alone to meet friends. He carried everything he might need—a little money, a handkerchief, his refillable water flask—in a little bag slung over one shoulder. When Tomo came to our house to play, he lined his shoes up by the door and hung up his jacket just so. Tomo never asked me or another adult to help him. Instead, when it was time to cook dinner he helped me without being asked. Tomo was so competent that I sometimes depended on him to prepare the salad or stir-fry some noodles while I took care of other things. Yet every night when Tomo went home at the end of the day, he took his bath and then fell asleep next to his aunt, who was helping to raise him. Tomo had slept next to his aunt nearly all his life. A mature, reliable, independent kid during the day, Tomo shared sleep with an adult at night.

Japan is full of kids like Tomo. After years of living there on and off, my husband and I (and even our kids) have noticed that most children—the same children who sleep with their parents every night—take care of themselves and their belongings, work out peer conflicts, and show mature social behavior and self-regulation at a young age. Japanese parents expect their kids to be independent by taking care of themselves and being socially responsible. They expect them to help contribute to the household or school community by being capable and self-reliant. And they don't worry that this is too much to expect of them, given the context of the twenty-four-hour give-and-take relationship they have with one another.

## THE SWEDISH WAY OF SLEEP

In Sweden, similarly, co-sleeping is regarded positively. It's considered so ordinary that it's not thought of consciously at all. The Swedes believe that letting a child share sleep with a parent, if he wants to, is good for him.

In a study of Swedish attitudes toward co-sleeping, researcher Barbara Welles-Nystrom found that nearly three-quarters of children co-slept with their parents at some point during the night. While nearly all children in the study had their own beds, flexibility marked nighttime sleep: many of them wandered into their parents' bed during the night and stayed there until they fell asleep (after that parents might take them back to their own bed, move to the child's bed themselves, or let them stay the night). Why do the Swedish tolerate—and embrace—practices that so many Americans would consider to cause a disrupted night of sleep? According to Welles-Nystrom, Swedish parental theories about co-sleeping say that "the child is a 'natural being' who needs a safe environment in which to develop. If parents take their cues from the child . . . and satisfy the child's needs, the child will develop normally and at its own speed." Swedish parents believe that co-sleeping is a normal phase that children will outgrow. They are fond of asking rhetorically, "Who has ever seen an adult sleeping together in the same bed as their parents?" Finally, Swedish parents believe children have a right to co-sleep if they want to. "The child is considered an individual with certain rights, which in this case include the right of access to the safety and comfort of the parents' body at any time of day or night," writes Welles-Nystrom in her article. She quotes parents: "We see so little of the children during the day that we all want to fill up our tanks with love at night sleeping together," said one mother in her study.

Swedish parents believe that if a child wants and desires the security of co-sleeping, this will only help him to be more secure and independent as he grows. Rather than worry about its impact on a child's developing autonomy, *they believe it actually helps to promote independence.* Swedish health care professionals share this belief as well, which normalizes the practice.

Intrigued, I asked Swedish families about their attitudes about sharing a bed. As I spoke to Ulrika, a mother of two, who Skyped with me from her home in Stockholm, I realized that some of my questions about sleeping with children were hard for her to understand, because co-sleeping is so unremarkable there that it was like I was asking if ice is cold or birds fly.

I asked if there is any stigma about co-sleeping with babies or children in Sweden. Ulrika told me, "My son hardly slept in his own bed until he was three years old. And I think this is true of most people. It's so normal here—from time to time your child wants to sleep in your bed, and you let them because they need to cuddle, talk to you, and feel comfortable."

You would be hard-pressed to find a parent in Sweden who has never slept with a child in bed, Ulrika explained. "It's normal, not judged or anything," she said. "What would be judged would be never letting your child sleep with you if he needs to."

I asked her whether Swedes sleep with their babies. Ulrika told me *of course they do.* At the hospital after the children were born, she got sleeping instructions that assumed the baby would be in her bed. "We learned that we shouldn't put really small babies under a blanket, so we would put them on top of the blanket, with a small blanket over them," Ulrika explained. "In Sweden breast-feeding is very important and if you have the baby in bed with you, you don't have to get up. It's much less tiring to the mother." When I asked if her babies were able to sleep through the night, Ulrika looked momentarily confused. In Sweden, apparently, there isn't a widespread belief that young babies should sleep through the night. If they are in bed, and breast-feeding, they won't be sleeping through the night, and that's okay. So Ulrika hadn't ever really thought about this idea before.

I then asked a final question: Do Swedes think that sleeping with their children will somehow prevent them from becoming independent? Here, Ulrika sat up a little straighter and spoke forcefully. "My kids have taken the subway since age nine to go to school and walked on their own since they were six or seven," she said. "Generally, the Swedish way of raising children is to make them independent, help them to learn to use their own judgment and not just listen to authority. It's about giving them security: the more certain they feel you are there for them and can rely on you, the more independent they become."

At this juncture, her thirteen-year-old son, Alex, wandered into the room. Brown-haired and friendly, Alex was very curious about the idea of someone interviewing his mother about co-sleeping, something that he and all his friends had done. I wondered if anyone ever made any negative comments to a boy who slept with his parents. He shook his head no—the idea had never occurred to him. How long did he co-sleep with them? He looked at his mother questioningly. "I slept in your bed until I was six, or seven, or eight." He looked at her again and they both thought about this a bit. Maybe ten or eleven, they concurred, if he had a bad dream.

I asked if Alex remembered what it was like. "I thought it was," he hesitated and searched for the right word in English . . . "security. It gave me security. It was kind of normal to be in your bed when I had a nightmare or something," he said, smiling shyly at his mother. As our conversation drew to a close, Ulrika added, "Rather than sitting up for half the night . . . you can just all relax together." She shrugged and smiled at the practicality of it all. "It makes it so much easier."

# BELIEFS ABOUT SLEEP BASED ON CULTURE, NOT SCIENCE

In America we are told that babies need a certain number of hours of sleep; a nightly bath, several books, and a lovey are part of the bedtime routine; daytime naps must continue until a certain age; babies sleep best in quiet, dark rooms by themselves.

Many cultures have idiosyncratic ideas about what sleep should look like, as Anastasya, an American mom married to a Danish man, discovered when she visited her husband's native Copenhagen with their infant son. In Scandinavia, it's customary for babies to take their naps outdoors despite the cold winters. (The Finnish government assures new mothers, "Many babies sleep better outdoors in the fresh air than in the bedroom. Sleeping outdoors is not dangerous for a baby.") Babies are bundled up and left in prams on terraces or outside of stores to sleep. In Denmark they're *really* bundled up: Danish babies sleep under a mountain of blankets, under down comforters called "dunes." This was a total surprise to Anastasya, as it would be to any American mom who's learned that babies must never sleep under a heavy blanket or have anything in their cribs or sleeping spaces at all—let alone sleep unattended, out of doors. When she first saw babies in these blanketed prams, she had to check the impulse to pull the blankets off. But being in Denmark gave her a chance to see her own cultural assumptions through fresh eyes. After that, her little boy, Oliver, began sleeping under a dune himself, with toys in his crib.

Most of our rituals, convictions, and rules about sleep are based in cultural beliefs, not scientific evidence. Numerous sleep researchers agree, for instance, that there's actually no evidence for how many hours a baby is supposed to sleep. When I asked Jodi Mindell, a clinical psychologist, professor at Saint Joseph's University, and one of the country's foremost sleep researchers, who has also written a popular sleep-training book, how many hours a baby should be sleeping, she replied, "Ahh, the question of the decade! Or maybe century. We really do not know what is the sleep 'need' for infants. We only know what children are getting at this point."

Most American infants and toddlers get a little less than thirteen hours of sleep a day. No matter how much sleep your child gets, it's easy to worry that he isn't getting enough. Curiously, over the decades the recommended amount of sleep has always been consistent at any given time: it's always been about thirty-seven minutes more than the actual amount of sleep children are getting. The number of hours that children sleep has declined over the years, but we have no evidence for how much sleep they really need. As adults, we valorize the eight-hour-a-night sleep. But in reality, sleep patterns vary—for adults and kids alike—throughout the world, and have throughout our history, encompassing anything from short little naps and nighttime fragments, to long siestas and late bedtimes. (And that solid eight-hour sleep is a modern construct that may not be what we were wired for.) These differences show us how fluid these so-called norms are. What we think is immutable, universal, or optimal about sleep actually looks different all around the world.

Bedtime habits are one of the most important ways we ritualize sleep. Bedtime routines are more complex when children are expected to sleep by themselves; it takes work to teach babies to sleep on their own. These complex bedtime routines serve a purpose: they mark the shift between communal daytime activities and the abrupt transition to sleeping alone. Ideally, the bedtime routine serves the purpose it's meant to: it is a reassuring signal to the child about what lies ahead. For some parents, though, the process might take lots of time and energy, especially if a child needs to go through many comforting steps before being able to fall asleep on his own, or is struggling with bedtime fears.

In some cultures there is no bedtime routine at all. Guatemalan Mayan babies, who share a room or co-sleep with parents and siblings and spend all day in close proximity with others, simply fall asleep when they are sleepy, and do not change into special sleep clothes, brush their teeth, or typically use any transitional objects. They just sleep. In communities where sleeping with others is normal and routine, there might not even be a bedtime. Children learn to sleep "at will," and can nod off flexibly under all sorts of circumstances to the murmur of activities and sounds in the background.

Transitional attachment objects also aren't common in cultures where children spend more time in physical touch with others—in co-sleeping cultures. The transitional object is a substitute for an adult care-giver, so many children don't find it necessary to have one if the adult caregiver is always there. We saw this in Japan, where we were struck by the sheer absence of any sort of attachment objects—we saw no children who clung to well-worn blankets or tattered stuffed animals. And we saw the reverse, coming back to the United States—how young children were highly attached to blankets and loveys, panicking when they got misplaced.

The obligatory before-bed book is not part of every culture's bed-time ritual. In Taiwan, picture books specifically about bedtime—featuring children mastering bedtime fears, saying good night one by one to objects, saying good night to a parent before falling asleep sur-rounded with stuffed animals or clutching a lovey—are almost always translations of Western imported books, because the idea that bedtime is a separate, distinct ritual just doesn't reflect the reality of bedtime for Taiwanese children. One popular American picture book even ends with a scene of the family dog sleeping with his (human) parents in their bed while the baby sleeps alone in another room—an unremarkable scene in many American homes, but truly startling to people from other cultures.

## GOOD MATCH BETWEEN PARENT EXPECTATIONS AND CHILD'S SLEEP PERSONALITY = BEST REST

As Ella and Jack anticipated the arrival of their first child, they won-dered about sleep. "I thought it was a little strange that people would go to sleep with their pets, but not their babies," Ella, a mom in Bellevue, Washington, admitted. Jack had been raised in a kibbutz in Israel where he slept communally with other children; while they weren't with their parents, they weren't alone either. Both eventually decided against putting the new baby in a room by himself, and decided to bed share, placing on the floor mattresses that would eventually accommodate two adults, their children, and the family's beloved dogs.

When co-sleeping is a common, endorsed cultural practice, it's associated with little stress and few problems. But when parents sleep with their kids only as a last, reluctant resort for solving sleep problems—ranging from repeated requests for a drink of water or one more trip to the bathroom, to persistent, crippling bedtime fears and extended, disruptive night waking (problems possibly created by separate sleep in the first place) these embedded attitudes cause understandable feelings of ambivalence and stress.

Co-sleeping after the fact—in response to preexisting sleep problems—is called "reactive co-sleeping." Reactive co-sleeping can lead to power struggles between parent and child. Reactive co-sleeping by definition doesn't exist in cultures where co-sleeping is the norm and practiced from the beginning of a child's life, but it does here; it's another reason co-sleeping is viewed negatively: people often think of sharing sleep with a child as a last-resort strategy used for managing problems such as sleep protesting or night waking. We rarely hear what parents elsewhere know: intentional co-sleeping is one viable option to prevent such problems from arising in the first place.

For all the cultural differences around children's sleep, one thing is certain—the very best sleep happens when there is what researchers call "goodness of fit": the right match between a child's sleep personality and parental expectations. We have a better chance of achieving this "goodness of fit" with our own children if we can open our minds up to all the ways children might sleep well, and if we expand the definition of what "normal" sleep might be.

Ella and Jack got something right when they modified their sleeping environment to accommodate the needs of a co-sleeping family. This is exactly how parents in co-sleeping cultures devise sleeping arrangements that ensure restful sleep for parent and baby: they'll put futons on the floor, prepare adjoining spaces for baby and mother that are separate from other family members, and give everyone room to spread out. Western co-sleeping is usually complicated by Western beds, which are high up off the floor and usually not wide enough for a family. This leads to the problems many associate with bed sharing: rolling on the baby, kicking, disrupted sleep, adult pillows and blankets dangerously close to the baby, baby falling off the side. How, really, could one be expected to get a good night's sleep?

Though she'd read that newborns slept constantly and through anything, Els and her partner, Lise, noticed that Sarah was different as soon as she was born. "When she was a week old, we took her out to meet friends, and I saw her eyes get bigger and bigger as she grew visibly more exhausted yet didn't want to go to sleep because what was going on was so interesting," Els told me. "This might have been my first inkling that baby books were not always right." Els made her peace with having a child who "never slept" by finally acknowledging that Sarah wasn't ever going to be one of those kids who slept long hours. Sarah simply wasn't wired to sleep like the baby our culture had conditioned her parents to expect.

Nina's parents, in Golden, Colorado, tried everything to get their baby to sleep better. Their pediatrician suggested patting her on the back. A sleep specialist they consulted told them to let her cry for "as long as it takes." The advice didn't work (they tried letting her cry once until Kurt went to get her, muttering, "This is ridiculous," as he picked his miserable baby up out of her crib). So Kurt and Cat moved their beds around to accommodate Nina's need for closeness. "She still needs a lot of touching and we lie down with her and her sister to put them to sleep," Cat told me. They now sleep well.

Lisa, Isabel's desperately sleep-deprived mother, doesn't regret having sleep trained her baby. "I was pretty crazy from sleep deprivation by that point. It was either that or, at some point, fall asleep while driving," she recalled to me. But she told me wistfully that she wondered if things would have been different if she had had more support. "We don't give new mothers any leeway to not be able to think straight. There are no studies on what happens with a mother who doesn't sleep for a year. I didn't have any support. I didn't have family in the area. I didn't have friends who knew how to help me. I think that's a typically American problem." She also wonders if some of her daughter's insecurities today stem from those early difficulties.

Even Dr. Richard Ferber, author of *Solve Your Child's Sleep Problems* and founder and former director of Boston Children's Hospital Center for Pediatric Sleep Disorders, whose name has become synonymous with the cry-it-out "Ferberizing" sleep-training method, now recognizes that there are many viable ways for a baby to sleep. Once a staunch proponent of babies' sleeping alone (even if a baby became so distressed he vomited), Ferber now states, "We've found that youngsters sleep very well in a variety of situations, as seen around the world. From a sleep perspective, we have little evidence for or against any of these arrangements."

Where should your baby sleep? Wherever he sleeps best. My Korean-born mother bought a crib for me because she thought that was the American way (though she confided in me recently that she rarely used it), and my parents did the "American" thing by providing my brothers and me each with our own room. Before having children, I thought I would do the same. Then we had our kids and found that we all slept best together. So David and I co-sleep with our kids, as growing numbers of American parents do.

# TWO

# BUY, BUY, BABY:
## Why Are We Drowning in Stuff?

Kathy, an expectant mom in Seattle, wasn't sure what she and her husband would need for their new baby. She did ample research, reaching out to her circle of more experienced, savvier friends for their personal recommendations, and trawling online lists for must-have items. Soon she came up with a list of necessities.

Kathy planned on breast-feeding, so she needed silk/wool washable nursing pads, nontoxic breast cream, an electric breast pump, and glass bottles with nontoxic, BPA-free nipples of various sizes (she'd be getting a nursing pillow once she sourced an appropriately flame-retardant-free one). She already knew which brand and style of brush she wanted to clean the bottles, though she hadn't yet decided which insulated bottle holder to buy. She had determined exactly what size and brand of diaper pail and washable diaper pail liner she'd use for their cloth diapers, though she and her husband were still not sure whether they'd be using a diaper delivery service or buying their own (it was such a hard decision for new parents, with more than fifteen brands to choose from, each more stylish than the next). But at least Kathy did know how much clothing they'd need to start off: ten organic cotton bodysuits or kimono shirts, ten pajamas with attached feet, four sleeping sacks, a fashionable, gauzy swaddling blanket, ten burp cloths, and ten bibs.

Kathy and her husband wanted a certain baby bath, which was twice the price of the kinds of baby baths for sale in Target, but it was worth the extra cost because of its unique and comfortable design. They planned to wash their baby in nontoxic bath wash and dry the baby off with a specialty organic-cotton hooded baby towel. A teething doll made of soft organic cotton would ease teething pain; it was safe to chew on and cuddly to boot. The baby would also have several nontoxic specialty pacifiers to choose from. A gentle animal mobile made of little hand-crocheted figures imported from India would hang above the Ikea crib and organic mattress and bedding to lull baby off to sleep, and a beech-wood rattle hand-carved in Germany would entertain baby during waking hours. Kathy had already decided on a nontoxic, phthalate-free bamboo-filled play mat, which had a colorful design that would promote brain development and encourage baby to crawl, and she had also chosen which French-language Baby Einstein DVDs their baby—who would be raised bilingually—would enjoy.

A few outstanding items remained to be added to the list: Would the baby need a bassinet or would the crib be sufficient? Would Kathy need a nursing stool? Should they get a diaper rash ointment made of extra-virgin coconut oil and calendula? What kind of mirror for the backseat would be best to help baby tolerate car rides? And though they'd already decided on which front pack and sling they would carry their baby in, they still needed to research a baby stroller and a car seat.

Kathy and her husband were an eco-friendly couple. As conscientious consumers, they knew about making careful choices for themselves, so it was natural for them to turn their formidable information-gathering skills to look for the best products for their baby. Kathy's choices reflected how carefully she considered things, and what thoughtful parents she and her husband wanted to be.

According to one study, the average American family gains 30 percent more possessions with the arrival of each child. For modern

American parents, providing a baby with food, clothing, shelter, and love is no longer enough. Today, good parenting has become defined by what you pick for your baby, whether you're buying premium organic wooden toys from a hip boutique store or stimulating, bright plastic learning toys from Walmart. We need to buy a lot of stuff for our baby in order to raise a happy, healthy, thriving child. Right?

## TOO MUCH STUFF

American parents face this paradox: our culture and media tell us that our children deserve the best, but those of us who strive to give our children that "best" often give them too much. It begins early. At our very first visit to the obstetrician's office, the waiting-room coffee table is stacked with magazines and pamphlets full of appealing advertisements for baby gear, educational toys, and adorable clothes. Even before our baby is born, we parents are well on our way to accumulating stuff: car seats, clothes, diapers, toys, mobiles, strollers, cribs, carriers, high chairs, and even flash cards. As our children get older, the gear they seem to need increases: Legos, dolls, art and craft supplies, bikes (and helmets) or scooters or skateboards, sporting equipment, books and clothes, electronic games, iPods, enrichment workbooks, trendy clothing, maybe even a cell phone. There might be a Wii in the living room, a trampoline in the backyard, stilts and Rollerblades on the porch. They accumulate all this before they've even graduated from elementary school. Then there are the vacation souvenirs, presents we bring home when we go out of town, and impulse buys from those spontaneous shopping trips. It's not only what we buy them ourselves: our kids also accumulate birthday presents from friends and family, holiday gifts from well-meaning grandparents, and special things from family friends.

We may not realize how much savvy marketers work to ensure that products for children entice us. We buy stuff because of the promise the purchase holds to enhance our children's lives. Persuasive, anxiety-inducing advertising convinces us that the very brands we buy will determine whether our babies will be smiley or colicky, whether our toddlers will be happy or throw tantrums, and whether our school-age children fail or succeed. The advertising coaxes us into believing that what we own defines the kind of parents we are (and the kind of kids we're raising), whether that's urban and hip, healthy and athletic, nature-loving and organic, worldly and adventurous, artsy and eclectic, or sports-loving and down-to-earth.

It's no surprise that the inside of so many American family homes looks like a retailer's warehouse, or enough goods, as one friend remarked wryly, to pay for a second mortgage for her home. According to one study, three-quarters of American families surveyed had stopped using their garages to park their cars, using them instead to house their excess stuff.

## WHY WE BUY

Children didn't used to be on the receiving end of as much spending as they are today. In early-nineteenth-century America, as in previous centuries, children were essential for the economic well-being of the family, and we had lots more of them. They helped out on the family farm, did real work in the family business, or generated extra income for the family by getting a job outside the home. Now we have far fewer children, and pay a great deal more attention to each. Our child-centric culture encourages us to view each and every child as, in the words of Princeton sociologist Viviana Zelizer, "economically worthless, but emotionally priceless."

The stereotypical mother of the post–World War II baby boom was encouraged to derive meaning from supporting her husband by maintaining a well-kept home. American mothers in the 1970s and 1980s strived to redefine the value of working motherhood. In contrast, many twenty-first-century American parents seek meaning in their lives and find purpose by making a career out of priming their children for success. Today, instead of being told we should wear high heels and pearls while vacuuming the house, we worry that by not buying something for our child that will help foster his unique interests, he won't live up to his potential. University of Pennsylvania sociologist Annette Lareau refers to this as "concerted cultivation," the middle- and upper-class parenting strategy of grooming one's own children to achieve excellence and success. Lareau argues that the way we spend money on our children—on their belongings, toys, books, clothes, and extracurricular activities—reflects our commitment to the idea that we should do whatever it takes to help each child cultivate his individual talents.

Kelly and her husband, James, understand this commitment. They live in an upscale community in California with their ten-year-old son and five-year-old daughter. Their son has been playing soccer since he was three years old (his parents pay for club soccer, indoor soccer, and Latin soccer), and he has a closet full of soccer gear: specialized cleats, ten different jerseys, and various other soccer gear, such as shin guards, headbands, water bottles, and soccer bags.

Their daughter also has a room filled with possessions that announce her interests. She sleeps in a French Art Deco–style bed; she has a collection of colorful, trendy "feathers" to clip in her hair, and her closet is full of fashionable clothes and jewelry. She wanted another American Girl doll last Christmas, but her parents drew the line at that since she already had two. Instead, in addition to gifts like a moving toy GoGo My Walkin' Pup, which walks and talks, a Barbie camper van, DVDs, Vans shoes, a makeup kit, a Polly Pocket set, two dresses, a Hello Kitty jacket, and art supplies, she was given a hundred-dollar gift certificate for a mani-pedi at a local spa/salon and a Build-A-Bear gift card.

Parents like Kelly and James strive to support their kids' development. They insist their son play sports and encourage their daughter's taste for fashion and toys that will help foster her imagination. And they're not alone. In their community they are surrounded by parents who cultivate their children's unique selves through classes, activities, and the right material goods. In their area, Kelly told me, "Parents just want the best for their kids."

Most parents, regardless of socioeconomic class, buy things for their kids because they see how the things kids own become tokens in their social worlds, according to Allison Pugh, a sociologist at the University of Virginia. Kids long for the things that will bring them social acceptance and approval among their peers, like name-brand jeans, trading cards, and the latest electronic games and gadgets. As parents we're keenly attuned to what will help our kids thrive and be happy.

Yet, though we buy into the culture of buying, we probably don't feel entirely good about it. I struggle with the toys our kids lost interest in soon after they got them, the impossibility of keeping the house free of clutter, the worry that our kids will get spoiled. Many of the American subjects of Pugh's research felt similarly ambivalent. They tried to steer their kids away from "inappropriate" toys and games, such as things that were not in good taste, expressed the wrong values, or weren't good for their development. Parents tried to shape and control their children's desires, but it took a lot of energy and didn't always work.

## I BUY, THEREFORE I'M HAPPY

In the United States, where we have more shopping centers than high schools, and where 93 percent of teenage girls listed shopping as their favorite activity in a survey, many Americans embrace a consumer-oriented lifestyle. We buy things for pleasure, indulgence, and to keep up with the Joneses. American children get an average of seventy new toys a year. "The messages that children encounter every day are that *the things they buy will make them happy*," says Susan Linn, author of *Consuming Kids: The Hostile Takeover of Childhood* and director of the Campaign for a Commercial-Free Childhood. "Their worth depends on what they own. They will not be happy unless they have the things that corporations value. And kids are spending a lot of time with those values, because commercialism has infiltrated so much of our lives."

This level of the commercialization of childhood isn't good for children. Having so much stuff, paradoxically, leave kids feeling empty. In her book *Born to Buy: The Commercialized Child and the New Con-*

*sumer Culture,* Boston College sociology professor Juliet Schor warns that recreational buying is harmful for all children. A consumer-oriented lifestyle is a significant cause of mental disorders such as depression, anxiety, or low self-esteem in children. Materialism has been associated with precocious sexuality, obesity, violence, eating disorders, and a propensity toward impulse buying. Even kids who are psychologically healthy are worse off when they're constantly thinking about what they own, want to buy, or what they long for. "Less involvement in consumer culture leads to healthier kids," Schor writes. Parents have only the best intentions when we buy so much stuff for our children. We don't realize how harmful it is.

Doesn't having money and being able to purchase the things we want make us happy? Yes and no. There is some evidence to suggest that financial security brings more life satisfaction. It's beneficial to know that you will be able to meet your basic needs for food, clothing, and shelter, now and in the future. But there's also considerable evidence that a constant pursuit of material fulfillment that goes beyond basic needs actually makes people unhappier. In fact, children of affluent families living in wealthy areas—whose parents have the means to buy them the things that they want—are unhappier than their peers in middle-class neighborhoods (and so are their parents). The satisfaction of buying what you want fades quickly, leading you to hanker after the next shiny new thing.

Consumerism can also harm children's connections with one another. Children have an uncanny sense about what they have and what they need to have to keep up with their peers. And through what social scientists call "invidious comparison," children begin to look down upon those who don't have the right possessions. When her son came home confused one day, saying that the children at school were wondering why the tooth fairy brought a vastly different sum of money to different homes, Hena, a mother of two in Washington, D.C., was disturbed when she realized how much kids compare notes on one another's lives. Our kids do all that whining, begging, and pleading because they are eager not to be left out of the materialist race. When children are highly aware that status is conveyed by what they own, they become more competitive.

Hena told me that when she was growing up, "There was very little emphasis and expense on the part of my parents to 'entertain' us. We were meant to keep ourselves entertained." She and her siblings were expected to read for pleasure or play games by themselves. Her parents felt no pressure to buy them the latest, greatest thing, such as a VCR, a PC, or an Atari game console.

It's harder for parents now, Hena noted ruefully. She remembers cleaning out her son's drawer once and finding so much stuff: rubber bouncy balls and erasers, debris from birthday goody bags, things he didn't care about. "I told my mom, 'These kids don't value things,' and she told me, 'It's because they have too much.'"

## IN JAPAN, LESS IS MORE

When we moved to Japan, I was mystified by the fact that children around us had so few gratuitous personal possessions. Our Japanese friends, in turn, were baffled by why our children had so much. Though we weren't able to take that much with us on our overseas move, our two young boys nevertheless had what seemed, once we arrived, to be a staggering amount of clothing, books, and especially toys: a wooden train set, toy cars, puzzles, toy musical instruments, art supplies, wooden blocks, Legos, dress-up costumes, and more. When my friend Sinae saw that each boy had a bicycle and scooter, in addition to a ride-on toy and a small red wagon they'd received as a gift, she laughed. "How many children do you have living here?"

In Japan, buying a lot of stuff for your children is considered indulgent. Despite the impression Americans may have of Japanese as avid, brand-conscious shoppers, most Japanese people around us lived simply and frugally. Wastefulness was frowned upon. Shopping bags should be saved to reuse many times, not recycled after one purchase. Paper with some blank space on it must be reused as well, cut up small, used as scrap paper. Japanese tend to be cautious spenders; prices are high in Japan, they live within their means, and personal debt is almost unheard of. Most purchases are made with cash, not on credit.

When it came to raising children, most parents I met felt that it was important to get kids accustomed to less from the start. It is better for their characters, their imagination, their resourcefulness, and their future lives not to experience immediate or excessive material gratification. It wasn't tasteful to spend money to accumulate lots of possessions for your child. Living modestly was a virtue that you wanted to teach your kids, something they could aspire to.

When this was the mindset surrounding you, you couldn't help being influenced by it. Daniel envied his many Japanese friends who had no family car (unlike us) because they made it seem so great that they got to walk everywhere and ride buses and trains. In contrast, a family car seemed boring. When he told his friends Yuya and Leon how many presents kids in the United States received at Christmas, they were incredulous. "I don't know what I'd do with all that," declared nine-year-old Leon. It wasn't even appealing.

Having less enabled kids to appreciate what they did have. One six-year-old girl we knew had only a dollhouse with animal figurines. Two young brothers we knew shared a box of action figures and a small car-and-track set. These few toys were well played with and cherished. We often heard the phrase *mono wo daiji ni suru*, which means to "take really good care of something." Japanese children were constantly reminded that possessions weren't disposable or replaceable, and to treat them with care and appreciation, like the leather backpack all kids receive when entering first grade and are expected to use throughout all six years of elementary school.

Japanese homes are far smaller than our own, and that limited space surely accounts for some of the reluctance to acquire. But we also encountered every day in small ways the notion that children didn't need to have so much. Once my friend handed one tiny packet of cookies to Mia and Anna, even though she had a few extra packets in her purse. She expected the girls to share the packet and knew that each child didn't need her own. From her perspective, she was doing me a favor by helping to reinforce satisfaction with less and a willingness to share. By contrast, American siblings are sometimes given toys at the same time, or even duplicate toys, to prevent bickering or competition or to just allow each individual child to enjoy his own thing for himself. Any adult who asks them to make do with less risks appearing ungenerous, even stingy. Children learn the phrase "Mine!" almost as soon as they learn to talk.

The Japanese I knew saw scarcity and sharing as one crucial key to cooperation and relationship building. They didn't feel bad about expecting several kids to share one toy. A private bedroom for a child isn't common. Children and adults alike loan things to each other because buying new is used as a last resort. These little everyday things help promote overall goals such as depending on one another, keeping consumption down, and sharing.

Such small, frequent reminders seemed key to taming what I'd thought was universal: a child's desire for more, more, more. The children we knew didn't exhibit the same desires as so many kids we knew back in the United States. They didn't make long holiday or birthday lists of gifts they wanted. They didn't pester their parents for things in stores. They didn't talk incessantly about the things they wanted. They were used to not getting things unless there was a really good reason.

I was used to birthday parties back home, which usually involved lots of kids, pizza and cake, and the crowning glory: a mountain of presents for the birthday child and bagged party favors for the little guests. When we were in Japan, there weren't any birthday parties. Several Japanese moms explained to me that it wasn't typical to celebrate a child's birthday with a party. Occasionally there might be one—one friend mentioned a particularly memorable one she had on her eighth birthday, and others remember celebrating a birthday with a friend or two—but they weren't de rigueur, annual events. Instead, in Japan birthdays are typically celebrated in a low-key way, at home with family, a meal, and a small cake. Japanese don't traditionally give much in the way of presents for birthdays or Christmas to children, though these days it's become common for families to give their kids a small gift like a book or an action figure.

It's not that the Japanese don't think children's birthdays are important. They just mark them differently. Our Japanese *yochien* (a multi-age school for kids ages three to six), like other *yochien*s, held a communal celebration for *all* the children who had a birthday that month. After a ceremony where they stood up together and each received a handmade card while the other children sang to them, there was a seasonal lunch prepared by parents at the school. The birthday china and tablecloths were brought out, and fresh flowers in small vases adorned the tables. For a Japanese child a birthday was special, not because of what kind of treat was brought to school or the presents he got, but because of the long-awaited, once-a-year-only ceremony and song, the chance to enjoy a moment of recognition together with other friends who shared the same birthday month, and the love and care of a homemade meal.

I noticed that at restaurants, Japanese children didn't seem dependent on toys to distract them as they waited for their meals. (Nor did restaurants hand out crayons and coloring pages to occupy children.) There were no parents pulling out supplies for the little ones in a frantic effort to keep them seated and entertained. It seemed to me that having less made kids more patient. Once I went to a very long, formal, adult-oriented evening event where some families brought their young kids along, and all they had to occupy them were a few sheets of origami. And most kids didn't bring much gear with them to parks or playgrounds.

After a few years in Japan, our kids too became accustomed to less being more. They could occupy themselves with a mere piece of paper— folding it, drawing on it, rolling it up, making jewelry or trinkets out of it. The neighborhood kids often entertained themselves without store-bought toys for hours as they made up variations on tag or hide-and-seek. A pair of socks or some wadded-up newspaper became a ball in a game of catch if there wasn't a real ball available. Children gathered on summer afternoons at the nearby park and fished for crawfish in the pond, devising little traps out of a bit of string, some empty plastic bottles, and tape. These handmade concoctions were more thrilling and gratifying than having brand new store-bought equipment. At school kids created handmade toys to sell at a pretend market—everything from candy and sushi, to flowers, jewelry, watches, and toys—all made of materials straight out of the recycling bin. While the activity was about consumption, children learned in a hands-on, creative way the value of reusing "trash."

The mindset the kids internalized through these daily activities was that you could do so much with so little. Scarcity fostered creative solutions. I wanted to know what parents did to promote this attitude in their kids at home, so I paid a visit to Naomi, a fellow mother at our *yochien*. I asked Naomi if her two children ever asked for things. "Of course they do," she laughed. But it was clear to me from spending time with them that they were remarkably content with what they had. I'd never seen them—or other Japanese children—whine or beg because they wanted to buy something. In her characteristically modest way, Naomi hesitated to consider she might have had anything to do with her children's restrained desire for stuff.

When I persisted, she gave me a few hints. It started, she thought, with instilling a deep awareness and appreciation in children of what they had. "When we go to the park, we don't take toys, buckets, or things like that," she told me. After all, she'd tell her kids, *there is so much already*; why would you need anything more? Kids learn to get hooked on the novelty of acquiring things when this is what they're used to. But they're not born addicted to constant acquisition. For Naomi's daughter Mori, there were the branches and leaves and rocks, there were flowers and bugs to play with and to appreciate. There were the other children to play with too.

As Naomi and Mori walked home from preschool every day, sometimes they'd stop by a store, and sometimes Mori would ask for a treat or a toy. There were times when Naomi would buy her what she wanted, but not always. Instead, she encouraged Mori to pick up something beautiful from the ground on their walk home to bring back to their apartment, maybe a lovely fallen flower, or a nut.

Research shows that simpler, open-ended playthings—things like a simple doll or wooden blocks—are best to foster a child's imagination and creativity. But in the United States, it's hard, if not impossible, to protect our children from the onslaught of single-purpose, branded toys on the market. In 2009 alone, $5.4 billion worth of branded toys were sold to American consumers. But these single-purpose toys circumscribe a child's imagination. Instead of creating their own complex worlds, children become passive players when the world is already predetermined by the manufacturer. But what struck me most in Japan was that children like Mori didn't need any purchased toys at all. There was so much for free right outside her door every day.

I looked around Naomi's sunlit apartment overlooking the Tokyo skyline. By Japanese standards, it was average sized—seven hundred square feet for herself, her husband, and their two children. It wasn't completely devoid of playthings—in one corner there was a small collection of stuffed animals and a few coloring books. Naomi showed me Mori's collection of treasures, which they displayed on a little ceramic plate near the front entrance. Today there was a branch with red berries clinging to it, a small pinecone, and a leaf. Once, Naomi recalled, a mother who had frequently spent time in the United States with her American husband's family asked her why she wasn't buying her kids toys when they were out shopping together, and that was her first inkling that in some cultures, giving kids their own new toys was kind of a normal way to entertain or pacify them. "But I don't think toys are really necessary," Naomi confided.

Naomi wasn't rigid or controlling. Her son got a modest allowance and bought what he wanted to from that—usually small items like trading cards or comic books. When he wanted to see a soccer game once, she had him do extra chores to earn the money to buy tickets. She stressed that it was really necessary to give him a feeling of control over his own life by letting him make small decisions about purchasing what he wanted to while he was young. This would also help him learn the value of money in incremental ways. "It's important to let him make his own decisions about what he wants to buy," she told me earnestly. Naomi encouraged him to pass his small purchases on to someone else to enjoy when he was done with them.

For every Japanese parent I knew, "reuse, reduce, recycle" wasn't a new notion. It was deeply ingrained in their culture and tied to notions of mutual dependence, not just with each other, but a reverence for living lightly on the earth too. Children carry their own handkerchief to dry their hands from the time they're in preschool. Our elementary school even held handkerchief checks. Teachers helped children get into the habit of using reusable cloth instead of paper towels until it was utterly ingrained.

Japanese moms in our area sought out children in the neighborhood to pass their children's clothing down to after it was outgrown. It wasn't solely a practical thing, about reducing waste or being frugal. It was also that it was special to wear a dress that a child they knew had worn. "The children feel much affection when they wear clothes already worn in, played in, by someone else," Naomi explained. It's nice both for the giver, generously passing something down, and the receiver, proud to wear something an admired older child had once worn. Now I understood the frequent clothing exchanges I'd seen in schoolyards at pickup. These clothes were infused with a personal history that connected people with one another in a way that donating used clothing anonymously to a charity, as we might do in the United States, cannot.

Though some Japanese, especially those who are more affluent or have spent time abroad, have started to emulate Western values and clutter their houses with stuff, it's easy to imagine how children who grow up in a society where there are few store-bought toys, but ample time and encouragement to make playthings, don't automatically need to buy things to feel satisfaction. As I walked home with a bag full of hand-me-down dresses for Anna that Naomi had pressed into my hands, I realized that in Japan, being a good parent meant teaching your children to be frugal, resourceful, and restrained in their desires. Being a good parent meant helping kids to understand that happiness can never be bought.

# FRENCH LESSONS IN DELAYED GRATIFICATION

In Japan, where we were surrounded by kids like Naomi's, it was easier for us to show our children the value in living less materialistically, even though it continued to be a work in progress for our family. Kate, an English mother who is raising two young children in France along with her French partner, understands how being surrounded by a different ethos makes the job of a parent easier in some ways. She noticed a striking contrast between France and the UK fairly early on in her stay in France. "I don't think there is this massive pressure to buy all the time," she told me. All families are different, but in general, she mused, in France, "I don't think value is found in what you purchase. I think it's found in your sense of family, how you bring your children up to be able to operate in the world like sentient adults."

Kate's partner used to quote a common French phrase: *C'est moi qui décide.* "It's me who decides." Kate posted the phrase on her refrigerator as a reminder to herself, once she saw that her children seemed just as happy when they didn't have so much focus on their wants and demands. She was always responsive to their emotional needs: fear, anger, sadness, but Kate also grew to recognize that it was possible to be responsive in these important ways while also taking the lead in shaping desires and wants. She told me that "Children need to learn how to become adults. That means learning that sometimes you have to wait. Sometimes you don't get what you want right away, the first moment you want it." This held true whether it was about emotional or material desires.

Another French parent, Gilles, agreed. His two boys, ages eight and five, have their share of material goods. They have toys that they love to play with and that foster open-ended, imaginative play. But his boys are not at all demanding—they are content with what they have. Their lives are satisfying—they read a lot, and have the opportunity to learn music and play sports. Still, Gilles tells me parents in France are subject to a lot of consumer pressure. There are always things one must buy: clothes, or prams and other baby gear. Some parents like to buy a lot more than others. But even so, there are some general differences between France and the United States, where the perceived image is that of the *bébé roi*, "child as king." Such a child must have everything, right away, in order to be *comblé*: satisfied and fulfilled in material and emotional ways.

In contrast, in France, there is an idea that "frustrating" children is good for them. *"On les fustre,"* Gilles said. "We frustrate them." French parents, he explained, deny their children things or make them wait for things they may want. Sometimes it means delaying gratification for years, maybe because it's not the right time, there's no money, or simply because the toy isn't considered appropriate. This is a pretty common approach in France that's widely understood to be for the child's bene-fit. If you don't teach a child to wait, or that they can't have every-thing, "they will never understand the kind of satisfaction that comes from waiting." If you give a child what he desires right away, then the child is at risk of becoming *boulimique*, always needing to have more, more, more.

Rachel, a Canadian mother who has spent time in France with her partner's French family, also experienced quite different expectations around indulging children with stuff. "The French Christmases we've shared there are nothing like the deluge of stuff we expect in North America," she told me. "Gifts are well chosen, well wrapped, and the ritual of opening them is watched by all, accompanied by a round of kisses and careful thank-yous. Then, the feast is the formal centerpiece of the event.

"But I think that ties into French discipline generally," she mused, "where all is to be thoroughly enjoyed—with strict limits and at the proper time, and where excess and gluttony are taboo. There is really something to be learned from this, at the table and at the toy store."

# THE TYRANNY OF CHOICE

Yet, one of the best things about contemporary culture is that we have so many choices. Paper or plastic, blue cheese or Thousand Island, BlackBerry or iPhone. Our children prepare to make important decisions when they're older by making smaller decisions now. Choice is good for our kids and good for us. Isn't it?

Actually, no. When we are faced with decisions about what to buy, our consumer habits actually affect our brains. Retailers are well aware of this brain science and seek to appeal to the side of our brains that loves novelty, while muffling the part of our brain that advises moderation. They employ a variety of strategies: everything from putting an expensive item next to the item they really want to sell you (thus making you think you're getting a bargain), to extending easy credit (which inhibits your cautious side, since plastic doesn't feel like "real money"), to cloaking items in a "halo" of attractive words ("wholesome," "educational"). The problem is that once we buy, the thrill soon dissipates and we're back on what researchers call a hedonic treadmill: like addicts, we seek to re-create that initial thrill by making additional purchases.

Few families in the world are as vulnerable to the desire to buy as American families are. Though commercialism is a modern, global phenomenon, it affects American children disproportionately because corporations have benefited from deregulation against marketing directly to children, which began in the 1980s under Ronald Reagan. The open access to marketing directly to children too young to distinguish reality from fantasy, combined with an explosion in digital media, has given marketers multiple platforms to gain access to the youngest consumers.

American children see more than 25,000 advertisements on television a year. Advertisements for junk food, soda, and branded or electronic toys can be found on cell phones, MP3 players, the Internet, video games, and e-readers. They can be seen in preschools and on school buses and even in report cards. Companies carefully research how children gain information, how much time they spend online, and who influences them the most.

Kids are uniquely vulnerable to marketing because they can't tell the difference between content that's informational or entertaining and content that's trying to sell them something, whether on television or on the Internet (and in fact, the Internet is even more effective for marketing to kids, because they are more actively engaged in their online experiences). By the age of two, they begin to recognize logos and associate them with the products that are being peddled, and by the time they go to elementary school they recognize hundreds of logos. The current generation of kids is the most brand-conscious ever, and teenagers talk about brands an average of 145 times per week, about twice as much as adults do.

In order to capture the youngest markets, corporations go directly between parents and their children. It's no coincidence that the American media often portray adults, especially parents, teachers, or other authority figures, as foolish, old-fashioned, and out of touch in comparison to sophisticated, cool, savvy kids. Marketing directly to kids by denigrating adults is a successful and popular strategy. It helps encourage young kids to be precociously mature and consider it normal to act disdainfully toward their own parents. That whining and nagging that kids do to get the things they want isn't happening just because they're spoiled, as parents might despair, but as the result of well-honed marketing strategies taking advantage of "pester power"—a proven way to sell consumer goods (and a clear contributor to family stress).

Family strife over consumer desires isn't a given, as harried American parents feel it must be. Children's well-being and their relationships with others are better in countries where corporate power is weaker, as Tim Kasser's research shows. Kasser, a psychology professor at Knox College and author of *The High Price of Materialism*, was traveling in the UK in 2007 when a major UNICEF report was released assessing the lives and well-being of children and adolescents in twenty-one wealthy industrialized nations. The UK ranked last, which made the news over there. (The United States ranked second to last, a point largely ignored here.) Kasser decided to use the UNICEF data in a cross-national study to evaluate whether cultural values and societal goals influenced how nations care for their children. He found that nations that value equality and harmony provide better lives for their kids than do nations that emphasize money, power, and achievement values associated with free-market-oriented economies, like America's. It's rather difficult, he told me on the phone, for a nation to be simultaneously corporate-friendly and promote the well-being of children, given that these two aims are often at odds.

"When people are focused on money, status, and power, they tend to be less happy," Kasser explained. This is true at the level of nations as well. Children living in nations that de-emphasized money values and prioritized egalitarian values enjoyed better well-being, and their families benefited from more generous parental leave policies and less advertising aimed at kids. "Nations that emphasize equality and love rather than money and power probably provide a variety of different kinds of supports for children and their families, like shorter work hours, adequate health care, well-funded schools, and family-friendly urban spaces, rather than focusing on activities like going shopping and making money," Kasser continued. "By doing so, it seems that their children are happier and healthier."

## HOW TO OWN LESS AND LIVE MORE

So what's a parent to do? How do we deal with formidable cultural forces, and limit what we buy for our children without making them feel deprived? What can we learn from other cultures where consumerism isn't so rampant? The first step is to recognize and trust that providing less for our kids really is a viable pathway to things that matter too, things—such as creativity, resourcefulness, moderation, self-restraint, and self-satisfaction—that kids carry with them far longer into their future lives than the material goods they ask for today.

When I had my first child, I got caught up in buying all the right things, because I believed that those right things would guarantee the best childhood for him. I wish I could talk to the uncertain new mom I was then and explain to her that all our little boy really needed was our love, attention, and time, and that despite the relentless advertising, there was no material object that I could have bought for him that would be worth as much as that.

Every child needs things within reason, but not every want is a need. Saying no is the hardest part of being a parent. But it's our job to set those boundaries so we can teach kids how to set them for themselves. If we say yes too often, we're depriving our kids: of knowing how to be satisfied with less; of freedom from unmanageable clutter; of the satisfaction of working toward and saving up for something they really want.

Global examples can teach us a valuable lesson for ourselves as well as our children. We don't need the best car, the latest iPod, or the fanciest dinnerware to be happy. And neither do our children. Although modern American culture tries to convince us that through buying stuff we can perfect our kids' performance, happiness, and overall self-esteem, we can be smarter than the corporations who care most about their profits. The best way to make our kids happy is by providing them with less.

# THREE

# GLOBAL FOOD RULES:
## How Parents Around the World
## Teach Their Kids to Eat

There are only a few foods that twelve-year-old Robbie from Pennsylvania is willing to eat. Mealtimes at home are a battle. His mother, Cathy, a concerned and determined parent, has tried many things over the years. When Robbie was little, he spat broccoli out on the table. Years later the only vegetable Robbie eats is mashed potatoes. He doesn't like fruit either. Cathy tries to keep unhealthy food to a minimum in her house, but at the same time she wants Robbie to eat. At five feet tall, he weighs eighty pounds, and she's worried he is undernourished. Even Robbie's doctor has told him he has to make better food choices.

These days his mom buys foods he will eat even though she knows they aren't healthy: kettle popcorn, Cheez-Its, toasted ravioli, Fruit Roll-Ups. It's a constant dance of providing him with food he *will* eat while also trying to urge him to eat better. Last week Cathy tried to entice him with a barbecue she prepared for the whole family—tomato, basil, and mozzarella salad; rice; grilled steak, chicken, and sausage; grilled vegetables; corn on the cob. When she looked at Robbie's plate, all he had taken was a small piece of meat.

Parents across America can relate to Cathy's struggles and her frustration. We all want our children to have healthy diets, but we don't know how to teach them to eat well, for a whole host of reasons. When our children refuse foods, we label them as picky eaters, believing that they won't ever change their habits. If one day they say they don't like tomatoes, we think that means they will never like tomatoes. In addition to having finicky eaters, many of us find it hard to make time to cook. We ourselves may have grown up eating Lucky Charms for breakfast, hamburgers and fries for lunch, and Kraft macaroni and cheese for dinner; and so many families lead such busy lives that we have no time for sit-down family dinners. The problem is compounded by the fact that convenience foods are often the ones children like best. Although we know it's better to make food from scratch and serve our kids fresh, whole foods, it's just so much easier and so much less of a struggle to buy ready-made foods. It's no wonder that so many American children, like Robbie, end up with spectacularly unhealthy eating habits. But isn't that just how most kids are?

As a culture, we don't do a great job supporting healthy eating or parents who want to feed their kids well. Evidence suggests that in the last few decades American children's diets, notoriously poor, have actually been getting worse. Nearly 40 percent of the calories American kids consume are empty calories—sugar and fat—and half of those are from junk and fast food. People in our nation eat more packaged food than people from any other country—lots of it frozen pizza and snack foods. Processed foods are full of unhealthy ingredients such as high-fructose corn syrup, which pumps our bodies full of more glucose than we can process, and petroleum-based artificial food dyes, which require warning labels in European countries. This kind of diet may even negatively affect our brains: A study of nearly four thousand children in the

UK (where kids are susceptible to similar food temptations as our own) found that eating a fat, sugar, or processed-food diet at age three was directly linked to lower IQ at age eight.

Food manufacturers spend enormous amounts of money to market their products to even the youngest eaters. "Dora!" a two-year-old cries when she sees her favorite explorer (and sidekick Boots) on a Yoplait Kids yogurt package. The labels are brightly colored and appealing, and the foods are advertised directly to children on television and the Internet. Supermarkets often put these kid-friendly foods at a child's eye level so a child will be more likely to take them off the shelves and put them in the grocery cart when a parent's back is turned. There are even popular Cheerios board books for toddlers that teach them to recognize the cereal brand while learning how to count or helping monkeys juggle by putting the cereal in the right spaces.

It's not just what kids eat, but how much. In the past thirty years, portion sizes have grown astronomically: a cookie today is 700 percent bigger than it was in the 1970s. Our kids get used to eating more—one study shows young children eat more when they're given larger portions. American children today eat almost two hundred more calories daily than they did in 1977, and most of this increase comes from unhealthy foods. Though the processed and unhealthy foods in the school cafeteria or school vending machines have gotten a lot of blame for American children's poor diets, a recent study shows that children's dietary habits are more likely to be formed outside school, in their homes and neighborhoods. Their diets get even worse as they get older and have more opportunities to eat on their own.

The price our children pay for their poor eating habits is dear. Today about one out of three kids is overweight or obese, which puts them at risk for a range of serious health issues. Our children are the first in centuries who might live shorter lives than their parents as a direct result of childhood obesity. Even children who aren't necessarily overeating or who don't look obese are suffering ill effects from unhealthy eating.

# ARE WE GIVING CHILDREN TOO MANY CHOICES ABOUT WHAT TO EAT?

Not all of us eat unhealthily. In fact, many parts of our country have become a friendly place for people following any sort of healthy diet: vegan, vegetarian, gluten-free, paleo, raw food. This sort of eating is marked by *personal choice*. It's the right to "have it your way." We cherish the right to eat what we want to, when we want to. This is a good thing for people with religion-based dietary restrictions or food allergies, who are usually met with sympathy and offered alternatives. But while America's strength is to have so many choices and such an emphasis on personal freedom, it can also be our downfall (in the food department, anyway).

When personal choice is the guiding principle for how we eat, it (understandably) feels hypocritical and wrong to tell children what to eat. But when children feel entitled to choose what and when they eat, and when they subsequently refuse to eat what the family is eating, dinnertime can become an unpleasant power struggle. In a study aptly titled "Why Is This a Battle Every Night? Negotiating Food and Eating in American Dinnertime Interaction," Amy Paugh of James Madison University and Carolina Izquierdo of UCLA pored over some 250 hours of videotape of five dual-income middle-class families in Southern California. Dialogue after dialogue described families struggling—ranging from a nearly seven-minute negotiation between two kids and their parents over milk versus lemonade (in the end, one child drank the two mixed together), to a prolonged back-and-forth where a parent asked her son what he wanted to eat as he was rooting around in the fridge, but then rejected his repeated request for Jell-O while trying to get him to eat tuna or salmon.

By offering many options (and then disapproving of what our children say they want) we run the risk of *socializing our kids to fight with us over eating*. Children are left "with no clear message of which choice is the 'healthy' one," write Paugh and Izquierdo, and our authority as parents diminishes. "These interactions point to an uneasiness with which these middle-class American parents approach issues of authority and control," they continue. We hate to seem too authoritative, but we don't know what to do when we don't like what our kids choose to eat.

I n our country, feeding our kids is marked by extremes. Lots of us rely heavily on the processed "kids'" foods so readily available in our supermarkets and convenience stores. It's common for young kids to eat a separate repertoire of kids' foods or even eat separately from the adults. Parents, short of time and convinced their children are picky eaters who will reject healthy options, simultaneously despair of and accept their child's choices and limited palate. Parents themselves often have no healthy food tradition to draw from, and they tell themselves that picky eating is normal and there's not much they can do about it, because that's how most children they know eat. Parenting magazines assure us that it's normal for young kids to be finicky and that kids will self-regulate and get the nutrition they need if adults leave them alone.

On the other hand, our unhealthy food culture compels well-meaning parents to be extremely vigilant about the foods their kids are allowed to eat, belying that healthily relaxed attitude toward food that we want to teach our kids to have. Any conscientious parent who opens a newspaper or magazine or surfs the Internet can't help worrying about what she—and her children—eat.

Susan, who was always careful about what her son ate and faithfully followed a diet consisting of lots of bone broth and fermented foods (both thought to be good to promote healthy gut flora and good digestion), methodically picked grains of sugar, one by one, off a muffin at a birthday party, before allowing it into her toddler's hands. As a new mom, I too tried to keep my toddler from eating artificial dyes, refined sugar, or white flour. But when I offered Susan and her son a bag of dried oranges that my mother had made for us, she bit into one, asked if it was organic, and when I told her I wasn't sure, spat it out with a horrified expression and handed the bag back to me.

Other parents I knew were constantly frustrated about their children's picky eating. They traded recipes for ways to sneak vegetables into everything from spaghetti sauce to brownies, complained that their children ate only white foods, made grazing bars by putting out different foods (fruits, vegetables, crackers, and pretzels) in ice cube trays so their kids didn't have to stop playing but could go back and forth to the table, picking and choosing what to eat, and lamented how difficult it was to get children to eat well. They talked about food in terms of its components: Were their kids getting enough bites of protein, enough fiber? These American parents (Susan and myself included) have nothing but the best intentions. We want to help our children develop healthy habits and good attitudes toward food. For good reason: rather than growing out of their eating habits, the habits children establish at a young age form their eating patterns for the rest of their lives.

## THE JAPANESE WAY OF EATING

Before we moved to Japan, we visited Tokyo several times and stayed with a friend and her two boys. Yuri, vivacious and cheerful, was a gourmet cook who made Japanese dishes from scratch in her small kitchen. She made a miso soup daily from freshly grated dried bonito (a fish popular in Japan) and kelp stock, and even sent me back to the United States with my own tools (and a gigantic hunk of dried bonito) so I could make the same thing. Daniel, at just eighteen months, loved her soup so much he would silently toddle back to her holding out his empty bowl to her to ask for more.

But even though her meals were all from scratch, with produce and meat or fish bought fresh in small amounts every day at the local market, when Japanese mothers got together at Yuri's house they were very relaxed about what their kids ate for afternoon snack. Once a neighborhood mother kindly handed three-year-old Benjamin a piece of candy as she was passing it out to other kids. He'd never had candy before. I took it away before he'd notice what it was, much to her astonishment. Japanese friends were amused by my attempt to keep Benjamin from tasting ice cream, at least until he was older.

My vigilance didn't make a lot of sense to them. Of course, food was important for health, but it was also meant for pleasure. As long as meals were wholesome and healthy and freshly made—what did a piece of candy or some ice cream during the afternoon really matter? The idea of monitoring what children were eating to this degree seemed strange to my Japanese friends. One of my friends referred to me as a super-healthy eater—not exactly a compliment. It seemed to imply I was obsessed and controlling. But I in turn felt confused by their laxness. Didn't they know that sugar was addictive? Didn't they worry about artificial food dyes?

Yet I suspected there was something to learn from the Japanese way of eating. After all, Japan has the lowest obesity rate in the world (4 percent, tied with South Korea) and is famed for its population's health and longevity. After I moved to Japan, I discovered that the whole concept of food and what purpose it served seemed different from the very beginning, starting with how babies were taught to eat.

One muggy summer morning I biked over to our neighborhood community center to meet Akiko, a serene mother of a plump and active toddler named Takeru.

Takeru was born in the United States, and the young family had just moved back to Japan a few weeks before. Akiko got a lot of feeding advice from her American pediatrician. She was told to start him on rice cereal and jarred fruits or vegetables like apples, and to give vitamins and iron supplements. She was a little surprised by these recommendations. Japanese aren't typically in the habit of taking daily vitamins or nutritional supplements and almost never give them to their children, because they strongly believe they should get their nourishment from the food they eat.

Akiko decided to start her baby on solids the Japanese way instead, relying on advice from friends and family back home. She introduced him to food around six months, though she still primarily breast-fed him—her friends had advised her not to rush into solids. Good first foods for a baby were rice porridge (made from real rice, boiled with lots of water), small bits of fish, and little bits of boiled pumpkin.

It wasn't just important to feed a baby seasonally, it would have been impossible not to. In Japan, many vegetables and fruits aren't available in grocery stores at all unless they're in season. You can't buy grapes in the winter, so they become a delicacy to look forward to when they come out in late summer for a brief time. The same goes for Asian pears, asparagus, and Japanese broad beans.

Vegetables, like bamboo, burdock root, carrot, or potato, were often simmered in a light broth made of kelp or anchovies called *dashi*, so that babies could get used to this taste, characteristic of Japanese cuisine. As Takeru grew, dishes would include bits of other foods: *hijiki* (a kind of seaweed), *natto* (fermented soybeans), and udon noodles.

What baby ate was important. But just as important was the attitude toward feeding a child. Eating in Japan is a communal matter, even for the youngest set. Babies should *never* eat alone. "We should give them the pleasure of feeling like part of the family when they eat," Akiko told me. Even when her baby was too young to eat solids, Akiko had always kept him with her and her husband at mealtimes, and as he got older he ate together with them. This was just a cardinal rule.

To make babies feel even more like a part of the family, parents give them the same foods as everyone else. Now I realized why we hardly ever saw children's menus in Japanese restaurants. From the time babies start eating, they're eating the same things as adults. The food is more lightly seasoned, or otherwise modified for the baby's age, but other than that, the basic ingredients are the same. If parents are eating a beef and potato stew, a baby might eat the same foods, a bit blander, and cut in small pieces. If parents are eating teriyaki salmon, pickled vegetables, rice, and miso soup, a toddler would eat similar things in smaller portions.

Akiko made her baby separate dishes sometimes. His favorites, at age eleven months, were pasta tossed with soybean powder, and little fish balls in broth. He also loved fermented soybeans and tomatoes, and usually had a bowl of miso soup with tofu and spring onions at dinner. In Japan presentation always matters; gifts are carefully wrapped, food is presented beautifully. This applies even to food for the youngest children. When food is appealingly prepared and laid out, with an ideal mix of colors and textures, Japanese parents say a baby will be more likely to eat it.

When we said good-bye, Akiko gave me a parting gift: a popular Japanese book about feeding babies, called *Meals to Feed Your Baby That Will Also Nurture His Heart.* It outlined some of the basic principles of feeding young children: help children to feel gratitude for the food that nourishes them. Be equally attentive to nurturing your child's heart as well as his body. Pleasant meals will help a child's heart to grow abundant and rich.

## THREE PROPER MEALS A DAY

In Japan the thinking is to introduce young kids to a wide variety of tastes and textures, teach them to appreciate food, teach them never to waste, and get them used to *structured mealtimes* and mealtime behavior. Unlike the casualness that we might see in the United States, infant and toddler feeding is a more serious, concerted business in Japan, and it's the adults who decide on the menu and wield the spoons.

At the *yochien*, wasting food was so frowned upon that children were expected to eat everything. If they didn't, teachers would let parents know, so they could adjust the amounts of food they packed in their children's lunches accordingly, and achieve the right balance of vegetables, rice, bits of fish or meat, and cut-up fruit that was healthy but also appealing to the individual child. While at first I found it intrusive and almost unbelievable that teachers were telling me how to feed my child, I grew to appreciate their involvement. It was so much easier to get our children to eat healthily when it was expected of them in environments other than our own. Parents and teachers were a team, helping to raise children who learned to eat.

We were surprised by the fact that so many people ate three square meals. Portions overall were small, but each meal was balanced and filling. There was often salad at breakfast, in addition to savory foods or soups, broiled fish, rice, and fermented pickles. Lunch was always hot, usually not a cold sandwich. Dinner was more of the same. It was important to satisfy more than just one's hunger: there was as much attention paid to aesthetics and presentation as to nutrition.

Strollers in Japan didn't usually have cup or snack holders, because kids weren't snacking while being strolled around. Random grazing and snacking, overall, was frowned upon as bad manners—as it is in many countries throughout the world—because of the general societal insistence on eating etiquette: not eating while standing or walking; not grabbing food, but waiting to be served; and eating without comment or complaint what was put in front of you. When food was eaten, it was an occasion. Kids sat down, their hands were wiped with a wet towel, and then they could eat. (Though I did frequently see small bits of candy distributed to toddlers to keep them quiet during PTA meetings.)

There were never any snacks served at our children's *yochien* except for occasional, seasonal treats: a green bean just plucked from the school garden (which children helped tend every day), a freshly harvested, roasted sweet potato after the annual sweet potato–harvesting field trip, or tart *natsumikan* (Japanese tangerine) gelatin that the teachers made once a year in the winter from the schoolyard's fruit tree, when tangerines burst into season. At first I thought of this as awfully austere. But our kids looked forward to these treats because they were rare and presented as a special privilege.

A typical school day for our three-year-olds stretched from nine to two, with nothing to eat during those hours but their *obento* lunch, since their meals were supposed to be substantial enough to sustain them. In *yochien*, children were taught carefully how to get out their lunches, spread out their lunch mats, sit with classmates at meals, and take the time to enjoy eating together and talking with each other and with their teachers, who were also modeling the art of sitting down to enjoy a meal. They were taught to wait until everyone was ready to begin eating. After saying *itadakimasu* (thank you for this food), everyone could start. Then the children were expected to wait at their seats until everyone was done with the meal.

I was used to a more casual approach, and sometimes I thought this formality was too much. Charming for a meal or two here or there, but every single time people sat to eat? But when I saw even my own kids feel at home with what I thought looked like so much formality and cere- mony, my mind opened to the possibility that there was something to be learned from a slower, more ritualistic attitude toward food. They *liked* it. It made eating an event, something special. It signaled, I'm worth a good, sit-down meal. I realized that making each meal an event provides a different kind of nourishment.

In the United States, it's typical for elementary kids to get no more than twenty-five minutes to eat, total—including the time it takes to stand in line and use the bathroom. Nutrition experts worry that feeling rushed is contributing to our nation's obesity problem. On Daniel's first day of American school after five years away, he had to be specifically told that it was okay to start eating as soon as he got his own lunch out. He'd been waiting for everyone to be seated, and was confused about why some kids were already unwrapping their sandwiches or bags of chips or pretzels and digging in. He also had to learn to eat a lot faster. He'd been used to forty-minute lunches every day, which is the typical time allotted in Japanese schools.

## "BE GRATEFUL FOR YOUR FOOD"

As a twenty-one-year-old exchange student living in Japan for the first time, I first heard the words "Don't leave even a single grain of rice in your rice bowl" from my host family in a small village in central Japan. It was hard for me not to leave grains of rice in my own bowl, because I was so accustomed to the widespread American notion that healthy eating meant giving yourself permission not to have to clean your plate. But my host family was eating rice they'd harvested themselves from a paddy in their front yard. They knew how much time and effort growing and harvesting each grain of rice entailed.

While our collective national memory of widespread food insecurity ends with the Depression, for older adults in Asia and Europe, starvation, hardship, and rationing are real, living memories of World War II and the difficulties of the decade that followed. One of my friends, raised as a child in Japan but now living in the United States, told me it still hurts her heart to see waste on American plates.

In Japan it was considered a *moral good* to teach kids to eat properly, and it was also an adult's job to teach children the concept of gratitude for every bit of food on their plates. All children were taught to think of the animal who provided the meat, the farmer who grew the produce, the person who made and served the food. They were taught to always remember the interconnected cycle that made it possible for them to eat this meal. Japanese encouraged children to eat everything they were served, to try everything they were given. To achieve this, parents served many different kinds of foods. They held spoons up to little mouths. They spoke highly of kids who ate anything. They said, "Just try one bite," or "Just try half." They encouraged little children to finish: one common phrase was "Let's eat everything" (but at the same time, portions were far smaller than they tend to be in the United States). I went to PTA meetings where parents sat around and one by one expressed their hope that their children would be able to accomplish the elementary-school milestone of being able to eat everything in their school lunch.

Paying so much attention to what children ate, and that they ate fully, well, and without complaint—such an ingrained attitude in the culture was difficult for me to understand. Don't they worry about eating disorders or food hang-ups? I wondered. Don't they care about respecting their children's personal choices? Wasn't this too much coaxing and pressure?

# BEING ABLE TO EAT ANYTHING—
# NOT EATING ANYTHING YOU WANT

Back home, I'd known moms like Regina and Diane who talked and thought a lot about how their children ate too. When they would get together, their conversations focused around what their children preferred. But it was different from the Japanese parents. For Regina and Diane, their quest was to figure out what their children liked so they could accommodate them. They looked at their children's tastes as innate and accepted there were certain foods they wouldn't eat. They strived to work around this. They didn't have high expectations that their kids would try new things, because understanding and respecting their children's individual desires and wishes was the mark of a good parent.

In Japan, there's a different mindset around food: A parent's job isn't to figure out how to meet the challenge of keeping her child's diet reasonably healthy while letting him eat anything he wants to. A good parent helps her children *learn to eat anything*, and she believes they can and will become good eaters, through high expectations, patience (you don't give up trying a new food after just a few times), beautifully crafted meals (like Japanese bentos), and lots of exposure to new foods. Kids could never learn to eat widely if parents didn't give them the chance. The kids couldn't just say they couldn't eat this or that, and expect the parents to just stop serving it. In Japan, parents didn't worry as much about trampling on their children's personal choice or individual inclinations. They were confident they were doing their kids a favor by teaching them to eat well. Kids spoke positively about and ate a wide variety of foods, from octopus balls to sushi, from red bean desserts to seaweed salad. Scores of children dug into their meals with gusto, without complaint, and really seemed to enjoy eating.

Of course everyone had preferences, things they loved as well as things that "weren't their favorites" (as they were taught to politely refer to dishes they didn't care for). But overall, the kids I saw were anything but picky eaters, and when all your friends were like this, you couldn't help being affected by it too. Children even coaxed one another to try new things. Instead of viewing it as normal to have a lot of preferences about your food, our kids started to see it as normal, admirable, and a sign of maturity to be *willing to try anything*.

The way kids eat in Japan and America is so different in so many ways that it's a constant topic of conversation among our kids, who are fascinated by the differences. "In America, you can eat your dessert first if you want to," Daniel once remarked soon after we'd moved back from Japan. "Well, of course, no one cares—it's your own lunch," Benjamin responded.

In America, food is an expression of who you are as an individual. But Syra, an American mother living in Japan, understands the peace that can come with not having to make constant decisions that define you and your singular values about eating, and the freedom that comes from knowing you are able to enjoy eating just about anything: "The set lunches in Japan have always tickled me. You just order one of them, and that's it. Ordering a meal in America can take ten minutes sometimes! While I appreciate being able to get blue cheese dressing on the side when I go home, I also love saying, 'I'll have the grilled fish,' and having everything decided for me."

## FOOD EDUCATION

I grew to learn that what made it easier for parents to raise healthy eaters was the consistent support that they got from others. It wasn't just up to them.

*Shokuiku*—"food education"—is woven throughout school life for every Japanese child. The national curriculum is standardized, so most kids experience the same kind of food education. Our kids helped tend the rooftop garden as preschoolers at *yochien*. All children grow their own tomatoes, eggplants, and cucumbers in first grade. They study soybeans for weeks during one language unit in third grade (by the time both our boys went through third grade at the local public elementary school, our whole family was thoroughly familiar with just how soybeans become soy sauce, miso, tofu, and fermented soybeans).

By fifth and sixth grades, children are learning cooking basics at school too. I watched cooking class one summer morning, arriving at school just as they'd started preparing their meal. The kids, wearing bandannas on their heads and aprons, were sitting in groups of four or five. Each table was outfitted with a gas burner, two gleaming chef's knives, a pile of vegetables, raw eggs, and a few assorted small bowls.

Today's assignment was boiled eggs and warm vegetable salad with dressing. After brief words of encouragement from the teacher, the room exploded into activity as the children were let loose. They quickly divvied up their tasks—some kids were busily chopping, others cooking or measuring ingredients, others were at the sinks washing up utensils and dishes. The room echoed with lively conversation and activity. As I watched them enjoy themselves so thoroughly, I understood why one survey of Japanese students shows that home ec is their second most favorite class, after physical education.

Kids in Japan have longer school days and a longer school year than U.S. kids. They even go to school every other Saturday morning. But overall, they have fewer hours of actual academic instruction than American kids do. The longer school days mean that there is room for extras in the schedule that many U.S. schools have cut back on. All Japanese schools, whether public or private, can afford the time to nurture skills they believe are important for the whole child—such as physical education, art, music, and self-reliance skills such as cooking, how to do laundry, and how to sew. "Food education" makes it possible for parents not to have to worry they must monitor their children's eating in order to keep them healthy. A 2012 study of fifth-grade children in Canada found that the more often the kids helped to prepare and cook meals, the more likely they were to eat vegetables and fruits and to feel they were capable of making healthy food choices.

Elementary-school lunch is the most important part of Japanese "food education." Lunch is an actual class, part of the Japanese national curriculum. It's a class to teach children where food comes from, how to enjoy a meal, and how to serve others. At our school, as at all Japanese elementary schools, a different group of children were in charge of serving lunch to their classmates each week. They donned a special outfit, hat, and mask, and dished out rice, soup, vegetables, and entrées in the classroom. Lunch is supposed to be a relaxing time, to learn how to enjoy eating together. Most days, sixth-graders presented a program over loudspeakers piping into each room—they told a joke or riddle, sang songs, or played some music. After lunch, when kids cleaned everything up, they flattened their milk cartons carefully before recycling them, and stuck their straws, and straw wrappers, in other bins. The children themselves wiped down the tables, swept the floors, and returned the food trolleys to the kitchen. Then they ran outside to play.

One day I stopped by the school to meet the school nutritionist and the school nurse. A truck had just rumbled down the narrow alleyway to the school to deliver the daily ration of fresh produce for lunch. Today's lunch would be summer vegetable curry, soup, and homemade sponge cake for dessert. Ms. Yoshida, the nutritionist, plans all the meals each month according to season. She likes to mix up the menu with a few selections of ethnic meals—Korean fried rice, or Indian curry, or Italian spaghetti, for instance—but she emphasizes regional Japanese culture too and serves rice three times a week. She includes plenty of variety to keep kids interested in their meals.

Ms. Yoshida and Ms. Noda, the school nurse, help the children to understand that what they eat helps their bodies grow. They take this role seriously. "Elementary school is when kids are really forming healthy habits for life," Ms. Noda told me. The kids see the three cooks at the school every day, cutting and cooking the ingredients that will become meals for one hundred students and all the teachers, through big windows in the hallway on the first floor that open up into the kitchen. This makes an impression—as it's meant to. "I can't believe," Benjamin would tell me in genuine amazement, "that three people make lunch for so many people every day."

After we spoke, I went to watch the school cooks myself. They'd just cut up a mountain of eggplant for the summer curry. There was homemade fish stock for the soup, and one person was whipping up, by hand, a daunting amount of sponge-cake batter to put in the oven.

In keeping with the idea that too many choices actually make it harder for kids to learn to eat widely, children are not offered choices at lunch. Our kids got used to this quickly. They just tried what they were given for lunch every day. "You'd think you're not going to like something, like these little beans covered in glazed pellets of crispy little fish," Daniel recalls, "but it's really good when you try it." Kids have second helpings if there is food left over, but only if they've tried everything. If there isn't enough for everyone to get a second helping, the kids play rock-paper-scissors to determine who got the rest. This got raucous when there was a popular dish on the menu.

Not choosing makes the moments when you do choose feel extra special. The boys and their classmates looked forward to the time, once a year on the last day before summer vacation began, when they'd get to eat a "select sorbet" at school lunch. In fact, they were asked to place their order a month before: Would it be apple, orange, or pineapple? They discussed their choices with their classmates. They looked forward to it over the next few weeks. It was exciting, alluring, and special because it wasn't an everyday thing.

## SWEDEN: MAKING CHOICES HELPS YOU PRACTICE HOW TO MAKE THE RIGHT CHOICES

In Japan, deciding some things for your children is a sign of parental love, a sign you're thinking about them and what's good for them. In Sweden, it is the opposite: parents show their children love by allowing them to choose for themselves. But both countries manage to raise children who eat better than most Americans.

Swedes tell me that it's common for people in their country to stop by the store for fresh ingredients before coming home and cooking dinner. Meals are slow, and shorter work hours and a decent work-life balance (one of the best in the world) make it easier for most families to take the time to cook together, to talk about food together. Swedes are healthy, even in comparison with other Nordic people: at birth a female can be expected to live to eighty-four years, and only one person in ten is obese.

When Mikaela, a Swedish teenager, was growing up, her mother always told her, "You can have anything you want from the fridge" (which was filled with healthy and nourishing foods). In Sweden, Mikaela told me, feeding children is about encouraging their autonomy, not monitoring them or evaluating everything they want to eat. Instead, kids are given a lot of freedom about what they eat. Her mother never told her to eat this or that only for snack.

But here's the thing: She was given choices, *but she'd never make wrong choices.* "You can have whatever you'd want for breakfast, because you'd never choose the wrong thing," she explained further. There is so much wisdom passed on to children about what good choices are, in addition to those options generally being wholesome ones, that, she said, they learn how to make good choices.

Kids are given a lot of choice from the time they are young. But parents and teachers guide those choices and constantly explain to kids what a good choice is. In the day care where Mikaela worked, even very young toddlers are given choices of breads, meats, cheeses, and vegetables, and assemble their own sandwiches. "In general, we ask the kids a lot of questions about what they would like before they can even talk," she explained to me. The teachers put the food out on the table, and then ask the children, "Would you like this bread, or that kind? Would you like butter on it? Would you like to have ham, or cheese, and cucumber?" A child who can't speak can point to what he wants. Choice and self-responsibility—*within a boundary of what are good choices*—underlie everything. They want kids to feel empowered so there isn't coaxing, or judging, or labeling of the child's choice as good or bad. They ask a lot of questions of the children because they want the kids to learn how to ask these questions of themselves eventually: What would I like to eat right now; what would be good for my body? Mikaela enthused, "I think this is a great way for children to learn how to make simple decisions early on and also be patient and calm around the table."

Teaching toddlers how to sit properly at a table is important. Kids don't start eating until everyone is seated, and are encouraged to stay at the table until everyone is done eating. "We generally try to make a routine of sitting down and having a nice time around the table even when very young," she explained.

We know that here, if you told children they could have anything they wanted for breakfast, you might risk their going out of control and choosing something like a Pop-Tart, or ice cream. But Mikaela told me that in Sweden, no one she knew would dream of having something like that for breakfast (and their family probably wouldn't have food like Pop-Tarts in the house in the first place), "because it's not what you do." You give children freedom of choice, knowing that they are regulating themselves through their knowledge about what really are good choices, and through the feeling of autonomy that comes from knowing their choices have always been genuinely respected—not watched over or monitored. You can trust a child's wisdom if you know he has internalized commonsense wisdom, such as what makes a healthy breakfast.

Mikaela cooks nearly every day together with her family. They always have a long, leisurely meal. Her family eats out rarely, as seldom as twice a year. Health is important, but moderation and pleasure are too. One of her favorite traditions as a child was getting pocket change for *lördagsgodis*, or "Saturday candy." In Sweden, it's long been a tradition for children to go to buy candy at the store on Saturday mornings. Candy stores are bursting with colorful and appealing choices: Swedish fish, chocolates, licorices, sour candies. Kids enjoy their candy later in the day while watching TV with their family. This was a cozy family memory for Mikaela. Because kids look forward to *lördagsgodis* every week, Mikaela explained, they don't hoard or sneak sweets during the week. In fact, Swedish children don't generally eat candy during the week. "You'd never think of having candy on a Wednesday!" she told me with a laugh.

# SOUTH KOREA: VEGETABLES IN ABUNDANCE

South Koreans tie with Japanese in having the lowest obesity rates in the world (at 4 percent). In South Korea, eating is a family event just as it is in Japan and Sweden. South Koreans take great pride in creating homemade side dishes and enjoying them with friends and family, cooking every meal from scratch, and using beautiful serving ware to show colorful Korean cuisine at its best. My parents grow their own vegetables, including Korean peppers and gourds, keep a collection of extra-sharp knives on hand in the kitchen, and when we grew up, there were often potluck gatherings with other Korean immigrant families who lived nearby to share homemade dishes, porridges, or sautés.

Korean tables are laden with dishes such as acorn jelly, barbecued beef, rice-cake soups, kimchi stews, and multiple tiny dishes of Buddhist-style mountain vegetables, followed by fruit, honey cakes, cinnamon tea, and bean cakes for dessert. Korean food is dizzyingly diverse and plentiful. It is distinctive for the variety of vegetables (fresh, pickled, or fermented) that accompany every meal.

Like most Korean children, Chaewon, a six-year-old from Seoul, has a notably healthy diet and active lifestyle. And like most Korean children I know, she loves to eat.

Her mother, Jinah, breast-fed Chaewon exclusively until she was six months old. Then Jinah started Chaewon on solid foods she made herself. "I fed her rice porridge—either with beef and broccoli, or with pumpkin, carrot, spinach, and shrimp," Jinah recalled. Jinah put a lot of different little things in Chaewon's porridge, because she wanted to get Chaewon started on recognizing different tastes by eating a variety of different things.

It must have worked. Now, at six years old, Chaewon's favorite dishes are broiled mackerel, bean-paste soup, bean sprouts, sautéed sesame leaves (a pungent-tasting leaf that is often used as a side dish or to make rice wraps), instant pickles made of chives, sautéed eggplants in soy sauce, little stir-fried anchovies, radish kimchi (spicy pickled radish, usually cut in cubes), and vegetable wraps (usually a big, plain piece of lettuce wrapped around rice and meat or fish, along with various pickles and condiments). In the winter, Chaewon likes to eat cabbage-wrapped pork. She doesn't complain about food, or whine about something she doesn't like. She's the rule, not the exception. There are so many kids like Chaewon that whenever I'm in South Korea I feel like I'm in a country of little gourmands.

Korean food is packed with flavor—especially the flavors of garlic, red pepper, and soy sauce and sesame oil. It's also very spicy. Like most Korean mothers, Jinah started her daughter on kimchi, the fiery Korean pickled cabbage, by first washing it in a bit of water. Some of the spice remains, just enough to get a toddler used to spicy food. This is how I learned to eat kimchi, and how our kids did too.

Snacks are simple. They might consist of an ear of corn or a roasted sweet potato. When we were young, my mother told my brothers and me that she walked to school with a hot potato in her pocket to keep her warm and, later on, enjoy as a snack. She told us this as she cooked her favorite childhood treats for us, or later for our children: plain broiled rice cakes dipped in soy sauce, or boiled potatoes mashed with butter and milk.

The most important principle of eating in Korea is to eat together as a family whenever possible, with everyone eating the same dishes, family style: a Korean dinner table is beautiful, with lots of small dishes, each filled with its own food, covering the table. My parents emphasized the importance of sitting down together at the table—even if my father got home too late from work to eat dinner with the rest of us, my mother tried to make sure we sat with him to keep him company. In Chaewon's family, dinner takes about an hour as they sit down and enjoy the food together. Most of the time, they have meat or a broiled fish or shrimp, at least eight different vegetable side dishes, and vegetable wraps along with rice and soup. After dinner, it's a Korean tradition to eat an abundant platter of fruit: Korean melon (a yellow melon with white flesh that has a mild flavor similar to a pear); watermelon in the summer; crisp apples, Asian pears, and persimmons in the fall.

Korean food is daunting to cook because of all the fresh ingredients and multiple side dishes. Although we love to eat Korean food (and I love to cook it), I rarely have the time to make a full-course meal on my own. This is where community comes into play. In Korea, where the cultural norm is to live near or with extended family, it's often the case someone can help cook a good meal, and relatives and friends will often make extra side dishes to trade with each other. If not, families do what they can to make sure they get a nourishing meal. (These days, I'm told, busy urban families who are far from relatives turn to home chef services offering regular deliveries of nutritious, home-cooked meals.) Whenever I visit my parents, a family friend will invariably drop by with a dish— sautéed seaweed salad, pumpkin porridge filled with rice dumplings, or a roasted salmon—especially made to welcome us and to help my parents feed us. For Koreans, food is an expression of love and care.

# FRANCE AND ITALY: TEACHING CHILDREN THAT FOOD IS SOMETHING TO ENJOY

The French, like the Japanese, take teaching children to enjoy food very seriously. "French parents believe that teaching your child to eat is as important as teaching them to read," Karen Le Billon, author of *French Kids Eat Everything*, explains.

Just as in Japan and other countries with traditional food cultures, there are specific times when French children eat, and the society as a whole frowns on random snacking. This French social stigma is so strong that snacking not only is privately discouraged—it's publicly warned against. TV snack ads appear with a banner that states, "For your health, avoid snacking between meals"—similar to warnings on cigarette cartons. Like me, Karen was a bit unmoored when she first moved abroad with her young children, who were two and four years old. "We had a much more permissive approach before moving to France, and the kids snacked more frequently," Karen explained. But her family soon came to appreciate how children aren't allowed to eat at any time and any place between meals, and even how the idea of giving kids personal choice over food is unheard of. Intriguingly, this structured approach to food actually enabled parents and children to avoid the power struggles and negotiations so common in our culture. "Kids don't get a choice about what to eat. But parents are not coercive," Karen continued. "Food is fun, and tasty, and a great source of pleasure." By teaching children to enjoy food, French parents teach them how to enjoy one of life's greatest pleasures. "The French believe that learning to eat is a form of citizenship training," she says. "It's about socializing, learning to share, and learning about national culture through food."

A parent's job of encouraging children to eat widely is much easier when you live in a country where eating a variety of foods is highly valued and there is ample time to share meals with others. The French workday accommodates leisurely meals: many stores shut for several hours at lunchtime, again around seven in the evening, and 90 percent of French kids eat together with their families at home. This is a country where, as one mom I know who raised her two daughters in France emphatically told me, "We *educate* our children about how to eat."

The way food is introduced to children in France helps shape their impressive palates. One study shows that French parents introduce their children to vegetables, for instance, in a strikingly different way than is recommended here. American parents are urged to space vegetables— or any new food we introduce—carefully apart (the "four-day rule") so we can spot signs of a food allergy. French parents routinely offer a greater variety of vegetables—typically six during the first month of weaning—and rotate them more frequently. Some mothers in the study made as many as twenty-seven changes in the vegetables they gave from day to day during the twenty-eight-day study. Their primary motivation in choosing their feeding strategies was *taste development*—not food allergies. This approach helps develop a mindset about food that everyone, from little children to adults, learns to hold dear: enjoying a very wide variety of delicious food is normal and expected.

Buttery *pain au chocolat* and a big bowl of café au lait for breakfast; steak au poivre with a side salad of white asparagus for lunch; cassoulet (a hearty meat and bean stew made with duck fat and pork sausage) for dinner. Americans don't think of French cooking—high as it is in butter, fat, meat, and white bread—as particularly healthy. But the French are slimmer and healthier than Americans. Despite their high-fat diet, they eat much smaller portions, pride themselves on moderation, and actually have lower rates of mortality from heart disease, greater longevity, and much lower obesity rates than do people in the United States. Since food is thought of as pleasurable, not guilt-inducing, individual foods aren't demonized. Learning to make choices in moderation is encouraged: although random grazing and snacking isn't condoned, individual foods or ingredients aren't treated as "bad." Karen told me, "They learn to treat treats as treats."

In France, social supports help provide nutritious school lunches to every child. When gourmet school lunches and food education are a mandatory part of school for everyone, learning how to partake in one of life's great pleasures isn't restricted to children of the elite, wealthy, or well educated. Freshly prepared three-course hot lunches are provided for six million children in the public school system, at a cost similar to our own, with subsidies for families who need financial support. In France, as in many other countries, the prevailing belief is that every child has the right to a high-quality, nutritious, and delicious lunch, and the quality of this lunch is the same for all (not the case in our own country, where income level often determines the quality of school lunch in a given location).

School lunch in France is a class in itself. Children get one and a half to two hours to eat a leisurely, three-course lunch, followed by recess. A typical menu for preschoolers in Versailles has children eating sliced radish and corn salad with vinaigrette dressing and black olive garnish, roasted guinea fowl, sautéed Provençal vegetables and wheat berries, Saint-Paulin cheese, vanilla flan, and wafers. The partnership between family and school means everyone is helping children hone the art of eating. Karen shared this quote from the website of a school near Paris:

> Mealtime is a particularly important moment in a child's day. Our responsibility is to provide children with healthy, balanced meals; to develop their sense of taste; to help children, complementing what they learn at home, to make good food choices without being influenced by trends, media, and marketing; and to teach them the relationship between eating habits and health. But above all else, we aim to enable children to spend joyful, convivial moments together, to learn a "savoir-vivre," to make time for communication, social exchange, and learning about society's rules—so that they can socialize and cultivate friendships.

The approach in Italian schools is similar. Jen, a Canadian mom of two, lived in Italy for several years when her children were younger. She vividly remembers how lunch was cooked on the premises every day at her children's Italian public school in a small town near Florence. She credits that experience with helping her children learn to eat well. "This school had no money for anything, but they had a cook, a kitchen, often a garden, and the kids got to pick the vegetables and bring them in," Jen recalled as we sat drinking coffee in a café in Cambridge, Massachusetts (her family lives in the United States now). "Sometimes they made minestrone with the cook. My son learned to eat real food there—cooked carrots, cooked peas, spinach, every day, made right there in the kitchen."

I asked Jen about children's meals, and she laughed at the idea that children would eat different foods than adults. "Kids have the opportunity to eat real food every day, with real flavors," she said. It's different in the United States, where she feels parents are trying too hard to meet children's needs—dietary and otherwise. "It's not their fault—we're being told we have to do all these complex things to provide for our kids, but don't realize how simple it can be," Jen continued. As she mulled over the fact that she never heard the term "picky eating" in Italy, she added, "I think that here, *kids learn to be suspicious of real food.*"

Jeannie Marshall, author of *The Simple Art of Feeding Kids: What Italy Taught Me About Why Children Need Real Food*, argues that when we raise kids to think of food as pleasure, we shape children's eating habits for better. "In Canada and the U.S., everyone has their own particular eating style (vegetarian, vegan, low-carb, gluten intolerant, lactose intolerant, organic only, raw food . . .)," Marshall explained to me in an e-mail exchange. "Even if some of these styles are actually healthy, they're still a form of picky eating." The individualized diets also can be a barrier to the shared experience of eating and enjoying food together, she pointed out.

On the other hand, shared eating experiences can be a great influence on our kids—when they see other adults and children enjoying food with gusto, eating widely and well seems normal. Marshall told me about a trip their family took to the beach with several Italian families, when her son Nico was four. They booked a big table at a beachside restaurant. One of the adults looked over the menu, quickly consulted with the others at the table, and then started ordering seafood antipasto, octopus salad, grilled calamari, little whole sardines that had been flash-fried in olive oil and then given a squirt of lemon, anchovies fried in an egg and flour batter, mussels, spaghetti with clams, and more. Everyone oohed and aahed over the food when it came to the table. The children helped themselves eagerly too. "I was so surprised to see Nico picking up sardines by the tail and then popping them into his mouth," Marshall remembered. "This is a culture of non-picky eaters."

## LESSONS FROM HOME

Despite a global rise in obesity, countries like Japan, South Korea, Italy, France, and Sweden continue to draw on cultural traditions that promote eating a variety of fresh whole foods, cooking from scratch with seasonal ingredients, and taking the time to enjoy eating together—both at school and at home. Parents in these countries, whose children enjoy better health outcomes and far lower obesity rates (with the exception of Italy) than in the United States, rely on age-old wisdom and cultural habits that have worked well for generations, rather than paying attention to ever-changing fad diets, aggressive marketing by food manufacturers, and nutritional "experts," which is what we tend to do in America.

But good eating can't be left up only to parents. Schools play a big part in fostering healthy eating choices and healthy eating habits. In Korea, a child at school would be served spicy chicken, noodles, soup, seasoned vegetables, and a persimmon; in Japan, perhaps a summer noodle salad in sesame dressing, cabbage and tofu soup, pickled vegetables, and a plum for dessert. Although First Lady Michelle Obama has been using her public role to promote healthy eating and nutritious foods in America's schools, for most kids in America, school lunch actually *undermines* healthy eating habits and reinforces poor diets.

Together with the First Lady, school lunch reformers across the country are working to improve the food we serve our children. At Fletcher-Maynard Academy, a public elementary school in East Cambridge, one-third of the small recess yard is taken up by a garden. In one corner is a native woodland area, decorated with small rocks painted by the children. Another section has gigantic planters where Japanese eggplant and sweet potatoes are growing. Raised beds hold tangles of bean, berry, tomato, corn, and squash plants. The children are cultivating peanuts, millet, grapes, and giant sunflowers as well. Just outside the school cars whiz by, hardly noticeable in the quiet of the garden.

Cambridge is one of the first cities in the nation to successfully turn back obesity. Almost ten years ago, after noticing that kids were increasingly overweight and unfit, a team from the Cambridge Public Health Department, the Institute for Community Health, and the Cambridge Public Schools began analyzing weight and fitness levels of K–8 students and reporting the results to families. The numbers were so alarming that they received federal funding to begin a multipronged attack on the obesity epidemic, strategically involving children in school gardening as well as providing them with more fruits and vegetables every day, healthier school lunches, and increased physical fitness opportunities.

On the day I visited the school, Alice Gugelmann of CitySprouts, a Cambridge nonprofit bringing sustainable school gardens to Cambridge public schools, was showing a group of excited, bouncy first-graders a corn plant and asking them what continent it originally came from. They took turns pulling the hard kernels off the cob. Then they lined up one by one to mill the corn. It came out in soft, downy flakes. Some of the children asked to taste it raw, and they walked away with it cupped in their hands. Their teacher passed chives out to each child—which some ate raw (the kids grew fond of chives as they watched them growing), and some waited for the polenta they were making with Alice's help, which was bubbling away in a pot on a little burner, to be passed out to each of them on a Popsicle stick. When the polenta was cooked, the children sat on a stone wall, swinging their legs and savoring their Popsicle sticks of polenta.

The first-grade teacher told me that improvements in school food—the school district has a multiyear grant to provide fresh fruits and vegetables to all the kids for snack and lunch—were even more effective because they were introduced to the kids along with the hands-on experiences they were having in the garden. This is a "very powerful combination," she said. "Their preferences have changed." Thanks to Cambridge's integrated program, rather than having no idea where their fruits and vegetables came from, the kids now recognize what they're eating in the cafeteria.

Researchers who have followed elementary and middle school students have found that parents of students in highly developed school food programs are more likely to say that school has changed their children's knowledge about healthy food choices, their preferences, and their eating habits. Children who have an opportunity to garden and talk about food are more likely to prefer fruits and vegetables, particularly green leafy vegetables, and eat nearly one and a half servings more of produce. The key component seems to be the combination of gardening integrated into the classroom.

Josefine Wendel and Dawn Olcott, nutritionists with the Cambridge Public Health Department who work with the School Food Service program, argue that Cambridge schools have achieved many of their goals—and impressive results—through a multifaceted and, most important, *slow* approach to change.

One of their most effective strategies was to use taste tests to introduce new foods to children, especially fruits and vegetables. Presentation was key. The taste tests were presented as a privilege—something fun to look forward to. Even so, the team was surprised by how much the students *loved* lightly steamed fresh broccoli. "Kids liked the crunchiness, the bright green color, and that it wasn't overcooked," said Olcott, noting that broccoli is still a popular menu item six years later. They also used what marketers and behavioral economists call "choice theory" to help children make sound decisions and choices in the face of temptation. To level the playing field, they tell me, those of us who present food to kids must be the marketers for healthy eating.

Research shows that paying attention to how food is presented to children can affect their choice of what to buy and eat. Seventy percent more kids will eat fruit if someone merely suggests they do, and putting the fruit in a fruit bowl rather than on a stainless steel tray more than doubles fruit sales. Broccoli at the beginning of the line encourages children to choose it, while, interestingly, putting a salad bar in front of the cash register nearly triples sales of salad. Placing low-fat milk in the front of the cases and chocolate milk in the back makes a difference. Feeling in control is important to our kids: giving them a choice between carrots and celery is more effective at getting them to eat the vegetables than making them take only carrots. Giving children choices, while also making sure those choices are positioned in such a way as to encourage healthy eating, works. As a result, Cambridge kids are beating back obesity and living healthier lives.

. . .

ome might argue that the culture of eating in Japan is too regimented (the lengths to which some adults go to convince a child to
clear his plate absolutely aren't for me) and France is too intolerant (try
ordering vegetarian in a French restaurant and you'll see what I mean).
Besides, our American lives are too busy for the long sit-down lunches
of other cultures; it's difficult to find fresh ingredients because our homes
are not within walking distance of little markets that make it easy for
parents in other countries to pick up small amounts of fresh ingredients
to cook an appealing evening supper; and it's discouraging to go to all
that effort to feed children with limited palates. These are valid argu-
ments that I understand well. Raising kids is exhausting, and treating
food as more than just fuel to get kids through the day can feel like an
added unnecessary burden. Even though I love to cook, I often find myself feeling tired and wondering what to make for dinner at the end of a
long day.

But the world of pleasurable, healthy eating is attainable for our
children and for ourselves. Once you get into the habit of eating well,
you realize that it's really not harder than eating poorly. It's just as fast
to rinse off a cucumber, peel a banana, or wash a handful of spinach as it
is to open a bag of chips. Strategies like cooking earlier, batch cooking
on weekends, or exchanging meals with friends can save time. A family
meal can be twenty minutes, but those twenty minutes are important
because they're spent together.

The idea that our children are picky eaters might just be a cultural
norm and a marketing strategy that doesn't have to bind us. It's possible
for us teach our children to eat well. As a friend told me, we wouldn't
offer our child just one kind of book if we wanted him to become an
avid reader: we can learn how to do the same with food.

Our family is hardly the paragon of perfect eating—but now I've
seen that isn't what really matters: a balanced approach is what helps
best to foster a healthy relationship with food, for ourselves and for

our children. Food is more than fuel; it's meant to be enjoyed and appreciated as a holistic experience. We can help our kids learn how to eat well just as we'd teach them any other life skill, so that they can share in the wider world alongside us, and enjoy all that food has to offer.

# PART 2

# The Raising
of Children

# FOUR

# FEELING GOOD:
## Can Self-Esteem Be Harmful?

Abigail, a first-time mom living near Washington, D.C., had hired a teenage babysitter, Imogen, to watch seven-month-old baby Samantha one afternoon a week so she could start to get back into her job as a blogger for a local website. Baby Samantha had wispy red hair and bright blue eyes and loved to smile.

Abigail was a conscientious mother who had read all the right baby books and had learned a lot about child development. She prepared a long and detailed list for Imogen to tell her what she needed to know about taking care of Samantha. She wanted Imogen to know about the things Samantha liked: her favorite toys, how she liked to be held, what kinds of things might cajole her if she got fussy. And she told Imogen to be sure to be positive and to praise the baby often, saying "Good girl!" or "Great job!" when she reached for a toy. Even a baby wasn't too young for praise.

Like Abigail, lots of parents hear that the key to raising confident and successful children is to make sure kids feel positive about themselves. It's why we praise babies for doing things they're intrinsically motivated to do anyway, what lies behind the urge to make our child's homework look perfect, or the habit of uttering that ubiquitous phrase, "Good job!" In one poll, 85 percent of American parents believed that praising their children was necessary to make them feel smart.

It's true that self-esteem has positive effects. It gives children resilience, staves off depression, and helps them to achieve more and withstand negative peer pressure. People with high self-esteem often have the confidence to take the initiative in starting new projects, speaking up about injustice, and being appropriately assertive. No one wants to raise a child who will become an adult who's down on himself or feels a lack of confidence. After decades of raised public awareness about the importance of self-esteem, American kids are now among the most self-confident in the world. The average American person now sees himself as above average. But have we been confusing an overinflated sense of self with true self-esteem, the kind that will really help our kids go far in life?

We may think that raising self-esteem is important because it boosts resilience (the ability to pick yourself up after failure and to grow from challenges and struggles rather than to give up and be defeated by them). Resilience is so crucial that it's now understood to be (along with self-control and motivation) as important as IQ in determining success. But it is not something our kids are born with naturally; resilience is an "acquired trait" that parents cultivate in their kids. The truth is that as a culture we have been focusing on shoring up our kids' self-esteem in ways that actually undermine the development of their resilience.

Telling our kids how great they are or how wonderfully they are doing can deter them from experiencing the challenges that help build resilience. An overinflated sense of self isn't what leads to happier, more competent, more confident children. Instead, it deprives children of the chance to build up the genuine reserves of self-confidence they'd get through mastering difficult tasks on their own. Not only do kids become afraid of failure; they might even feel worse about themselves: kids who are praised for being "smart" feel less intelligent when they make mistakes. When their self-worth and very identity depends on being smart, they are at risk of being less able to persevere through challenges, like James, a bright preschooler from New York, who gets upset when he gets an answer wrong or stumbles while trying to read a challenging sentence. Kids like James, whose parents have been telling him how smart he is since before he was old enough to talk, take failure personally. For James, a wrong answer isn't just a wrong answer. It is a blow to his self-image.

Kathy, a fourth-grade teacher, often saw the effects of overpraise in her students. She remembered when one student's mom took her to task for not putting "enough positive praise and stars" on his work when she corrected it. While Kathy offered specific, concrete feedback ("You are remembering to carry your numbers!" or "Your neat work is easy to read") and alerted her students to their wrong answers by circling them, Robert's mother insisted that Kathy put a star on every problem he got correct so that "he would feel better about his efforts." Kathy told me, "I felt pressure to put artificial praise on his papers." She felt it gave Robert a false sense of his progress.

Julia, an infectiously enthusiastic music teacher in a Boston suburb, loves helping little ones develop a lifelong fondness for music. What she doesn't love is the way parents in her classes constantly praise their children. Julia told me that parents seem to think that heaping on praise helps improve children's self-esteem, no matter how well a child can really do. But Julia doesn't believe this. "Self-esteem doesn't come from other people telling you how wonderful you are," she insisted. "It comes from overcoming something, from having done hard work, from persisting." Julia worries about what kind of message we are really sending children with our indiscriminate praise. "In some cases," Julia said, "I could swear that the constant stream of praise has had the paradoxical effect of convincing a child, 'I must be pretty weak and useless; otherwise why does my parent spend so much energy trying to convince me of the opposite?'"

# WHY WE PRAISE OUR KIDS SO MUCH

Where did this idea come from: that we could actually make our kids feel good about themselves by praising them a lot (even when they hadn't done anything particularly praiseworthy)? It came from the idea that by doing things like this, we could raise their self-esteem, and help them to have better lives.

Self-esteem was first mentioned in 1890 by the psychologist William James, who defined it as something that grows when you achieve a goal that is important to you. But it wasn't until decades later that self-esteem became a dominant psychological concept, when theorists began to write about the link between parenting and education and self-esteem in the 1960s. In combination with a growing new image of American children as precious, fragile, and vulnerable, by the late 1980s the idea of self-esteem as a magic bullet that would prevent any number of psychological disorders, from depression to eating disorders, was firmly entrenched. For the first time ever, parents were being told that the way they parented—whether they praised their children or not—could make a crucial difference in how much self-esteem their kids had, and thus how successful and happy they would be.

On the surface, the campaign to raise our kids' self-esteem worked. Jean Twenge, a psychology professor at San Diego State University, collected data showing that self-esteem among children dramatically increased during the 1980s and 1990s. By the mid-1990s, Twenge argues, "it was everywhere." Self-esteem became a familiar theme in books, on talk shows, in schools, parenting literature, television shows for young kids, and even coloring books. Television shows like *Blue's Clues* tell children, "You sure are smart!" Popular toddler apps shower preverbal kids with praise for every flick of their finger on the screen.

In her book *Generation Me*, Twenge writes that this emphasis on self-esteem has profoundly impacted our youth, teaching small children to always put themselves first. For this generation, focusing on the individual is about "moving through the world beholden to few social rules and with the unshakable belief" in your own importance, writes Twenge. "We simply take it for granted that we should all feel good about ourselves, we are all special, and we all deserve to follow our dreams."

But the earliest proponents of raising self-esteem to ensure children have a successful, productive future actually believed this could be done best through a child-rearing style that employed clear rules and limits. Research backs this up: it is parents who allow children freedom and independence within clearly set guidelines, while treating children with respect and love (as opposed to being top-down dictators) who tend to raise confident adults. But self-esteem transformed into another notion: it became less about gaining confidence and resilience through goals you set and achieved, and more about our right to be happy and feel good no matter what.

The fact is that excessive self-esteem can do more harm than good. At the same time, parents became convinced that criticizing their children could harm them. People with high self-esteem don't always make good leaders; humility is more of a key trait than self-esteem. People with unstable high self-esteem—a combination of narcissism and high self-esteem—are more fragile and defensive, and prone to anger and aggression. Bullies often have high self-esteem (as did Adolf Hitler), and kids with high self-esteem who also have antisocial tendencies can twist their perceptions of themselves or other children. Addicted to feeling good, they achieve this by belittling others. Self-esteem isn't a panacea for everything. One scholar even pointed out that people with low self-esteem actually "may do better, because they often try harder."

In an article in the *Los Angeles Times* in 2005, psychologist Roy Baumeister, once a forceful and outspoken champion of fostering children's self-esteem, regretted his earlier assertions. His review of the data brought him to a totally different conclusion. "After all these years, I'm sorry to say, my recommendation is this: Forget about self-esteem and concentrate more on self-control and self-discipline. Recent work suggests this would be good for the individual and good for society—and might even be able to fill some of those promises that self-esteem once made but could not keep."

## DOESN'T EVERYONE CARE ABOUT SELF-ESTEEM?

In contrast to the United States, in most other countries the debate over self-esteem never happened. Some researchers even think that the idea of self-esteem—especially as something that adults are responsible for cultivating in their kids—hardly exists in other parts of the world.

A comparative study of Euro-American and Taiwanese mothers' beliefs about self-esteem found that their different cultural beliefs led them to hold very different goals for their kids. Bathed as they were in a wash of parenting books, media, and television that constantly emphasized the importance of self-esteem, the Euro-American mothers in the study—especially the middle-class mothers—believed it was a crucial thing to foster. Self-maximization (reaching one's potential) and self-confidence were qualities they wished to cultivate in their children. These mothers valued abundant praise and encouragement, discussing their children's feelings and emotional states with them, showing their kids physical affection, and providing their children with opportunities to experience success. They dreamed of unlimited opportunities and capabilities for their kids.

By contrast, the Taiwanese families studied did not value self-esteem or self-affirmation at all. Instead, they focused on things like "values" and "morals." Parents and grandparents (in Taiwan, both generations often help raise young children) were focused on "an explicitly self-critical stance that was part of a larger concern with children's moral education." To them what was important was "allowing children to grow naturally, assiduously correcting their misdeeds," and "watching them to figure out what kind of personality they have." Adults saw themselves as moral guides and guardians, providing children with stories grounded in real life to help teach them the right way to do things, but they also saw their children as natural beings. Like American mothers, they looked at children as individuals. But unlike their American counterparts, they were more interested in looking to their individuality to help guide them in disciplining them.

In a culture like ours, speaking well of things you're proud of is completely expected. It's seen as a positive sign of confidence. "Get your parents—they're going to want to see what I made!" one boy excitedly told our kids after he had created something on our computer on a play-date. This boy had a good self-image; he was certain that people would be interested in seeing what he'd accomplished. When Melissa, a school art teacher in California, complimented a mother on her child, the mother gushed enthusiastically, "Yes, isn't he great? And just wait until my twins start kindergarten next year—you're going to love them too!"

This kind of candor can be refreshingly direct. You know where the other person stands and what they think. There's no false modesty here.

In Japan, in contrast, speaking well about yourself like this is considered bad manners. We laughed when an American boy overheard us speaking Japanese and asked us how to say "I'm awesome!" in Japanese. It was a very understandable question for an American child to ask. But there's no Japanese translation, because it isn't something a Japanese child would ever say.

In Japan children learn from a very young age that modesty is a virtue. Asking Japanese children to talk about what they are good at can be like pulling teeth. The kids I know are animated and well-spoken, but I rarely heard them talk about the things they thought they were really good at—unless they truly were good at them. In Japan, children typically do not participate in a bunch of different extracurricular activities. Instead they usually concentrate on one thing, like piano or soccer. Their thinking is: It takes commitment to achieve a level of mastery that is praiseworthy.

My friend Riko was an accomplished classical guitarist—what was equally remarkable was that she hadn't learned guitar until she was in her thirties. But she would never say anything about her abilities that wasn't self-effacing, because she considered herself to be still learning, not quite there. If I'd taken her literally I would have thought she was a terrible musician. Much of the time, with the Japanese people I knew, I had to get used to reading between the lines. They knew who they were and what they could do. They didn't feel a need to share their accomplishments with others for validation or recognition.

In several other cultures, children grow up learning that to be humble is a virtue. Rebecca, who grew up in Sweden, where the concept of *lagom*, or "just enough," prevails, recalls how safe it felt for her to be a child there because you did not have to be special—you could safely blend in and not feel singled out. "In general, I think Swedes put more emphasis on being a good person—doing the right thing, being good stewards of the environment—over making a name for oneself," she told me.

Elin, a Swedish teenager who recently spent a year in the United States, told me that self-satisfaction and positive self-regard, in Sweden, come from being ordinary, not from excelling. She told me that her American host father said that when he was young, his father had encouraged him to dream big by saying, "You can be whatever you want to be!" Elin thought this was such a surprising thing to say to a child. "My parents wouldn't typically say that," she told me. "You reach for something that makes sense. You try hard, but there's no urging to go for the extreme. Having a good-enough life—just enough travel, toys, food—is all you need—just good enough so that you and your kids have it well, without going over the top."

In Germany there is a similar thinking about what kind of encouragement will best help a child. Gerhild, a German mother who has been living in the United States for the past several years, told me that one thing that really jumped out at her was how "American parents are so friendly to their children." Gerhild was talking about the specific child-directed praise, proactive encouragement, and cheerful verbal engagement that it's so common to see. She noticed a lot of making people feel good, not wanting to hurt feelings, giving lots of choices and alternatives and speaking gingerly, not frankly. In Germany, a child wouldn't be given so many options, so many choices, and catered to in such a person-alized way, Gerhild said. "We aren't afraid to say *nein.*"

In the United States, it is controversial for teachers to use red ink to critique their students' work. Can you criticize children in Germany? "Definitely. We are very willing to hurt children's feelings," she said, laughing. A kind and loving mother, Gerhild clarified, "What I experience here is that children get compliments for poor work. If they do a craft, even if it's not really very nicely done, they will still get a compliment—an overwhelming compliment." In Germany, by contrast, adults believe that children are strong enough to hear accurate feedback—the good and the bad. Constructive feedback won't crush them. It will help them do better next time. Praise, when it does come, is well earned.

There is some confusing cross-cultural data on self-esteem, self-confidence, and performance. The cultural differences between the United States and countries like Japan, Sweden, and Germany help explain this confusion: How would you accurately measure self-confidence when in some places, it's not something you ever talk about or display—it's just the way you are?

What we do know is this: American mothers tend to overestimate their children's abilities, while Chinese and Japanese mothers tend to underestimate them. American children fall into the same trap. Seventy percent of American college freshmen reported that their academic ability was above average or in the top 10 percent.

A Brookings Institution report found that American eighth-graders are more confident about their math skills than their peers in other nations, even though their scores are lower. Thirty-nine percent of American eighth-graders felt they did "well" at math, even though the least confident Singaporean student outperformed the most confident American one. In fact, the ten countries in which students reported the least self-confidence about math skills had the highest scores—countries such as Japan, where only 4 percent feel as though they usually do well in math.

This aligns with other research on cultural learning attitudes.

Overall, American students feel more self-satisfaction with how they are doing academically, while Asian students evaluate themselves by assessing where they can continue to improve. U.S. schools often emphasize feeling good about yourself, "believing in yourself," teaching that's relevant to real life, and enjoyment. This is something many parents want for their kids too. But "happiness is not everything," the report concluded, "and by simply producing contented students, good results do not automatically follow." Yet the notion that students who feel good about themselves will achieve more is alluring.

Research shows that self-esteem and achievement are correlated. But there are no findings that prove causation. Instead, the self-esteem could be a result of the good feelings that come from doing well. One Norwegian study, looking at six hundred third- and sixth-graders and then again one and a half years later, found that while students who did well in school had higher self-esteem, the following year—due presumably to their achievement—the opposite was not true: initial high self-esteem did not lead to better academic results. High self-esteem in sixth grade actually predicted lower academic achievement in seventh grade. Another study suggests that intentional attempts to raise self-esteem among low-performing students may have taken away their incentive to work harder. Without the incentive, students might have been normally inclined to try to work harder to feel better about themselves, but when they were made to feel good about themselves even without achievement, they lost their reason to make an effort.

It's not that making our children unhappy or taking their confidence down a notch or two would lead to better outcomes. But these results cast doubt on the beloved notion that happiness and feeling good about oneself are crucial to engage kids in their studies. The truth is that happiness, high confidence, and self-esteem don't automatically lead to achievement. Another truth is that successful achievement can lead to happiness and positive self-regard.

# WHY AREN'T AMERICAN CHILDREN HAPPIER?

Despite their high confidence levels, American children aren't even as happy as you would expect them to be after so much focus on their happiness. In *The Optimistic Child*, University of Pennsylvania psychologist Martin Seligman explains, "America has seen thirty years of a concerted effort to bolster the self-esteem of its kids. . . . But something striking has happened to the self-esteem of American children during the era of raising our children to feel good. They have never been more depressed." Rates of depression among young people are far greater than they were in generations past, more young people struggle in college or their first jobs because they expect things to come easily to them, and empathy among young people has declined as narcissism has risen.

It turns out that when parents and educators send children the message that their needs and their individual happiness and dreams are more important than other things, like being a compassionate, ethical, hardworking person, it makes them unhappy. People who have been told to put themselves and their needs first feel empty and discontented, and dissatisfied with themselves because they feel they deserve to be special rather than accepting and understanding the ways that our ordinariness connects us to other human beings.

There's a fine line between feeling good about yourself, and being narcissistic or entitled; between finding your own path through life, and trampling on others. There's ample evidence showing that our fulfilling and harmonious relationships with one another make us happy. If, as a child, you become used to being the center of attention and believe you deserve to be special, you compromise your ability to engage in the healthy give-and-take that human relationships require.

# HOW JAPANESE PARENTS BUILD SELF-ESTEEM

In Japan, we discovered, parents might not *talk* about self-esteem. But they want their kids to feel proud and competent, just as American parents do. They just have a different notion about what makes children feel good about themselves, gives them confidence, and motivates them.

Chiemi, a Japanese mom living in Tokyo whose two children often played with ours, told me that in Japan there's a popular saying, "Heavy work in youth makes for a quiet old age." In other words, working and putting forth effort and facing challenges while you are young will pay off throughout the rest of your life.

Chiemi took this to heart when raising her kids. She constantly encouraged her kids to grow through their own experience. She expected that they carry their own bags and be responsible for their own things, get themselves from place to place by themselves, and do errands that would help her, such as distributing flyers for an upcoming school event. While in our family David and I would often demonstrate our caring by doing things for our kids, Chiemi demonstrated her caring by having her kids do things for themselves.

One day, when her son Taka was seven, he wondered aloud why seawater is so salty. Chiemi could have had him look up the answer in a book, or even told him the answer herself, and been done in less than five minutes. But she thought the answer would have more meaning to him if he challenged himself. "I suggested that he boil seawater while we were staying at my parents' house," near the sea. Not only that—he carried the seawater himself in a small bucket on the half-mile walk back from the sea to their home. She thought that if Taka went through the entire experience all by himself, this would bring him wisdom as well as confidence. Once they got home, Taka boiled the water and saw that there was white residue at the bottom of the pot when the water boiled away. He tasted it and was thrilled to discover that it was actually salt. Seawater was salty because it had salt in it!

"In Japan, many people think that the effort you make is more important than the result," Chiemi explained to me carefully. "This is because we believe that making an effort, facing troubles, and overcoming them really help make you grow. I think this experience brought him much confidence that he can achieve if he thinks and puts forth the right kind of effort."

Japanese children are accustomed to being held to high standards— not always standards of individual achievement as we might assume, but of strength of character, or their ability to persistently put forth effort no matter what challenges come their way. Many Japanese parents believe that everything that will make for a successful life originates from this ability—an ability we would call resilience. How much effort you put into things shows that you aren't complacent, that you will keep trying, that you will try to grow, that you will be able to face things in life. These are the things that parents and teachers praise Japanese children for: their sincere effort and willingness to persevere.

All Japanese public elementary students learn to swim at school throughout the summer. At the start of summer, each elementary school holds an annual "pool opening" ceremony. At our school, after the adults give their speeches, a child from each grade stands up and gives a speech about his swimming goals for the upcoming summer. There are thirteen levels that children can aim for, with increasingly challenging requirements, and the kids usually spend their elementary school years moving up through the levels.

The first- and second-graders' goals are typically modest ones: "to get used to putting my face in the water," "to be able to swim across the pool and back." As they get older, the speeches invariably include a lot of frank and earnest reflection on what goals the student didn't meet last year, and how that felt. "Last year, I remember I couldn't get to the next level because I was too slow, and I remember how frustrated and disappointed I was. This year, I really want to try harder and make that goal.

I'm going to do my best!" a fifth-grade girl announced. A sixth-grade boy, tall and confident, said he was disappointed that he wasn't able to reach the highest level the year before, because he had missed the requirements (to swim fifty meters of freestyle in forty-five seconds, and the breaststroke in fifty seconds), sometimes by a few seconds. Here he stood, announcing in minute detail all his failures to 150 parents, teachers, and students. He ended with a declaration that he would try his best this year, followed by an earnest bow of appreciation to everyone for listening to his speech.

These kids do not worry about keeping up appearances. They're not at all afraid that focusing on what they can't do will tear down their confidence or make them look bad or incompetent.

It takes confidence to be able to face your shortcomings. The process of self-reflection is called *hansei*, and everyone—from Japanese elementary-school children to adults—does it. People tell me it reflects how much the Japanese value things like constant self-improvement, industriousness, and taking a frank look at your own shortcomings in order to improve yourself. It also reflects something else: an acceptance that life contains moments of difficulty and adversity as well as moments of contentment and ease. Cultural psychologists have noted that one difference between East Asian cultures like Japan and our own is that, in East Asia, success and failure are viewed as part of a continuum, a natural and harmonious cycle and process that is just a part of life. This is a lesson children absorb too, and it makes it easier for them to accept successes and failures with equanimity and resilience.

Students reflect frequently, especially after a big event, like the annual sports day, or a field trip, or a class presentation, but also after more ordinary moments. On many class handouts our kids received at school there was a space to write down, "what I can do better next time; what I'll try to work harder on next time." Children are taught the habit of *always remaining attentive to how they can improve.* (By contrast, children in our country are typically asked to reflect on what they did well.)

Chie, a confident and outspoken Japanese college student from Hokkaido, Japan's northernmost island, explained to me why it is so common—and not a sign of poor self-image or poor confidence the way we might misconstrue it—to talk about your mistakes and failures. The point of this is not just to make kids think, "What did we do wrong?" though, to a Westerner's eyes, it can sometimes feel like there is too much of this. They also reflect on and analyze what they might have done right—what might have helped them to succeed. *Hansei* lets people look at themselves objectively, and gives them tools to look at the next goal. "In a lot of different ways, *hansei* helps us to move to a higher level," said Chie enthusiastically. It's about honing self-awareness, with the goal of your improved future self in mind.

"Strict" parenting is considered good in Japan. It shows a parent cares about holding a child to high enough standards that he will persevere. Unlike here, where a strict adult might convey a sense of menace or even seem somewhat punitive, in Japan being strict mostly just means having standards and expectations. The Japanese believe that knowing that someone believes in you enough to be strict toward you gives you confidence. "In Japan, if a parent isn't strict, then we feel like they have given up on us," Chie explained. "When someone is strict, it feels like they care about what we are doing, and how we are going to turn out." She says that she and her friends viewed it as motivating. "If my goal is limited, then there's nothing I long to reach. But to be able to continue to reach and stretch means there's no limit to how far we can go."

Jim Stigler, a professor of psychology at UCLA, noticed as a graduate student doing research in Japan in 1979 that Japanese teaching methods were very different from American ones. While in America it was usually the best kid who wrote his math problems on the board in front of the class, in Japan it was a child who was struggling who was invited to the board—and struggle he did, in front of the entire class. While this was surprising to Stigler (who expected the child to burst into tears at any moment), it's a common Japanese teaching technique to let students struggle, make mistakes, even if in front of everyone. Like Stigler, we would probably worry that a child singled out this way would feel terrible about himself, because we have a folk belief that sees struggle as something smart kids shouldn't have to do. In Japan and other Asian cultures, on the other hand, according to Stigler, struggle is an "opportunity"; this isn't a child being singled out and humiliated for having low ability. It's a child who is helping his whole class to learn. The child Stigler watched completed his problem with calm persistence.

This view of what it takes to succeed lies at the heart of many differences we ourselves saw in Japanese classrooms. While American teachers believe individual differences of ability are an "obstacle" to teaching well and should be met by tailoring to each student, "Japanese teachers view individual differences as a natural characteristic of a *group*," Stigler and his coauthor, James Hiebert, write in their book *The Teaching Gap*. These differences are a resource to be used, not something that gets in the way: seeing how other students learn or the mistakes they make in their individual approaches "allows students to compare them and construct connections among them." Teachers anticipate and actually plan on children making many mistakes, through which they will eventually collaboratively arrive at a deeper understanding of the problem. It would be considered wrong in Japan to tailor the curriculum to individual students, because it would be seen as "unfairly limiting and as prejudging what students are capable of learning." Every student should be given the same chance.

The underlying message kids get in Japan is that *they are stronger than we think*. Instead of striving to make sure their kids get individualized attention, Japanese parents praise their kids for trying hard, guide their children toward their own personal best, and have faith in their strengths and abilities. All children are considered capable of achieving great things, and on the whole, there is something to learn here: Not only do Japanese children report being happier in school than their counterparts in most other developed nations, but Japan does a much better job of bringing most of its children up to a high level of achievement than our own country does.

# HOW CULTURES VIEW
# HUMAN POTENTIAL

"My son is so gifted at math," Ellie, a mother of two young boys, told me as we sat in a playground watching our kids play. "I just don't understand why his teachers don't challenge him better." While Ellie was frustrated with her son's teachers, a Japanese mother might feel her son needed to try harder.

This isn't surprising. The way we view human potential—what our kids are capable of—is shaped by cultural views about effort versus talent. Some cultures believe ability to achieve is something that children are born with. Others believe that your innate talents are all but irrelevant and that achievement comes primarily from hard work. Studies show cultural differences in the way people view whether you can change things like your "intelligence" or "goodness" or not.

This cultural difference starts in childhood. One Yale study looked at Japanese and American children's beliefs about traits ranging from intelligence to eyesight. Japanese kids tended to hold a more optimistic belief overall that traits could genuinely change for the better through deliberate effort, instead of believing they were inborn and couldn't change much. American children were also optimistic about change being possible when they were very young, but as they got older, they seemed to absorb cultural messages that people were born as they were, and held the belief that effort could achieve superficial changes but wasn't able to alter who a person really was.

As a society we are attracted to innate traits, to talent, giftedness, and effortless achievements, because this fits in so well with the ideal of the individual genius, a more appealing idea than hours of practice, struggle, and hard work. In our country we hear parents talk about kids who have a knack for math, or are very artistic, or have a learning disability—both positive and negative traits—which are considered inborn, to be worked around/worked with, and are unique and individual.

It's not surprising that American psychologists and educators fervently embraced the IQ test, more than any other culture has. Alina Tugend, in her book *Better by Mistake*, attributes this to our cultural fondness for the idea that intelligence was something that could be measured, something that was fixed and unchanging.

But researchers are discovering that perseverance is one of the most important keys to success and achievement. In one study, Angela L. Duckworth of the University of Pennsylvania questioned why "some individuals accomplish more than others of equal intelligence." It was clear that other attributes besides raw intelligence made for success. Duckworth and her colleagues compiled a test called the Grit Scale and measured how undergraduates at the University of Pennsylvania and incoming cadets at West Point (among other subjects) rated themselves on qualities such as being persistent in pursuing goals, finishing what they started, overcoming setbacks to conquer an important challenge, and working diligently. Scoring high on the Grit Scale was associated with a high GPA, and the Grit Scale accurately predicted which West Point cadets made it through the rigorous summer program. The researchers concluded that "grit"—persistence and passion for goals—may be as important to achievement as talent.

In Japan, there is less labeling. In school, students aren't separated according to ability. There is no "gifted" education, and most learning-disabled children are integrated into the regular classroom. Instead of dividing kids up, there is a pervasive belief—reinforced in school—that it's less about what you're born with than what you do. Up to a certain point *everyone* is capable of cultivating skills, even in art or music. So, while in America art and music are looked at as things for all kids to dabble in, but serious training or cultivation is reserved for kids who show talent, in East Asia there is a common belief that anyone can and should be able to achieve a certain degree of mastery in a variety of areas, whether it be mathematics, art, music, or physical education. It just takes effort.

Japanese schools make this possible by providing ample time, from preschool on, for kids to practice a lot of gym, art, music, and other activities. Contrary to the stereotype most of us probably hold of Asian schooling, Japanese elementary schools are surprisingly boisterous places (with noise and laughter at levels often well above those tolerated in Western schools), full of lively groups of children engaging in many different activities together. The result is not just well-rounded exposure but finely honed skills in areas as disparate as sketching, jumping rope, developing pitch and singing in tune, playing the piano and recorder, even using a paper cutter.

A qualitative study of world-class achievers (in fields as varied as music, sports, neurology, math, chess, and sculpting) showed that very few of them had been regarded as prodigies by the adults in their lives. Accomplishment came from hard work and long hours, day after day, for ten to fifteen years. A body of recent research confirms that genius-level prowess at anything comes from hours and hours of dedicated, concentrated practice that helps build myelin connections in the brain.

A belief in effort rather than talent pays off, because developing skills *does* take time. There's just no other way around it, no magical shortcut.

We were always struck in Japan by the children's performances in school plays or concerts. Children as young as age three were expected to memorize long dialogues and lyrics, perform before others, and sing in perfect tune, and they usually lived up to these expectations in ways I, and other Western parents, found remarkable. In fact, at first we were a little unnerved. We thought young kids needed to have more room for self-expression.

But we grew to realize high performance was within reach of anyone if you thought about it as the result of practice and effort. Self-expression was good, but so was giving children a chance to discover the excellence that they were capable of. The reason they performed so well was that everyone not only believed it to be possible, but recognized that mastering anything takes time and diligent practice. Children practiced for school concerts for hours a week, sometimes even before school.

Teachers and parents were certain that practice would lead to proficiency, and conveyed their confidence in children's ability to rise to the occasion by taking the performances so seriously.

Those hours of practice, the results achieved through sincere, serious effort: these are the kinds of things that parents in countries like Japan think that self-esteem comes from. It's no surprise that in a Japanese national survey, "effort" was chosen as the most well-liked word, followed by "perseverance." When you work hard, overcome challenges, and achieve something, this gives you the confidence that you have the ability to shape your future. These are the kinds of experiences that make you resilient.

Elena, a middle school math teacher in Washington, would agree. Elena was born in Latvia, raised and educated in Lithuania, and came to this country when she was thirty years old with her husband and two daughters; they were political refugees. Where she was raised, people believed human potential was limited only by how much (or little) you were willing to work. Self-esteem came from hard work and nothing else. It was shocking for her to come here and find American parents who focused on their children's self-esteem itself rather than setting high goals for their children.

An experienced teacher, Elena believes children aren't fragile; in fact, they learn new things fast and adapt to new situations better than adults. But, she told me, "We can *make* them fragile by not teaching them how to overcome difficulties and struggle in order to achieve great results. We have to lead them through this process."

She never lets her students think of themselves as incapable or stupid at math. Anyone can become good at math if they work at it. "I teach them it's okay to make mistakes, because math is difficult and there's always more to learn. Even if you're not born great at math, you can work hard to be *good* at math. You can learn to overcome difficulties, learn from your mistakes, and be ready for new challenges."

Elena praises her students when they have worked hard and really accomplished something. Once she asked her geometry class students to solve a difficult problem for extra credit. One student stayed after school to work on the challenge. Elena remembers how after ten minutes of struggling on it, he ran up to her screaming, "I found the formula!" He was so excited he could hardly talk.

"Congratulations—you did it!" Elena shared his joy. After that hard work and struggle, he had a genuinely well-earned feeling of true self-esteem and confidence—what every parent wants for her child.

What a lot of parents don't see is what happens when we boost our kids too much. If we let "making kids feel good" be our guiding principle, we are buying short-term goodwill at the expense of their future resilience.

"I see people terrified of having their kids make mistakes or get hurt physically or emotionally or fail," says Kelly Webster, cofounder of the Island School, a private school in Bainbridge Island, Washington. "But, if you don't mess up, how do you ever learn how to fix anything?" Webster tries to reassure parents who worry their children might not fit in socially or might get physically hurt. She reminds them that life is littered with obstacles and difficulties. "You can go ahead of your child and move the rocks and get the fallen branches off and chase the bumblebees away. But at some point you won't be there anymore. So our school philosophy was, let's teach children to move the rocks. Or go over the branches. Or avoid the bumblebees. Let's teach them to do it by themselves." Webster worries that if we don't let our kids mess up they can't then overcome challenges or setbacks. "Try, try, and try—that's how we learn. Kids feel very proud when they solve a problem, but I don't think we let children solve problems anymore."

Webster told me a parable she'd heard about a school class that had a chrysalis in the classroom. The kids were watching the butterfly emerge. "If you ever have seen a butterfly come out, it's a very difficult procedure. It's painful. They have to struggle." Thinking the butterfly needed help, one child cut the little string so the butterfly could get out more quickly, but then the butterfly died. The teacher explained to the small, sad student that the struggle is necessary: it develops the wings so that when the butterfly finally emerges, it can fly. "We have to let our children struggle, because it's just how you learn, how you get strength, how you become an individual," Webster told me.

She worries that in our country, we've become afraid to let kids struggle. That means we're raising children who don't trust themselves. "The message we want to give our kids is: I know you can do it," says Webster. "Because if we don't, we're actually giving them another message: 'I don't really think you can do this, so I'm going to do it for you.'"

## GROWTH MINDSET GROWS POTENTIAL

The mindset you see in Japan and other effort-oriented cultures is something that Carol Dweck, a Stanford psychology professor, has researched for decades. Dweck, who is also the author of a popular book, *Mindset: The New Psychology of Success*, is well-known for her robust and compelling studies on the detrimental effects of praise and her research on children's resilience. Her work highlights how American parents' good intentions might be undermining our children's ability to achieve.

Dweck has defined two different kinds of mindsets: a *fixed* mindset and a *growth* mindset. People who have a fixed mindset have a fixed idea of traits they have—intelligence, for example, or even lovability. They view these as something stable and unchangeable. A child who is told he is very smart, for instance, will begin to define himself through this label.

While this sounds like it would be a good thing, even so-called positive labels can be harmful when they give a child a fixed view of himself, since it is a view he must protect. That child may become worried about taking risks or risking failure, because being smart is part of his self-identity. Why attempt something that could reveal you to others as less smart and threaten your sense of self? This fear makes people shy away from seeming too earnest or making too much of an effort in the face of challenge. But since our culture tends to downplay effort and practice as the building blocks of mastery, kids and adults can get anxious and depressed and lose motivation when they have to try not to look like they're trying too hard. Failure would be just too large a threat to their fragile self-esteem.

Dweck is certain that an effort-first, or growth, mindset motivates you to face challenges. A child who has growth mindset may have been praised and encouraged as well, but more for the qualities that are within her control— qualities of growth—such as the ability to work hard, to try hard, to practice, and to face setbacks and to give things another try. This is why the kids at the Japanese elementary-school pool-opening ceremony could stand up and publicly list their failures. Not only is there nothing to hide, it's actually seen as a positive thing to be able to assess yourself so you can continue to grow. A growth mindset helps a child see new challenges as opportunities to improve and learn, not as loaded with the threat of judgment, or as losing an aspect of her identity. A child with a growth mindset, who does not see her qualities as fixed or as the most important thing about herself, can develop the capability to view failure as a route to success. It's a recognition that success comes from trying hard, not from taking the easy road or waiting for things to fall in our laps.

In one of Dweck's most well-known studies, she set out to see whether the motivation of four hundred fifth-grade students to face future challenges could be altered by the kind of praise they heard. All the children were given nonverbal IQ puzzles that weren't too hard so they'd all do pretty well on them. After the test, some of the children were pulled aside and praised for their intelligence. "Wow, you got a really good score. You must be really smart at this." Others were praised for their effort: "Wow, you got a really good score. You must have worked really hard."

Both groups were then given the chance to try a new, more challenging test. Those in the first group—the ones who had been praised for having a special gift (intelligence)—tended to reject the chance to try the harder test. They had a fixed mindset, and didn't want to try something that would potentially expose their limitations. In contrast, 90 percent of the kids in the second group wanted to take the second challenge! Having been praised for the effort they put in, in a way that fostered growth mindset, they viewed challenge differently.

The way they'd been spoken to even affected how they felt about taking harder tests. The children primed with fixed mindsets didn't find them fun, and thought the difficulties they encountered showed that they were not smart. The struggle deflated them. Meanwhile, the "effort kids" thought the difficulties meant they should keep trying. They didn't look at their effortful performance as failure. They focused on the gratification that comes from hard work. Their motivation came from within: It was intrinsic motivation, not dependent on how others labeled them. It made the difference between feeling internal mastery or helplessness.

By phone, Dweck told me she personally has memories of a very different kind of upbringing from that of children today: "We were expected to be self-sufficient. Doing homework was our job. It was our responsibility. We scheduled our own play, and if we took music lessons we practiced, and the parents were there for guiding and as resources, but their lives were their lives and our lives were separate. Overlapping, but separate."

Now, Dweck says, there is a sense in America, especially among some parents, that you can control things. "You have these really high-achieving parents who feel like, okay, I can control everything, and I can make my child perfect." A simple formula developed for how you make your child perfect, and it sank in: Making children feel good = making children confident.

Many parents have told Dweck that they saw their kids as fragile, believing that meant they needed more praise and even less honest feedback. "There is an idea now that a good parent is always telling their children how smart and talented and wonderful they are," said Dweck. "Parents take too much responsibility and try to ensure their child never has a moment of a bad feeling, of inconvenience, of failure to get what they want."

Instead, Dweck's research shows, a good parent doesn't undermine her child's motivation through empty praise and encouragement. She scaffolds her child's ability to face challenges and even accept failure as something that anyone can grow from.

It's a hard thing to change. But it's possible. "You don't have to be this harsh autocrat, but you don't have to be this overpraising, undercritiquing marshmallow," Dweck explained earnestly when I mentioned how challenging it sometimes feels to get the balance right. "You can set very high standards, give very honest feedback, in the context of loving and learning." If this makes your child anxious, then something is wrong. You're going too quickly. You can't change things drastically overnight. "You can't set the highest standards right away if you've been doing the overpraising. You have to start teaching children the joys of challenges and how their brains change and grow when they take on difficult tasks. They have to start enjoying the improvement that they experience when they put forth effort. And then in that context you start setting higher standards, once they enjoy learning and understand challenge."

Dweck doesn't say to abandon praise completely. Instead, she is urging us to find the sweet spot, a way to provide kids with the kind of feedback that will promote children's resilience, growth, and confidence. And the key to this is to be found, not in blanket praise, but in *which* behavior or traits we praise, and *how*. Parents and teachers have found that simply using phrases such as, "You can grow your intelligence," empowers kids to believe that getting better at something is within their reach. Any child can make the effort to grow his intelligence—if he believes it's possible, that it's not fixed, but something that can change through effort. If someone isn't good at something now, that doesn't mean he never will be. It just means he isn't, *yet*.

## NEVER-ENDING EFFORT

There is a lot for us to learn from a mindset where people trust that children genuinely thrive from the rewards that sincere effort brings.

We believe kids who feel good about themselves do well; others believe that doing well is what makes you feel good. So parents in other cultures encourage their kids to be diligent and make an effort, even if it's hard—especially if it's hard. This is the approach that research shows actually leads to resilience, persistence, and perseverance—the true building blocks for future success.

At the same time, I've seen the downside to the "effort first" mindset, when taken to an extreme, and it's this: it can be so relentless. It's clear that more children achieve well across the board when effort is valued: but what happens to those few—and there always are some—who fall behind? Talent is limited, but there's no limit to effort. When one can always do better, *there's no end point*. When everyone is held to the same high standards without much regard for individual situations and circumstances, it's inevitable some of us simply won't be able to meet them.

In a country like Japan, special needs, exceptional situations, or temporary hardships are rarely a sufficient excuse for not being able to try as hard as other people, other students, other parents: an ideal that can be exhausting. In America, even if a child can't do well at something, we are encouraged to seek out and validate the things he *does* have a knack for, and help him to form a view of himself based on his unique strengths. So while it's tempting to idealize Japan's emphasis on effort, and easy to find the shortcomings in the American tendency to overpraise and underexpect, I've come to realize that both cultures have their benefits, and finding this sweet spot may be the best way to motivate our kids.

I understand how overpraising my children can make them focus on pleasing me rather than the joy of accomplishing something for themselves, can harm their self-confidence, and can prevent them from feeling how good it is to meet and overcome challenges, while warm parenting and paying attention to the effort they put into a project provides the right kind of boost. Our years in Japan, where we watched children become confident through meeting challenges big and small that I would never have thought to ask of my own kids before, opened my eyes to the valuable lessons we can learn from cultures that let kids know that everyone struggles and makes mistakes, but that's how they become better.

# FIVE

# HOVERPARENTING:

## How Can We Foster Self-Control?

he kids in Megan's fourth-grade classroom were excited. They were about to present their final research projects for the year. Each student chose a topic, read a nonfiction book about that topic, compiled a binder of notes and research, and created a display board with information to share with the other kids. This was a challenging project with lots of dimensions. Megan, an experienced teacher, knew these presentations would be a great learning opportunity for her students. She looked forward to seeing the results.

One of Megan's students was a little boy named Aidan. His mother, Heather, always helped him out: she typed his assignments for him, kept on top of his homework, and came to school frequently to discuss Aidan's progress.

Aidan's presentation, on tornadoes, wasn't very good. He was stiff and spoke in a monotone, even though this was a topic he'd chosen and loved. The rest of the class looked as bored as he did. Usually loud and boisterous, Aidan mumbled through his explanations about twisters.

Though he wasn't taking medication, he spoke as though he were on sedatives.

After the presentations were over, Megan asked the children to write about what they had learned from the multiweek project. She felt disheartened when she read Aidan's reflection. Aidan wrote, "Well, my mom did a lot of the work, so not as much as if I had done it by myself." Megan was struck by his honesty and perceptiveness. Aidan was unable to have the chance to work hard and experience his own learning because his mother had taken over his project.

Throughout the thirteen years she has been teaching elementary school in the United States, Megan has seen this kind of thing often: parents stepping in with the intention of helping their children do well and feel good about themselves. The result is projects that are superficially well done but ultimately meaningless. "The kids don't even know how to talk about them! They're embarrassed," Megan told me. "That is one thing I wish all parents knew. Kids *know* when they don't do their own work, and they lose pride over it when the class is sharing."

Most of us probably think that good parenting and involved parenting are the same thing. Research confirms that caring, involved parents have children who do better on a variety of measures—they are more apt to succeed in school, have fewer emotional problems, show more positive attitudes, and are less prone to teen alcohol use. Their self-esteem is higher and even their motivation is more sustained. The involvement looks different depending on the family—for some it may mean signing up for the PTA, for others it means packing a healthy lunch every day—but social scientists tell us that parental involvement is a good thing.

So if some involvement is good, more must be even better, right? We believe a good parent is watchful over her child's safety, his body, and his feelings, makes sure his disagreements with friends are resolved fairly and peacefully, reaches out to his teacher if he has a problem at school, helps him with homework, and always escorts him where he needs to go so he can stay completely safe.

But it turns out there is a fine line between involvement and codependency, between reasonable, supportive guidance and hoverparenting, between protecting our kids and impeding their ability to learn essential life skills.

In fact, the wrong kind of parental involvement can make our kids feel like they're not in control of their own lives. If we take over tasks our children could be doing, even if they are kind of stressful or a challenge, when we are over-involved and do not allow a child his own autonomy, we can make a child anxious by giving him the message that he isn't capable of doing things himself. We orient our children to ourselves, instead of to their own growth and accomplishments. Our over-involvement can also make it harder for our kids to cope with stress, or lead them to resist trying new things.

Being an involved parent begins early. We talk to our newborns, coo at them, make eye contact with them, name objects for them, and even show them flash cards, purportedly to stimulate brain development. We make sure our babies have lots of rattles, soft Lamaze toys, crib mobiles, and baby gyms. After all, experts tell us that babies need lots of stimulation and engagement, and long-term studies have shown that the more a parent responds to a baby's attempts at communication, the more advanced the child will be at language skills when he is older. Yet while being interactive with a baby has many benefits, well-meaning parents may inadvertently take all this engagement too far.

What most American parents don't realize is that too much involvement, though it comes from a sincerely loving place, can backfire even with babies. Jennifer Lansford, a research professor at Duke University's Center for Child and Family Policy, explains that over-involvement derails young children. "One of the most important things for parents when interacting with infants is to be sensitive to their cues," Lansford said. "Sometimes you will see American parents who are trying to be overly engaged with an infant—but it's actually distressing for the infant. They'll be fussing or crying or trying to break that eye contact, and that should be a signal to the parent to back off."

Lansford is concerned that when parents ignore babies' cues in infancy, the problem continues into childhood: "Children need to be able to engage with other children and entertain themselves. There is tremendous value in giving children more space."

## LETTING CHILDREN WORK IT OUT

When Benjamin and Daniel were toddlers, we lived in New York City. We spent many hours at a nearby playground. Like the other parents around me, I tried to be prepared and attentive. I would get up mid-conversation to help my boys negotiate and share if I sensed trouble was brewing; I parceled out snacks, helped them on the swings, and generally watched over my kids.

My Japanese friend Sachiko, who often joined us with her four-year-old, wasn't watchful at all. In fact, she seemed to ignore her little boy's behavior. Sometimes he would grab toys from other kids, push them down the slide, or shout at them when they were taking too long on the swings. Sachiko seemed a little too relaxed about these things, and that bothered me even more than her son's behavior. I felt like she wasn't doing her job. It was as if she just didn't understand that being aware and right on top of things was what good parents did.

Then my friend Aiko visited us from Japan. Aiko's son Yoshi taught Benjamin to sword fight. Four-year-old Benjamin, who had never held a toy weapon of any sort in his life (we were a proudly "weapon-free" home), was delighted when Yoshi pulled out the toy swords he'd brought. The boys sparred in the living room while Aiko and I drank tea in the kitchen. When the shouting escalated, I went over to redirect their play and make sure they were okay. Aiko finally put her hand on my arm when I was about to jump in the fray again and said in a quiet voice, *Christine, Kodomo de yaru yo.* "The kids will work it out."

Would the kids really work it out? Was Aiko's a smart insight or a prescription for bullying, to say nothing of cuts, scrapes, and hurt feelings? While I had always thought Aiko was a parent well worth emulating (her son was extremely polite, well behaved, and compassionate), what my friend said went against my motherly instincts. I felt like my sons were too little to be left to work things out with other kids by themselves; it was all so unpredictable, and they were so young. They needed my guidance.

When Benjamin was five, we moved to Japan. At his kindergarten in New York City, he had been expected to sit still and focus on letters and numbers. Kindness and empathy were frequently discussed in morning meeting, and any rough behavior was swiftly curtailed, so that all the kids could learn in a safe environment. We expected school in Japan would be similar.

The day after we arrived in Tokyo, we headed to Benjamin's new school, a kindergarten for kids ages three to six (in Japan, preschool and kindergarten are taught together in a multi-age setting called a *yochien*). As we approached, we saw children everywhere in a little schoolyard filled with dirt and trees. They were running, digging, shouting, jumping rope, playing tag or soccer, building huge towers with blocks, and climbing high. The school was a beehive of activity. We thought it must be recess, but later realized we were wrong. This was how children spent the bulk of their hours at school. For nearly five hours a day, they ran around playing freely with what appeared to me to be startlingly little direction or guidance. Children could do whatever they wanted: join in a group of kids doing origami, go out to the sandbox or swings, search for bugs in the bushes, take off all their clothes and squish their toes in the mud. They could go indoors, they could go outdoors. They had the run of the school.

Adults didn't impose their notions of correct behavior onto the children's natural, boisterous play. Play fighting was not discouraged. It was considered to be a normal stage of early childhood. Teachers even taught the kids to make their own swords and guns (out of rolled-up newspapers) to use in their imaginary battles, something we found simply unbelievable in a country known for its pacifism and low crime rates (homicide by gun is virtually unheard of). We'd just arrived from a country where weapon play was often frowned upon. Melanie, a mom I knew back home, remembered feeling deeply ashamed when her five-year-old's teacher chided her for his interest in guns. "She acted like I was an irresponsible parent raising a criminal," Melanie told me, "just because my son had a dart Nerf gun at home."

In Japanese *yochien*s, skirmishes between children weren't nipped in the bud by adults; rather, kindergarten was regarded as a time—*the* time—in life for kids to experiment socially in a fully engaged, unhindered way; not only to play but also to fight and to cry.

We soon discovered that many Japanese parents had a different view about childhood than we were used to. For one thing, parents I knew spoke of fighting as *a rite of passage*, declaring that skirmishes with friends helped children build resilience, like little inoculations, and were filled with all sorts of social lessons. "Children grow through fighting and making up," people would say. My first reaction was, *Fighting? Are you kidding me? We should be teaching our children not to fight in the first place.*

But in parent-education workshops held throughout the year, the *yochien* teachers explained that fighting, crying, and making up again were normal ways of figuring out how to get along. They insisted it was important *not* to interfere in this natural process, but to let children hone their innate abilities to work things out on their own. The teachers didn't see aggression as a sign of aberrant behavior or the mark of a "problem child" who would grow into a violent adult, but something normal that arose in childhood and would naturally fade when it had been allowed to run its course.

We were a little shocked that hitting wasn't taken so seriously. Many Western researchers looking at Japanese preschools have noticed the same thing. In her book *Learning to Go to School in Japan*, American researcher Lois Peak observes that "Japanese teachers do not consider hitting as a 'crime' or a demonstration of antisocial tendencies. Rather, it indicates social immaturity and frustration at an inability to verbalize one's feelings." If they intervene, they do so to help kids figure out what happened, to try to get the kids to mutually understand one another's position. Peak also quotes from the Tokyo Board of Education's parent booklet: "Fights between children are an important experience in acquiring proper social attitudes and behavior. . . . Through fighting, children come to understand others' viewpoints and learn tolerance, self-restraint, and self-assertiveness."

This was really hard for me to understand. I simply couldn't endorse what I thought of as a lack of supervision when I watched little children shove each other, grab things from one another, or speak unkindly without anyone calling them on it. In America, I had always learned it was important to *prevent* kids from being aggressive or unkind to each other, and if conflict happened to immediately let them know why it was wrong. I'd learned that parents should sit down and carefully explain things to a three- or four-year-old who might have hurt a friend's feelings or balked at sharing a toy.

Whatever form our reaction took—a time-out, a talking-to, a snack to counteract fallen blood sugar—the important thing was there was always a reaction. The parents I'd known in America always stepped in and intervened when a young child "misbehaved." They parceled out pleas or threats, punishment or "natural consequences." If they didn't do something, the people around them would wonder why they were letting their child get out of control.

Our ways weren't always effective. Many parents, including me, often dealt with their children's whining and protesting, by ignoring them. And this kind of disciplining took so much time and energy—lots of talking, explaining, placating. and negotiating. But at least the parents were paying attention. Even if I'd wanted to be more relaxed, I felt tremendous peer pressure from other parents to do the acceptable thing—keep children under control.

But as we settled into life in Tokyo, it became more noticeable (and embarrassing) to be the only parent who stood close to the playing kids and who went in to break up a budding argument. I also started noticing something else: While other children bounced up quickly after getting hurt, my kids' automatic reaction was to turn to me first. Instead of being able to gauge whether they could handle small setbacks on their own, they needed my reassurance that they were okay.

## AGE-APPROPRIATE EXPECTATIONS

As I talked to other parents from other countries, I realized Japan was not the only country with a relaxed, tolerant attitude toward children. Laura's family moved from Switzerland to Sweden when her son was three. In Switzerland, she'd been accustomed to keeping her active toddler under control—quiet and demure in public places, which often wasn't easy. In Sweden, the first time they visited a park, her son began running off, shrieking at top volume like the normal child he was. "I kept going *sh, sh, sh,*" Laura recalls, "constantly shushing him. Then I looked around and noticed no other parents were shushing their kids. I thought . . . we're in another world here. I had so internalized that children should never be loud in public, even in parks and in playgrounds. It was eye-opening to realize no one was shushing their kids here."

Lots of American parents worry that their children won't outgrow spunkiness or misbehavior without an adult's help, intervention, guidance, or punishment ("consequences"). We do not realize that this unrealistic fear is a hidden relic of the Puritan view of childhood as a period requiring strict moral molding and taming, even the breaking of a child's will to override a naturally sinful nature. "I just don't want my son to grow up to be a thief," one distraught mom said after she discovered her four-year-old had "stolen" a coveted toy from his sister. We're anxious that if we don't take the lead in shaping our children's natures by disciplining them, making sure they share, and protecting them from bad influences, they will never develop a moral compass.

In contrast, the Japanese have a more relaxed attitude toward misbehavior. Some researchers attribute the "often-observed public misbehavior of Japanese children" (who, it turns out, are famed for their carefree rambunctiousness) to a cultural belief that young children are semi-divine, still partly rooted in the spiritual world and thus too young for discipline. Another belief is that babies are born pure, untainted, and good—even superior to adults. For most of my Japanese friends, it was simply about believing that all children have basically good intentions and that we can best support them in their growth by holding age-appropriate expectations. People don't curtail young children's joy and exuberance because they don't think they need to: children are who they are, not creatures who must be shaped and tamed.

Parents like Nobuko, a mother of two boys, talked about how important it was that young children feel *nobinobi*—at ease and carefree. Other moms talked tolerantly, even smilingly, of a child who was an *itazura-ko*—a little prankster or mischief maker. A mischievous child was nothing to be ashamed of or hide; aggression wasn't something to feel so mortified by. Misbehavior among children in Japan was not an early sign of a life of crime, but a sign that they were still little kids.

I was still doubtful. Wasn't it strange that there was no teacher watching what the kids were looking at near the rabbit hutch? Weren't those shovels and sticks dangerous? That girl climbing up and standing on top of the jungle gym could fall! And how come no one went to see why that boy was crying over there?

George Bear, a professor of education at the University of Delaware, has researched what kinds of morals Japanese and American children internalize when it comes to misbehavior. In one study, Bear compared American and Japanese fourth- and fifth-graders and their thoughts on hitting, fighting, talking badly about someone, or spreading rumors. He found that when the children were asked why they should not do these acts, there was a stark difference in their responses. Ninety-two percent of the American children talked about not wanting to get caught, or not wanting to get in trouble with a teacher or parent. In other words, they focused on what would happen to them; it was the external guidelines that shaped their actions. The vast majority (90 percent) of Japanese children, on the other hand, did not talk about punishment or getting in trouble. They said they shouldn't misbehave because it would hurt a friend's feelings, it would be wrong, it would hurt the group. They focused on the consequences to others.

In another study, Bear found that American kids were much more likely than Japanese kids to blame other people for their own behavior. Remember the difference between fixed and growth mindset from the last chapter? Research shows how people blame others for their own behavior when they have a self-image to protect. Despite the lack of early intervention of perceived misbehavior, having been raised within an overall climate of expectations that emphasized things like empathy and responsibility, mistakes and remorse, more than external rules and consequences, Japanese children had a stronger internal moral compass than their American peers.

Bear's studies are part of a body of research that shows that Japanese children show fewer behavioral problems than kids in the United States. And this is even despite the fact that Japanese discipline is characterized by what one American researcher, Catherine Lewis, calls a "muted adult authority." "Teachers attribute positive motives to children, making it very hard for children to develop an identity as 'bad' children," she writes in her classic book *Educating Hearts and Minds: Reflections on Japanese Preschool and Elementary Education*. Japanese teachers see less value in meting out immediate consequences and punishment than in taking a longer-term view. The point of discipline is to help shape a character that you believe to be intrinsically good and well intentioned, and fostering a child's "understanding," not "compliance," is the ultimate goal. The best way to motivate children to behave or try to get along with others is to enhance their feelings of belonging, not make them feel bad.

To be sure, this approach appears surprisingly lax to anyone used to a swifter and more decisive adult response. It is common in Japanese elementary schools for teachers to wait quietly for as long as it takes the class monitors (a job rotated among the children) to get their peers settled down. With younger classes, I saw this could take a while, even ten or twenty minutes. Teachers didn't intervene in the process, which was sometimes uncomfortable to watch. When I first watched this, I could hardly restrain myself from charging to the front of the room and calling the class to order myself. But I eventually found out that non-intervention was a deliberate strategy based on the notion that children shouldn't learn how to obey just because adults told them to. Teachers wanted kids to learn self-control for themselves. Even if this took time.

## "BELIEVE IN YOUR CHILD'S STRENGTH"

While our children played in the alley outside their Tokyo home, Maiko and her husband, Hidekazu, parents at our *yochien*, told me that when they had their first child, Michi, they too had reservations about taking a hands-off approach. "I wanted him to do things perfectly, and to change things for him," Maiko explained. "If Michi didn't get along well with a friend, I wanted to step in. But once he started going to *yochien*, our teacher Yokota-sensei told me, 'Believe in your child's strength. Let him try to figure out how to make up after a fight, on his own. Through this experience, he'll grow.'"

Maiko took Yokota-sensei's advice to heart. "We believe that if kids act out, it's because they're tired, or it's because they're children! Children will be children." Her attitude reflects a deeply rooted cultural notion: trust in children's innate positive desire to learn and adapt socially. That desire to adapt and get along is what will motivate kids to mature more efficiently than adults hurrying them along.

It turns out the American mom who was afraid her son would grow up to be a thief need not have worried. Although we sometimes feel driven to perfect our children's social experiences because we fear that bad behavior is a window into a troubled future, one large-scale study drawing on data from six studies (looking at 34,000 children) concluded that how well behaved a child is at the start of kindergarten, or, conversely, how ill behaved, fidgety, or disruptive, is unrelated to how well they do in third grade, despite the widely believed American assumption that disruptive, fidgety kids will lag behind their peers. The Japanese seem to understand better than we do that we shouldn't jump to judge or label a child, because their most characteristic actions today will be gone by tomorrow. Teachers reassured parents that we shouldn't forget that children are *still growing up*. "Growth and change," Yasoshima-sensei, our seasoned, serene head *yochien* teacher, often told us parents, "is the *only* thing we can be certain of with young children. They are always, always changing."

The most important principle, Yasoshima-sensei told me on a summer day when I sat down with her for a longer talk over tea, was that teachers should be constantly attentive and aware of what's going on, but hold themselves back from getting involved in a situation too soon. If they see trouble brewing—two kids who were starting to fight with each other—they try not to react immediately. You had to *give them that moment* and sit on your own discomfort or desire to rescue the child from the situation, because, she asserted, "This experience is good for them."

We weren't talking *Lord of the Flies* here. But the teachers did not interfere unless things became imminently dangerous. Otherwise, she told me, they would be interfering with the children's *growth* by being overly involved. Being too involved deprives the kids of experiencing the good feelings that come only from mastering the situation on their own.

There's a fine line between giving kids space and letting children bully each other, and Yasoshima-sensei urged her teachers to get to know each child well. Teachers always wore comfortable clothes and were active, frequently involved in a vigorous game of tag or soccer with a group of kids somewhere in the *yochien* yard. A teacher who takes the time to bond with and understand each child well develops a sense for when a situation can be resolved without adult intervention, versus when things really are about to spin out of control.

When Yasoshima-sensei was young, neighborhood children of all ages would play in the narrow alleyways between Japanese homes while their mothers kept their windows open, knowing what was going on without being right on top of things. Nowadays, like many kids around the world, kids have less free time, and with Japan's low birthrate, fewer siblings and playmates than in previous generations. But what Japanese *yochien*s tried to do was to re-create the atmosphere of the alleyways, where children were each other's best social teachers. As we watched our children's classmates grow up over the years, we saw the merit in their having had time and space in early childhood to be with children with all sorts of personalities, without adults closely mediating their relationships. These children had had years of daily, raw practice in what humans need to do to get along.

## KIDS GAIN MORE WHEN WE DO LESS

Experiencing and resolving conflicts is a cognitively demanding and essential part of childhood development. Because peers are harder on each other than adults, peer play gives kids even more opportunity for challenge, negotiation, and growth than they have when we adults are playing with them. Peer play gives kids powerful opportunities to learn how to resolve conflicts, how to read other kids' verbal and nonverbal cues, and how to interact with different personalities and play styles. As they accumulate positive experiences negotiating interactions with other kids, they feel a genuine sense of accomplishment.

Our concerns about play fighting eventually dissipated. Pretend play, including play fighting, actually helps children be less aggressive in real life. (It turns out even gun play has a purpose: researchers believe it helps children to read each other's facial cues and body language, figure out their place in a group, and modulate themselves accordingly.) By allowing kids to practice being villains or superheroes, pretend play gives children a chance to try on different characters and experience the world from different points of view. We saw bigger kids hold themselves back from using their full strength, to equalize the playing field between themselves and a younger classmate. We saw younger kids model their behavior after older ones and act more maturely so they could all play together enjoyably.

A child who climbs so high in a tree that the next branch he reaches for breaks learns on his own how high is too high. Many Japanese adults believe excessive cautioning from grown-ups ("Be careful," "Stop running," "Play nicely," "Slow down") undermines a child's growth. This is because someone else—the adult in charge—is the one who is determining and setting those limits for him, rather than letting him learn through the messiness of making his own mistakes, or by seeing how his peers react, or having a chance to feel his feelings for himself. One American friend of mine started to get up to run to her daughter when she saw the little girl stumble during a race at her Japanese elementary school's sports competition and fall flat to the ground. Two Japanese moms on either side of her held her back. They believed her little girl would really want to experience the good feeling of getting herself up and finishing the race on her own. (They were right.)

Research tells us that our personality—who we believe ourselves to be—is shaped by how we see ourselves, and in turn is shaped by how we believe the world sees us. If the people around us trust that we will grow and mature in time, we feel less pressure than if we believe that we need to hurry up and change because we're not acceptable right now as we are. I felt certain that one of Benjamin's classmates, who often stood up and walked around the first-grade classroom, disturbing his classmates and fooling around, would never change unless teachers took him by hand and explained to him how important it was for him to sit down and learn and not disturb people. In my mind, he needed frequent discipline and consistent consequences, which, from what I could see, he wasn't getting. Over the years, though, I watched him grow into a self-controlled, mature kid, just like the rest of his class, without the kind of overt discipline I had felt so sure he needed.

In the Japanese system, our children became surprisingly resilient. Our boys learned to brush off encounters with less-than-pleasant children with little more than a philosophical shrug—that's just how some kids were. They stopped expecting me to rescue them from every uncomfortable situation, stopping first to see if they could handle things on their own. Spending time with other children instead of with accommodating adults helped our kids learn patience and self-regulation. It wasn't that they had to tamp down their feelings to seem cool in front of their friends. It was more that they had chance after chance to learn how gratifying it could be to get over a minor incident and get right back to playing, rather than to prolong their distress with a lot of adult attentiveness and concern. An adult's solicitous concern, framed this way, became an *interruption*.

Of course, my kids, like all kids, have breakdowns and plenty of fragile moments. They know they can come to me at any time for comfort or support. I want them to know I'm in their corner and always here for them, and I still listen to my internal radar about what might be too much for them. But in Japan I learned that my children weren't quite as fragile as I thought and that they didn't need me to crowd them. They gained more by my doing less.

## THE INVISIBLE FENCE

A father of three at a park in Buffalo, New York, forbade his three-year-old from jumping on the play structure's swinging bridge because it was "too dangerous." When the boy jumped up and down anyway, his father put him in a time-out. Brittany and her husband, living in Manchester, Connecticut, admit that they used to be overprotective. They cautioned their three young kids (a toddler, a three-year-old, and a seven-year-old) about being careful, hovered over them at the playground, and generally kept an eye on them. Like the parents around them, they thought they were just protecting their kids.

Then Brittany and her young family moved to Sweden. They knew they were joining a much-touted family-friendly society, but they assumed its reputation had to do with its public policies like universal health insurance and child care. They soon found that there was a side to life in Sweden that no tourist guide could have prepared them for: the way that even very small children were permitted to play and wander freely.

Brittany noticed things that she would never have seen back home. She saw children as young as three or four climbing up high trees and onto playhouse roofs, playing in the woods without an adult, and riding bikes around the neighborhood on their own. The first time she saw a three-year-old high up in a tree, she started to look for the teacher to let her know. Then she noticed another parent stopping to chat with the child, before heading toward the school. It was clear the other parents weren't concerned. Usually they kept an eye on the children from afar and rarely offered directions or warnings the way parents Brittany knew back home always did. "That's when I realized I was seeing the world differently from them. I think of myself as open-minded . . . and here I was wanting to go tell a child to come down from a tree."

Yes, children might fall from those trees, but they had a chance to learn what their bodies were capable of. For the first time, Brittany realized, she was seeing children who were given space to explore and tune in to their own instincts about what they could do, instead of "relying on rules that we shout from the sidelines."

In Sweden, her boys played on elaborate two-story structures built into the ice on a hillside; they scavenged by themselves in the woods; they ate wild roots pulled from the ground by their friends. (Brittany says she drew the line at mushrooms.) Most surprising of all, her three-year-old's school had no fence. How could kids understand boundaries at such a young age? Why weren't the kids just dashing off into the woods beyond?

But, like the trees, it had to do with having a different view of what kids were capable of, and how you fostered these capabilities. Swedish adults didn't just let kids wander off into the wilderness without any preparation or guidance. In fact, there was lots of guidance. Teachers talked to their students about how far they could go, and explained where those boundaries were. They were certain that kids would learn if adults only communicated with them, and respected their ability to understand. But they didn't want a real fence; they wanted their kids to develop a feeling of an internal sense of control. True enough, kids just never went beyond what Brittany eventually grew to think of as something implicit in Swedish parenting culture: an "invisible fence," constructed from trust.

Nothing in life is without risk, of course. But the mentality that seems to prevail in the United States is that *no* level of risk should ever be acceptable, that it's our job to make sure nothing ever happens (and our fault if anything does). When Brittany and her husband moved back to Connecticut three years later, the boys were really surprised that at their new school in America, they weren't allowed to pick up a stick on the playground. It might poke someone in the eye; someone could fall on it and get hurt. Trying to eliminate all possible risk isn't just stifling; without the right sense of proportion and reasonableness, an environment filled with rules gives a false sense of control.

## RISK-TAKING SERVES A PURPOSE

Parents in many other countries think that a reasonable amount of risk taking is actually crucial for the development of a healthy, self-confident, independent child. In Linja playground in Helsinki, Finland, as I chatted with Veera, Anita, Michele, and Elina, all mothers of young children, I noticed with surprise how far away some of their toddlers wandered. The mothers remained unconcerned. The park was fenced, and the children were within eyesight, though one of them was no more than a pea-size blob on the horizon on a slope beyond the border of the playground itself.

Some researchers believe there's an evolutionary reason why our kids like to take risks, like wandering far away or climbing high trees. Ellen Hansen Sandseter, a psychologist at Queen Maud University College in central Norway, has been conducting research in Norwegian, Australian, and English playgrounds and schools for thirteen years, observing and interviewing parents, teachers, and children. She found that children naturally seek exhilarating risky play, such as exploring heights, experiencing high speeds, handling dangerous tools, being near dangerous elements such as fire or water, doing rough-and-tumble play, and wandering far away from their caregivers. Her work indicates that kids evolved to be drawn to risky play because of how it exposes them to physical challenges, and then "habituates" them to their fears. Kids get used to and learn how to manage their fears a little at a time by seeking out risky experiences that push their personal boundaries just a bit. Kids are driven to these behaviors because it's almost like a natural form of cognitive therapy—helping them to get used to and overcome their anxieties.

No parent or teacher anywhere is saying that we should not take risks into consideration. But the questions we ought to be asking ourselves are these: Are we looking at risk in the correct way? Could the way we view risks actually be creating new risks for our kids?

Researchers worry more about what they dub "surplus safety"—a situation in which we're so concerned about protecting kids from perceived risks (such as minor injuries) that we actually put them at risk of other risks (for instance, the very real risk of obesity from sedentary indoor play). There is growing evidence that, far from protecting children from injuries, children are at increased risk of more broken limbs on our modern, safety-first playgrounds. When an environment is too sterile and safe, children may be driven to truly unsafe behavior. The greatest risk factor for playground accidents is that children will become bored by the limits of the playground and try to increase the challenges they crave by, say, twisting the chains of a swing, standing on that swing, or walking on top of a climbing structure. Another danger is that they will become complacent and unaware of their own movements, because everything is so standardized (like rungs of a ladder spaced the same distance apart).

If adults are always in the way, we come between children and their inner voice. But we won't always be able to be there for them. Sandseter points out that what's *really* dangerous is if, say, we let a fifteen- or sixteen-year-old boy loose who hasn't had incremental practice over the years, who has always had adults around him, directing him and telling him what's safe and unsafe. "That's when kids really are at risk," Sandseter warned.

Some of the kids Sandseter talked to described their feelings while doing something risky as "scary/funny." By overcoming physical challenges, not only do they build up skills, but they feel good about having mastered something and they learn to emotionally cope with those complicated feelings or anxieties. If they don't have that chance to experience these small risks, though (because of an overly protective parent, say, or a too-safe playing environment), they won't be able to become physically competent and safe. "Allowing children to handle risks on their own with their own bodies, their own minds, and through their own assessment and courage, *is the most important safety protection you can give a child*," Sandseter told me.

Norwegians believe in what one parenting expert calls the blessings of a skinned knee. It is good for a child to endure a little hardship, to not be protected all the time, to come home with a scraped knee, a bruise, the bumps and scratches that are a sign they've played vigorously and are having a robust childhood. "We have a notion that children have to freeze a bit, have to be a bit hungry, have to learn how to master all the cold snow we have here," Sandseter informed me. "It's a toughening notion," one that, she acknowledges, is not very common in Anglo-American culture. David Lancy, a professor of anthropology at Utah State University, agrees. As a culture, he notes, we've become more disengaged from nature except in a controlled way (think the zoo). We don't value dirt and scrapes, whereas parents in other countries "think those things are important and essential."

What we don't realize is that risk taking also fosters qualities we as a culture value highly, such as adventurousness and an entrepreneurial, can-do spirit. Studies show that when kids face a task that is stressful or a little bit hard, parent-child interactions make a difference in how well children fare. Even as they are trying to do the opposite, nervous parents inadvertently foster anxiety in their child. Anxious children tend to have parents who are "more involved, try to take over the task, are overly involved and don't allow the child his own autonomy," Donna Pincus, an associate professor at Boston University and author of *Growing Up Brave: Expert Strategies for Helping Your Child Overcome Fear, Stress, and Anxiety*, explained to me. "These parents could be falling into 'traps' which research has shown fosters more anxiety—such as being overly protective, or overly reassuring."

It's natural to want to reassure our kids—it's instinctual when we see them in distress—but rushing to our children gives them the message that they can't do things on their own and predisposes them to avoid challenges in the future. On the other hand, a parent who encourages her child to stretch beyond her comfort level and allows that child to face challenges alone (going alone to a big birthday party with a bunch of new children, for instance) is giving her child a positive message about how to cope with things. "If you are trying to help a child develop coping skills, the better way isn't to hover over everything. *It's to take a step back,*" Pincus explained. "Bravery doesn't mean never feeling fear. A parent who lets her child experience some stressful things in life is giving her child the tools to develop a way of facing challenges."

## CONFLICTED ABOUT INDEPENDENCE

Americans hold independence in the highest esteem. We admire the free spirit who knows herself and what she wants, and in particular we value verbal independence—a child's ability to tell us what he thinks. Yet we may not realize how much we often impose rules on kids and involve ourselves in children's lives in a way that undermines their independence.

This phenomenon is known as "dependency conflict." But who has the conflict, the parent, or the kid, or both? Thomas Weisner, a professor in the departments of anthropology and psychiatry at UCLA, explained to me that dependency conflict is the simultaneous process of both "pushing a child to be autonomous or separate and do things on their own, while at the same time telling the child that the parent is judging, evaluating, or watching what the child does, which sends the opposite message. It ties the child to the parent. The parent is, in fact, the person who is controlling the child. A paradigmatic example is a five-year-old on a playground," Weisner said. "The mother says go off and play, meet other children. When the child gets a few feet away, she calls out, 'Hi, I'm right here! I'm watching you! Don't worry!'"

Weisner told me lots of American parents are ambivalent about how independent our kids should be. We want for our kids to separate from us (only in some ways or some contexts), and don't want them to be too separate (again, only in some ways and contexts). Kids react to this and feel ambivalent too. On the one hand, they have that natural desire to explore, to play in the park like normal kids with their parents there, but they also know they have to please their parents or manage them somehow. "And one of the things a child learns from observing the parent is that *attention seeking is important*," Weisner told me. "Parents want the child to pay attention to them. They want the child to orient to them."

In other words, we're raising independent children, but we're also raising dependent children. If we are constantly engaging with them, checking in with them, and eliciting reassurances that they are doing fine, we're undercutting their autonomy because they have to pay attention to us. And they become dependent on their need to have us pay attention to them too.

This form of dependency seems unique to a particular style of child-rearing in our culture. Gilda Morelli of Boston College researched attention-seeking behavior (sparked by her observation that phone calls with a mother of young children were punctuated by frequent interruptions), comparing American toddlers living in Salt Lake City with children of an African forager tribe, the Efe. On average, the American toddlers were far more likely to interrupt an adult conversation between their caregiver and a researcher-interviewer than the Efe children were.

In contrast to the Efe children's silent gestural bids for quiet assistance, over a quarter of the American children's interruptions "were for the sole purpose of singling themselves out for social recognition." Sometimes the American children even grasped their caregiver's face between their hands to turn her toward them. Because these interruptions were also usually verbal, the Salt Lake City caregivers had to interrupt their own conversations to respond.

The child who can speak up for himself, get attention, and make his needs known clearly is far more likely to thrive as an adult in America. But as many of us know, raising kids who have an insatiable need for attention can also make for aggravating and stressful moments. The solution: to find a middle ground so that American children can be expressive, individualistic, and creative but also fearless and resilient, learning to stand on their own two feet without the constant need for adult intervention and attention.

## HOVERING LESS HELPS KIDS BUILD SELF-CONTROL

Is it our job to protect and control our children? Or is it our job to hone *their* self-control?

Most cultures believe kids need space to develop mastery and autonomy and self-reliance. But kids in America, who typically don't experience many genuinely adult-free moments, aren't often able to have the space they need to find out who they are and what they are capable of, and to develop that self-control and judgment they'll need as they grow older.

But if we wait too long to give kids that chance, we risk their not being capable when we finally deem them ready, because they haven't had enough experience listening to their inner judgment if they've been listening to ours all along. As parents, we're unknowingly depriving ourselves too. You can't really know what amazing things your child can do until you let him try.

Katherine, a mother of three young children living in the Boston area, was protective and solicitous toward her children. But one day, after checking in on her kids every twenty minutes as they played outside in the snow, she realized her kids might never have the kind of childhood she had had, where she had experienced the joy of doing things on her own, and where some of her happiest memories were of moments free from adult eyes. She knew it was time for things to change. "You know," she mused to me, "I sort of learned to be a parent by watching parents who were around me." When they were parents who were anxious and invested, she was too. It helped when her son made friends with kids in the neighborhood whose parents worked late and couldn't watch their children like hawks. Those kids had more freedom of movement and her boy wanted to join them.

The first time he left the house alone, she watched the clock, and wondered if she should drive out and look for him. But a few hours after he left, he opened the door, and came back in, beaming and satisfied, "and it was the most amazing feeling. We had crossed this bridge that I wanted to cross for so long! He could do it. *I* could do it."

Sometimes Katherine's protective instincts still kick in. There's an alley near their house that her husband taught her son about, a shortcut back home. She wanted to warn her son never to go down that alley, to always take the long way instead. But she stopped herself. "I don't want to be coloring his childhood with so many fears. Twenty years from now, I want him to remember this alley as a place he went to, that he didn't see as scary."

We do not do our children any favors when we do their homework for them, mediate their friendships, and hover too close to them as they play. If we want them to be independent, we also have to trust them, let them make mistakes, and realize it's okay for them to skin their knees. We want to pave our children's way, but there are some things that we simply can't teach them and that they'll learn for themselves, through experience.

Teachers at the Little School, a progressive independent school in Bellevue, Washington, lay a rope on the ground to teach their three-year-old preschoolers where the boundary is when they're playing outside. As they get older, and the kids show they've developed the self-control and judgment they need to stay safe, the rope boundary progressively widens, and eventually is replaced by a mere ribbon on a tree in the woods. It seems to me that this rope is an apt metaphor for a middle ground we American parents can keep in mind. Children are driven to become competent masters of their world. They don't need high fences, which deprive them of the chance to exercise their own judgment and hone self-control. Nor can they thrive in the absence of any boundaries at all, which no parent anywhere would feel comfortable with. The three-year-olds learn, with a couple of reminders and a lot of practice and trust, where the boundary is.

In our front yard there is a stately beech tree with lots of branches, perfect for climbing. Our kids like to swing themselves into it, settling down to wait for visitors, read, or be found by a pursuer during a game of hide-and-go-seek. Each child finds the right spot: Benjamin, confident and athletic and twelve years old, climbs high in the tree's branches. Daniel, ten, who tends to play it safe, likes to perch somewhere in the middle. Six-year-old Mia, still learning and cautious, feels good being on a lower branch, and three-year-old Anna, who can't reach that high yet, digs with her fingernails, her little shovel, or a choice stick near the trunk of the tree.

How high, or how low, our kids climb is for them to decide. I now know I can't make that judgment better than they can. But it's taken time for me to believe that when kids are given leeway to trust their instincts, they don't tend to take on more than they are capable of. It's taken time for me to understand that, if they're not allowed to take some risks now, they won't develop the judgment I'd need to be able to trust them to stay safe later on.

I still have my limits: they're not allowed to climb when it's just rained and they can't get a good grip on the branches. And I remind them to avoid the weak spots. But the doubts I used to have about letting them climb at all (*Should they be doing this? Isn't it dangerous? How much should I allow?*) have mostly fallen silent now.

There are parents who visit and ask us not to let anyone climb the tree when their kids come over, and I understand. That's the limit that they've set for their own children and that I have no problem accommodating. But part of me, deep down, can't help wishing their children too could share in the experience of scrambling up the tree, straining to get to the next branch, figuring out how high is high enough, and triumphing in a task well accomplished as they sit on their roost and look at the world—which has suddenly gotten smaller—down below.

SIX

# QUALITY TIME:
## The Value of Unstructured Play

ulia and her daughter, Daisy, always enjoyed spending time with their friends Miguel and Jane and their children, Cassie and Grace. Only a few years apart in age, the three girls got along really well. When they were preschoolers there were lots of playground dates and potluck dinners. As all the girls grew older, though, everyone was getting busier, and once they were all in school it became harder to meet up. While Julia sensed that Daisy needed plenty of downtime and made it a priority to help her daughter have time to herself, Miguel and Jane increasingly scheduled after-school enrichment activities in their girls' lives.

On Tuesdays after school, Cassie had gymnastics. Grace had flute on Wednesdays. Then there was a specialized dance class about an hour's drive from their house in the early evening on Wednesdays. The girls were both involved in children's theater, which met twice a week (on Mondays and Fridays), that their parents hoped would help them to feel more self-expressive. They also took art classes on Saturdays, to unleash their creativity. These activities were very important to their parents, who strongly believed no financial or time sacrifice was too much for the best enrichment. Miguel and Jane were proud of their decision to forgo things for themselves, like a larger home or newer car, in order to provide these opportunities for their daughters. The girls and their education came first. Miguel and Jane spent much of their time driving their daughters to activities and keeping track of their complicated schedules. They spent at least an hour and a half a day in the car, often eating their meals as they drove. Homework was often done in the car too.

On the rare occasions the two families managed to meet up like they used to, Miguel expressed his worries to Julia. He couldn't stop wondering whether he was shortchanging the girls by not giving them more opportunities to maximize their potential. Grace seemed to be incredibly gifted at music, but was the flute enough? "What if she has some amazing hidden talent that isn't cultivated because she hasn't had the chance to try another instrument?" he wondered anxiously. He thought Grace had the potential to become world-famous. If that was what she was capable of, that was what he wanted for her. Trying to reassure him, Julia told Miguel she hadn't done any extracurriculars when she was the girls' age (as a child, she'd been living abroad, in a country where it wasn't typical to have parent-scheduled activities after school), and that even without an adult introducing her formally to this or that, she'd found her own interests and things she loved to do. She was an avid knitter and antique-book lover, and had a fulfilling life in teaching after getting an advanced degree in early modern European history.

Instead of being reassured, Miguel feared that perhaps the girls needed a stint abroad to help expose them to more stimulating, interesting, and unique experiences.

When she came home from these get-togethers, Julia also found herself second-guessing her own decisions. Daisy, nine years old, took piano lessons, and that was all. But given Julia's long commute home and Daisy's love of homebody activities, it didn't make sense to add more activities or time in the car to the schedule right now. Julia was surrounded by parents like Miguel and Jane who did more, paid for more, believed in scheduling every spare minute for their children so they'd be fulfilled, active, and enriched—even though it came at great parental sacrifice. With parents like this around her, Julia frequently wondered: "How much is too much? How little is too little?" Was she really doing her best for Daisy, in the end, by giving her so much free time to play, or would Daisy be better off with a variety of activities to pursue?

## WHY AMERICAN KIDS DON'T PLAY LIKE THEY USED TO

Many American parents today struggle to figure out the right balance of structured and unstructured time for their children's free hours. Free time is hard to justify when there are so many things our kids could be doing: sports, music, art, supplemental math, acting, sewing, woodworking. Middle-class and affluent parents see others around them whose kids are pursuing interesting (but expensive!) activities. When they don't schedule their children's free time, their kids have no one to play with in the neighborhood, because everyone is at soccer practice or music lessons.

Parents who grew up in the 1950s, 1960s, and 1970s had a very different childhood, full of unstructured time outdoors with other kids. Those afternoons were free of adult involvement, high in imagination, and low in any measurable "productivity." That sort of childhood play is increasingly rare now. Between 1981 (when I was thirteen years old) and 1997 (shortly before I had my first child), the amount of outdoor free play children had fell by 50 percent. Nowadays their free time decreases even more as they get older. One survey found that 79 percent of middle and high school students participate in some sort of activities during the weekdays or on the weekends; 57 percent have an extracurricular activity every day or almost every day. As scheduled activities have increased, the amount of outdoor time children enjoy has plummeted. Today, the average American child is spending only between four and seven minutes in unstructured outdoor play.

There are fewer kids ringing the bell to see if little Johnny can come outside, or riding around the neighborhood on their bikes till dinner-time. "Playdates" and enrichment classes are now a normal way for children to spend "free" time. At the same time, electronic media use has been skyrocketing among the youngest set. A 2009 Kaiser Family Foundation study found that, on average, kids spend more than seven and a half hours a day using electronic media (including multitasking, it actually adds up to a stunning ten hours and forty-five minutes).

Is it a good thing that our children have more stimulating gadgets to play with and more opportunities for enrichment? Didn't we play so much as kids because our parents were busy and there wasn't anything else for us to do?

Childhood play is how kids construct meaning and make sense of the world when they are little, and discover what they love as they grow. Play is a springboard for creativity: as kids pretend and make up their own games, they create possibilities out of thin air. Pretend play is an especially crucial way to hone human intelligence because of how it enables kids to envision possibilities. The more kids play, the more practice they gain at mastering what ultimately are the competencies kids need for the twenty-first century: the ability to create, to innovate, and to make unexpected connections. The more practice children have losing themselves in play, the better they become at finding their way back to that creative place again.

The lack of unstructured free play—especially outdoors—is taking its toll on our children's mental and physical health. Obesity has tripled in the past thirty years; antidepressant use in American children is on the rise; and the use of psychotropic medication to counteract attention deficit disorders has also skyrocketed (the United States consumes 80 percent of the world's supply of Ritalin). There is a growing vitamin D deficiency in American children, who also suffer more from poor distance vision and hyperactivity than ever before. The less children play, the more their self-regulation has dropped: an American five-year-old today is as self-regulated as a three-year-old from the 1940s.

Contrary to what parents like Miguel believe, it is *unstructured* play that enhances a child's ability to learn. Pretend play is crucial for developing self-regulation, which is one of the most important capacities a child needs to thrive in school. Make-believe play is, after all, rule-based play. Kids come up with the rules themselves and must remember to keep the play consistent and coherent. As children repeat scenarios based on their real-life experiences, they hone their internal ability to control themselves and behave in socially acceptable ways so they can keep the play going.

Open-ended pretend play also helps children make sense of their social world. When a child pretends that a block is a car or a stick in a blanket is a sleeping baby, he's exercising his ability to make deliberate choices and create something imaginative. Kids love language-rich, socially enticing, and engaging play for a reason: these are the sorts of experiences that are developmentally appropriate for them, that help grow their brains and prepare them for the kind of learning they'll be doing in school.

Children at play are like avid little social scientists: their pretend interactions with peers help them build their knowledge of how others will react to what they say or do. As we saw in the last chapter, peer play provides kids with powerful opportunities to learn about conflict and resolution, verbal and nonverbal communication strategies, and the range of different personalities out there. Kids feel competent and confident when they see how successful they are at getting along with others. These good feelings help children to feel positive about school. Ultimately, kids who feel good about themselves and school are better able to learn and retain information.

## CHILDHOOD ISN'T A RACE

We're told those first few years are crucial, not to be wasted. Media-stoked pressure after a flurry of groundbreaking brain research in the 1980s and 1990s led lots of parents to believe this means that there is only a small window of time—the first three years—in which to help children get on the road to success. While this message was aimed primarily at disadvantaged children (for whom early intervention and stim-ulation are important), this awareness created a strong cultural message that "the earlier, the more, the better" we push our children, the more we maximize their cognitive development. Playing Mozart to our babies would help make them more intelligent. Babies and toddlers were capa-ble of learning to read, if only we would teach them how.

The role of adults during a child's early years is very important, but children's brains continue to grow throughout childhood (and even well beyond). There is no evidence that a child's brain benefits from a par-ent's attempt to speed things up. Reading to our young children every day is a good thing, but that doesn't mean that flash cards and Mozart CDs are even better. One researcher who participated in the study about the benefits of classical music that sparked the "Mozart Effect" mania later noted that there was no compelling evidence that listening to Mo-zart could make babies smarter. Besides, the study had been about col-lege students, not babies.

Yet the myriad "smart baby" products and early-learning toys and apps targeted at parents continue to reinforce the message that earlier is better for future success, and that if you aren't careful, your child will be left behind. Invested parents, like Sarah, a mom of four in South Da-kota, find educational toys to be the perfect bridge between play and learning. All her kids used them and learned reading, math, spelling, and numbers at a very young age. "I felt good that they were learning and they were happy, because it was fun," she told me. Sarah's right—it's good when our kids make a positive connection between learning and play. The problem comes when parents believe that the more they work at play—guiding, structuring, facilitating, scheduling, or providing the right kinds of toys—the better off their kids will be.

It's now common for academic instruction to begin before elemen-tary school: American children are typically taught letters, numbers, and even science starting in preschool, and kindergarten teachers are often constrained by curricula dictated by standardized tests—their classes are now more focused on literacy and math skills than on learning through imaginative play.

But educators are seeing that too much time spent on early enrichment actually takes time away from the unstructured play children need in order to develop life skills and imagination critical for school readiness. Invested parents are tempted to enroll their smallest children in extracurricular activities for the sake of their future success, but Steven D. Levitt at the University of Chicago found that there wasn't evidence that parent-dictated activities correlate with academic success. In fact, the zeal with which some parents try to prepare kids for the future can backfire. Researchers found that early-learning centers, which promise to give infants, toddlers, and preschoolers an academic head start, produced children who eventually had more difficulties: anxiety about tests, lowered creativity, and less of a liking for academics. Many studies show that "artificial stimulation"—early learning that is developmentally inappropriate—can be counterproductive and even hinder children's development. One well-known study showed that the more babies watched educational baby videos, the more their vocabulary acquisition dropped.

Focusing on "school readiness" isn't without costs. Numerous studies have demonstrated that when preschools are not "developmentally appropriate" (play-focused) but instead are focused directly on academics, children fare less well: they experience more behavioral issues, stress, and anxiety, and do not do better academically. We also know that early academic instruction doesn't necessarily benefit the cause of literacy. One cross-cultural study of European children indicated that children who learned to read when they were five had more trouble than children who learned to read when they were seven.

This may be because the complex areas of the brain that are necessary for learning to read aren't adequately developed until a child is between five and seven years old—the minimum age at which people in many countries expect their kids to begin learning how to read. Although some kids show an interest in reading or literacy at a younger age (one of my four kids happens to be like this), and it's appropriate to support that interest when it emerges, many researchers agree there shouldn't be a blanket expectation that all children begin formally learning how to read in preschool or even kindergarten, *especially if it takes away from time to play.*

Highly scheduled lives and early academics aren't what our children's brains evolved to need. "It's clear from our look at the brain's evolutionary history that it's not been designed to be stuffed into classrooms, sat in front of television sets, handed battery-operated dollhouses, and told how to play ball," Gabrielle Principe tells us in her book *Your Brain on Childhood.* An associate professor of psychology at Ursinus College in Pennsylvania, Principe argues that we actually disrupt our children's brain development when we interrupt, proscribe, or deprive them of open-ended free play.

On the other hand, experiences that are developmentally appropriate *grow* the brain. Open-ended play and downtime are both important and productive for children. It may look like children playing are not doing much—nothing that you can score, tally, or keep track of. But kids who play freely and abundantly—kids who are engaging in open-ended play that is self-determined and involves give-and-take with one another—are actually building skills in perspective taking, self-direction, and creative thinking.

Peter Gray, an evolutionary psychologist at Boston College, has extensively researched play and self-directed learning. He told me that anthropologists who have studied diverse traditional societies have found certain commonalities no matter where they conducted their fieldwork. "In these societies, children are expected to be playing and exploring joyfully and learning what they need to know to become adults in that culture." Through play, "children are practicing the kinds of skills they will need to develop: how to get along with their peers, how to solve their own problems, and how to regulate their own emotions, such as anger or fear."

Just as we saw in the last chapter, the skills that help children to get along with others are best learned with minimal adult supervision. Our modern lives, with children spending so many hours in organized, structured, adult-led learning or activities, concern Gray. "There's been a measurable rise in childhood anxiety, depression, narcissism, and measurable declines in empathy as well over the last forty to fifty years—the years during which free outdoor play has declined dramatically," he said. "The kind of emotional regulation that is necessary for psychological resilience has declined in young people."

But many parents feel a lot of pressure to keep kids on track cognitively or even give them an edge. One third-grade teacher, at a school for the gifted in New York, told me how dismayed she was to hear the mother of a little boy in her class proudly tell her that she wasn't signing her son up for any "fun stuff" during summer vacation, only academics, because she wanted to be sure he'd be able to skip a math grade the following year. "He was actually in need of support, not acceleration," the teacher confided, "and an unstructured summer to just have fun would have been exactly what he needed so he could focus on his work later."

Unstructured time to play is anything but frivolous—it prepares kids for life. A professor at a prestigious local college told me she was worried that her students were increasingly at a loss because they hadn't learned "how to think." The vast majority of her students spent so much time being groomed for college acceptance and doing scheduled activities to help them get into college that they had never taken time to pursue their own unique interests. When she first started teaching more than twenty years ago, she'd seen kids come in with passions of their own, who had read up on, say, Roman history, for years and came to college excited to learn more. But today's students have had no downtime to develop those passions. They're skilled, she told me, at trying to figure out what they have to do to get good grades, but any real initiative or love of learning just isn't there. The self-motivation, passion, interest, and original thinking that she saw in the past are gone in today's students.

Instead, this professor sees more kids who are highly accomplished, but less confident, less quirky, and less self-directed. They are marching to someone else's drumbeat, looking to adults for guidance in how to feel or what to do, unable to think for themselves. At the end of the semester when she asks her students what their favorite book during the course has been, they all invariably pick the same one—not because it is the best book of the semester, but because they do not feel comfortable having their own opinion. To her dismay, she and her fellow professors are finding they have to "deprogram" their new students every year in a way they have never had to before, helping them to recognize that forming their own opinions—not ones that they thought they ought to hold to satisfy the teacher—is intellectually valuable.

## HOW PLAY BUILDS CREATIVITY AND PASSION

We Americans tend to stereotype Japanese children as rigid rule-followers, and there were certainly aspects of Japanese childhood—and its outcomes (especially as kids get older)—that my husband and I couldn't feel entirely comfortable with. But we were especially impressed by how free play was privileged in the early years in a way you would be hard-pressed to find in America today, where academics have trickled down to preschool. Japanese parents and teachers hone children's ability to be self-motivated and self-directed through play in early childhood. Researchers comparing preschools in Japan, China, and the United States in 1989 surveyed parents in the three countries and found that while 67 percent of the Chinese parents and more than half of the American parents believed preschool was crucial to give their children an academic head start, only 2 percent of Japanese parents believed this. "The reason we want children to play so much," said Yasoshima-sensei, my children's Japanese *yochien* teacher, "is because it helps them learn what their interests are and *who they are.*"

Sometimes children's play in Japan didn't look like the kind of play I was used to seeing. I was mystified by all the young children I saw in every park practicing making *doro-dango,* little balls made of mud. Narumi, a quiet, wide-eyed girl I first met when she was three, and her little friends would make small balls of dirt by rolling a mixture of sand and mud between their palms over and over, repeatedly. To me this play made no sense; *doro-dango* weren't even like the humble mud pie, a prop in an imaginary scenario. Other expatriates living in Japan shared my skepticism: one British parent I knew even took her six-year-old out of Japanese *yochien* so he could spend his time learning to read instead of "making mud balls all the time."

Yasoshima-sensei told me that, actually, there was a kind of learning going on that adults might not recognize. But this is how humans learn: through experience that's meaningful to them, freely and autonomously chosen.

Kids making mud balls learned much about the world in a tactile way that no book could teach them. They were learning about the properties of mud: how mud changes when it is wet, or when it is dry, how much water to use, how much force to apply as they roll it over and over in their little palms. They were learning how to cultivate patience, concentration, perseverance, and self-control as they dealt with frustration over the occasional failed or cracked mud ball. They practiced conflict resolution as they dealt with children who might accidentally step on and crush their mud balls. They felt task satisfaction when they watched the little mud balls pile up. And they gained the respect of their peers, and learned about cooperation, as they crouched side by side to make these little balls.

But the most important thing was that this play, whether kids were making mud balls, playing house or tag, or looking for bugs in the garden, was *self-directed*. These were tasks they set out for themselves, not dictated or controlled by adults. One day I sat down next to a few children to try making the mud balls myself and the kids looked at me oddly: this wasn't something that *adults* did. By practicing their mud balls, they were taking learning and growing into their own hands. By playing freely with friends for hours at kindergarten, by deciding for themselves what they would do with each minute of those hours of play, they were experiencing how it feels to carve out your own autonomy and independence. The hours kids spent at *yochien* were filled with endless activity and purpose. As a Japanese college student reminisced aloud to me, "I still remember *yochien* very well. Every morning I would arrive at school and think, 'Oh! What should I do today?' *The choice of what to do that day, all those hours, was all up to me.*"

## PLAY AROUND THE WORLD

Even after leaving Japan, we returned there every summer, and Daniel, Benjamin, and Mia rejoined their former schools for two months (in Japan, and throughout Asia, summer vacation doesn't typically begin until the end of July). During Benjamin's sixth-grade summer, he joined a committee of kids who would teach the whole school a game to play at their weekly community time. Their job was to come up with a game that would foster community spirit.

After a lot of lively discussion for an hour in the classroom, the kids decided on one of the many variations on tag that are so popular there. They came up with a version that would appeal to the little first-graders, but engage the sixth-graders too. Fundamentally it was simple: children tried to run from one wall to another without getting tagged. But of course, it wouldn't be fun unless they changed the rules and made their own modifications. They debated and negotiated the rules and decided on interesting variations (there was considerable, vigorous debate over which specific arm signals would tell other players whether a child was "frozen" or "tagged"). That Friday's community time was a huge success.

Like Benjamin's classmates in Japan, kids all over the world make up their own games and variations of games. Mark Bekoff, an evolutionary biologist at the University of Denver, thinks there's a reason why young animals play so many different kinds of games. He calls it the "flexibility hypothesis" and speculates that the sheer variety of different ways that young mammals play is to help train their brains to be flexible and adaptable and to face the unexpected. Similarly, the endless number of ways children can play might have evolved because of the benefits kids get from honing an equally wide variety of skills. Not only do Japanese kids play a lot of games, but they play games that they often come up with by themselves—variations on simple, classic games they already know, like tag, soccer, or jump rope, with few or no props.

It's not just sentimental nostalgia to lament the disappearance of pickup games like marbles, jump rope, and other spontaneous child-organized games. One study has shown that how well children play games like this predicts how well they will adjust to school. Researchers believe that games where children actively make up, negotiate, and break their own rules are a crucial way for them to exercise and develop important aspects of their cognition. Humans evolved to live successfully in groups: we can think of these games as nature's way to ensure that kids get the brain exercise they were intended to have.

Play has other characteristics that cross cultures. Object play is universal: toddlers in all cultures play with objects and go through a stage when they pick up and play with objects with avid curiosity: tasting, touching, gazing, and then eventually imagining them to be other than they are. All children use repeated pretend play to help them make sense of the rules and social expectations of their own culture. This might look different in different places: children playing at pounding grain in Botswana, doing the end-of-the-year household cleaning in Japan, or pretending to go to the grocery store in the United States, for instance—but all this play derives from the same impulse.

But some aspects are more culturally dictated. In most American middle-class families, child's play revolves around toys—carefully calibrated for certain ages and stages to help foster child development and maximize cognitive skills. We even often segregate children's playmates by age. Many American parents, in a somewhat unique twist not seen in most other cultures, frequently sit and actually play together with their children. This was a great surprise to AnnKatrine, a German mother who is now raising her two young daughters near Boston. Whenever they would have social visits with other families back home, adults had coffee and cake while the children played in another part of the house. In contrast, when getting together with parents in the United States, the American parents seemed more involved in guiding and facilitating their children's play than she was used to, talking to them pointedly about the toys they were playing with. ("That's a blue truck! Blue. Truck.") Every moment, even in play, was a teaching moment for adults to guide kids through.

We hold dear the idea that it's important to spend "quality time" with our kids or provide good opportunities for them, in part because it will help them to develop and learn. But that's because cognitive intelligence is one of the traits that we, as a culture, prize, and it's not one all cultures share such an interest in cultivating in their own young kids.

In Sweden, there aren't a lot of parents who are concerned that they should be involved in facilitating and making sure their children are playing the right way to build a foundation for later learning. The Swedes' laissez-faire attitude can have benefits in a wide realm of areas. One Swedish teenager, Mikaela, valued having free time in the afternoon to just hang out with her brother. From the time she was seven and he was eight, they were left on their own all afternoon before their parents came home from work. "I loved playing with my brother, making up games, playing on swings, climbing trees, doing nothing," she told me.

Having to structure her own time helped Mikaela learn how to get along with her brother—while they played with other kids too, he was the one playmate consistently there day after day. "Things wouldn't be very fun until we were friendly again. You have more of a sense of the whole story—the before and after, how conflict works." But if you have activity after activity, you have to endure that discomfort for only a little bit of time, and then you're off to go somewhere else. Mikaela wondered whether having lots of structured activities could distract a child from facing the consequences of his own actions on others—the child wouldn't have enough time to work relationships out.

Naoko, a Japanese mother spending two years abroad in the United States with her husband and two sons, was surprised by some of the cultural differences surrounding the playdate. When she first moved to her new town north of New York City, she accidentally committed some social faux pas, like the time she arranged to host a playdate for her son with another child's mother and then spontaneously invited one of the kids' other friends to join them. When the first child's mother got upset at her for doing that, she realized, "Okay, maybe this is an American rule I need to learn. . . ."

In Japan, parents didn't arrange playdates for school-age kids. It was up to the kids to decide among themselves who they wanted to play with and where—it could be one child, it could be many, and they could be flowing in and out between their house, another house, or the park. Parents didn't have interesting and stimulating activities ready. In Japan kids spontaneously decided what to do, whether it was to turn cardboard boxes into a "camp" site and pretend to go on an expedition, play tag or hide-and-seek, make up some new, complicated version of rock-paper-scissors, or just hang out. At the end of the afternoon, there wasn't a parent popping her head into the kids' room and saying, "It's five o'clock—get ready, your dad will be here to pick you up soon." Instead, kids were responsible for keeping track of time by themselves and getting themselves home by the time they'd promised their parents they'd be home.

Like other Westerners in Japan, we were sometimes surprised by how students were given so much freedom and time alone in their classrooms or on the playground to come up with games or activities without a teacher to moderate, but their teachers knew something we could learn from: children everywhere like to make up their own games and rules, it's important for them to be able to do this, and with enough practice they'll become skillful at negotiating the games among themselves. Letting kids have the responsibility for making up their own games or keeping track of their free time is part of how adults in Japan give kids the message that they are in charge of their own play, and aren't required to look to grown-ups to tell them how to play, when to play, or with whom it's appropriate to play.

## HOW ACTIVE PLAY BOOSTS LEARNING

At a public elementary school in Tokyo on a brisk autumn morning, children thundered down the stairs and out the back door to the schoolyard for recess. Some third- and fourth-grade boys grabbed a ball and started an intense impromptu soccer game, while one group of girls was intent on practicing riding unicycles—a popular activity in Japanese schools. Other kids twirled brightly colored hula hoops, practiced on the uneven bars, or just hung out together, talking. As soon as the bell rang, they ran back in for their next class. They'd be back out here after lunch for another half an hour of free play.

After classes ended for the day at 2:40, a bunch of kids returned to the playground. Most Japanese elementary schools keep the playground available for another few hours of play at the end of the day, giving kids additional time to get physical exercise and fresh air and time with friends. When the last bell chimed to let the kids know the playground was closing, there was a happy hubbub as the kids gathered up their bags, put on their school hats, and walked home in the late-afternoon sunlight.

In Japan, recess is as standard in school as math, reading, or lunch. Recess is frequent—usually there is a little break after every fifty-minute class period, and then two longer recesses during the day.

Naperville Community Unit School District 203 in Illinois, pro-filed in John J. Ratey's book *Spark*, is a particularly inspiring example of how physical movement enhances cognitive ability. School officials implemented a district-wide PE curriculum that focuses on fitness as op-posed to sports, and then had students take some of their hardest subjects after exercising. As a result, Naperville students achieved stunning re-sults on the Trends in International Mathematics and Science Study (TIMSS), a standardized test administered every four years to students worldwide. In 1999 it was given in thirty-eight countries, and Naperville students scored *first* in the world in science, and sixth in math—behind only math superstars such as Singapore, Korea, Taiwan, Hong Kong, and Japan. This is remarkable, since Naperville students are a cross-sampling of ordinary American students. The stunning results from Na-perville echo other studies suggesting a strong link between exercise and learning. Researchers from Harvard and other universities reported in 2009 that the more physical fitness tests children passed, the better they did on academic tests.

Research confirms that a day that includes breaks for physical exer-cise is beneficial to productivity. Active, playful breaks during the day also help children retain and assimilate what they are learning. Children who alternate intense bursts of study with frequent playful breaks (the way kids do in Japan) pay more attention to classroom tasks immediately afterward. And a study published in *Pediatrics* looking at about 11,000 children ages eight and nine found that those who had more than fifteen minutes of recess a day behaved better in class than those who did not.

These breaks are crucial to boosting a child's attention. They also help children avoid cognitive interference, a term referring to distraction caused by unrelated thoughts. For example, a child who has been focusing on challenging spelling words might find it hard to transition right to math. But a quick recess in which he can clear his head, run around, let off steam, and play with friends will leave him refreshed and ready to switch gears back in the classroom. A recent Centers for Disease Control and Prevention review of fifty studies found that not only do we have no evidence that recess negatively affects learning, but there is "substantial evidence" that physical activity benefits grades, test scores, and academic achievement, and can positively affect concentration and classroom behavior. A 2013 policy statement by the American Academy of Pediatrics states unequivocally that "recess is a crucial and necessary component of a child's development," and has unique, irreplaceable benefits for children's cognitive, emotional, and physical health.

But in spite of all the persuasive research showing its benefits, American children get less recess than their peers in many other countries. Scandinavian nations, famous for their emphasis on early-childhood play, late-start academics, and plenty of outdoor recess for kids at all ages, were recently ranked among the most creative nations in the world. The United States ranks high on that list as well: innovation and creativity have long been hallmark traits of American society. But evidence suggests that American creativity is at risk. Americans have been showing a decline in creativity over the past two decades, according to results on the Torrance Test for Creative Thinking. If we are to maintain our creative edge in the future, we want to be attentive to how our children are spending their time now.

Before our move to Japan, Benjamin had had no more than twenty minutes to play outdoors every day when he was in full-day preschool and fifteen minutes during full-day kindergarten in New York City. But he had lots of company. Thirty percent of American children studied in a recent *Pediatrics* journal study were found to have little or no recess at all. Recess is often taken away as punishment for misbehavior ("recess deprivation"), when it is exactly what would help let off some steam. Even more disturbingly, underserved schools often get the least amount of recess, compounding their students' difficulties with school.

Recess itself isn't just an aid to learning; it is itself educational. Free play during recess is cognitively beneficial, as children who play with one another need to juggle and incorporate another person's perspectives and views. This is a challenging but important cognitive task for them to master, and is one of the building blocks for future creativity, which requires the ability to step outside your own limited experience of the world. Studies show that peers, rather than adults, contribute to more sophisticated imaginary play, because their stories and suggestions help to collectively take the play to a new and higher level.

In our country, school administrations and teachers are under pressure to provide visible, measurable academic results, often compelling them to cut back on recess to make more room for academics. But the neuroscience of play has shown that this is the wrong approach. It's especially counterproductive since today's students need to develop twenty-first-century skills that require the sort of initiative and creativity that they develop through play.

## DISCOVERY AND WONDER THROUGH OUTDOOR PLAY

Rebecca, a Danish graduate student in education, has been doing her internship at a "forest kindergarten," located in western Denmark. The kindergarten is for students ages three to six and is located on the edge of a forest; a small, icy bay lies on the other side.

One winter day, since the sun in this northern country was too low to get through the treetops of the forest at this time of year, they headed to the bay to catch every bit of sunlight. "On our way, some of the children talked about swimming in the sea, because of the sun, and the teacher just smiled in response," Rebecca told me. The teacher did not correct or admonish the children, she did not tell them it was too cold, or make rules that kids not go near the water, or warn them about the dangers of the ice. They collected stones and shells on the beach. When one of the girls said that she wanted to go into the water, the teacher explained, "We'll have to break the ice on the sea and there will only be a small towel to use after you come out." The little girl nodded and took off all her clothes. Some of the other children followed her initiative, the teacher quietly watching.

"We broke the ice a bit and the children put their feet in the freezing water—they were screaming and laughing and I got ready to dry their feet and help them to put on their clothes as soon as they got out," Rebecca remembered. "None of them went further out in the sea, and they definitely learned about the temperature of Danish waters in winter. The children said they feel tough like the Vikings—I was quite impressed by their courage."

These kids play outdoors for hours, in all kinds of weather, every day if possible. They feel safe in nature, exploring and experimenting, learning about the world. "I've noticed how physically mature the children are, and how they come up with games and activities without any toys. In the forest there's just what nature offers, and they have to be creative and active to have a good time," Rebecca enthused. "There is no such thing as bad weather," she added (a phrase I would hear many times from many Nordic parents), "only bad clothing."


On the outskirts of Düsseldorf, Germany, there is a forest school, similar to the one in Denmark, that I visited one spring morning. The forest there is utterly silent except for the sound of wind in the trees, birds singing, and the crunching of leaves and branches under our feet. Trees reach high up to the sky.

Far off in the distance, twenty-two-month-old Anna and my Korean-German aunt (who lives in Düsseldorf) and I saw flashes of color: children moving through the forest. We heard human sounds: quiet murmuring voices, and then some laughter or occasional shouts. As we drew closer, we saw about fifteen children, ages three to six (German kindergartens, like Japanese and Danish ones, are mixed-age), and a few adults, all dressed in rugged, durable clothing—hooded jackets, kerchiefs or hats for their heads, rain boots for the muddy forest floor. Nearby was a small trailer that served as a shed to hold supplies—books, tools, and so forth. There were hooks on the outside where the children hung their little bags. There were a few small tables and chairs near the trailer, as well as a small sandbox.

Everyone gathered, sitting around a clearing on some logs and beginning the day with songs, accompanied by a teacher strumming a guitar. For about fifteen minutes there was singing, then a story. When circle time finished, the children ran off into the forest to play. Some dug with shovels, a few scattered to the sandbox, and others dispersed farther into the woods, within eyesight, but off on their own. All they had was a few tools, all of nature, and each other. They looked small under the tall trees.

One of the teachers, Wolfgang, a tall young man with long blond hair wearing a blue and gray hooded sweatshirt, came up to me. "They are building a castle for the beetles in the sandbox," he told me, indicating some children gathered nearby. He pointed out a rope hanging from a tree with a large, sturdy branch suspended on it. The children had made it themselves—two of the children had used a saw to cut the branch to the right length. They now used it as a challenging sort of seesaw—more difficult to balance on than a conventional one, but that was exactly where its merit lay. "What I think is important—the big difference from a playground—is that it's not fixed. It's not just moving in one direction, so the children have to learn to control their own bodies much more," declared Wolfgang. It's also important that the children have come up with ideas for structures. There's no teacher saying, "Hey, let's make a seesaw today!" Teachers scaffold the children's play by helping to bring their ideas to life, but children feel the power of coming up with ideas from their own imaginations.

There are about seven hundred forest kindergartens in Germany, where children spend all four or so hours of their preschool day outside, and the number of the schools is increasing. In Germany, there is a strong notion that children ought to spend as much time as possible outside tramping about in the dirt, getting muddy, and being as close to nature as possible (one mother near Berlin told me her grandmother actually brought dirt and sand into the house for the children to play in). Parents who send their children to a forest school say they value not just the time spent outdoors and the heightened bond with nature that results, but the simplicity of the daily schedule and the way their children become confident about what their own bodies can do. A study comparing Swedish forest kindergarten students and city kindergarten students showed the forest kindergarten students were able to play for longer, concentrate better, and get along better with their peers, in part due to having fewer space constraints and more freedom. They were also less irritable with peers.

"We want to allow them as much as possible. We try to forbid as little as possible to give them as much freedom as we can," Wolfgang told me when we came upon a five-year-old boy in a red sweatshirt carving a stick with a pocketknife, lips pursed in concentration. It's not unusual to see an unsupervised child wielding a knife here, though he assured me that the teachers show the children how to carve safely, with the movements going away from the body. Other children have been involved in other kinds of play throughout the morning: a little girl, Lina, showed me a beetle she'd discovered, several kids were using water from the pump in some form of imaginary play, and Friedeliche, one of the other teachers, offered me a cup of elderberry juice several children had squeezed from berries and mixed with water. The kids sat and ate a midmorning breakfast. It wasn't as though the children were completely divorced from the modern world. As they chatted with one another throughout the meal, I saw a few kids pretending to talk on cell phones with their sandwiches.

After breakfast, the class got ready for an excursion. They gathered supplies: a hammer and tools in a little wagon, their packs. Slowly everyone began to leave, moving at a pace that was just right for the children to stop and look at something or chat with each other. The children, rather than the teachers, were the ones who dictated the pace of this walk, just as they had decided upon their own play throughout the morning.

In a school like a forest kindergarten, the basic premise is that children, left to their own devices and only minimal adult guidance, will be able to create their own meaningful experiences for themselves. There are no stations, because there is no room to divide up into predetermined spaces; there's no book corner, art center, or pretend play area. Time is fluid too; the day isn't divided up into many different activities—circle time, science, library, reading, playtime. Nor are children divided up by age or constricted by rules about behaving safely in a small, shared space. Instead, it's left to the children to make their own learning, do what they will with their day, make their own props, approach their peers and invite them to play. Children are given space to think what they would like to do and the encouragement to act on it.

Just about all German kindergartens are play-based now. In the 1970s there was a wave of early-learning reform in Germany. Most kindergartens were transformed into schools that emphasized cognitive academic skills instead of play. But subsequent research showed that not only were there no cognitive gains when ten-year-old graduates of these kindergartens were compared with peers who attended play-based schools, there were actually deficits. Children who had spent their early years playing were actually better at math and reading. They were also better adjusted, socially and emotionally, than their peers. And they excelled in areas such as creativity, intelligence, and industriousness. As a result, the German government abandoned these educational reforms and kindergartens reverted to their play-based origins.

# FINDING THE RIGHT BALANCE

Most parents, myself included, know how frustrating it is to hear a child start to pester, whining, "I'm bored," "There's nothing to do." While too much structured activity isn't the right answer for this common dilemma, many children thrive on a busy schedule, and there's no doubt for many families going to activities is a positive experience that provides them with quality time to talk and connect, or shared interests to get excited about. I love and share the widespread belief that the parent-and-child relationship benefits from quality time spent together. The reliance of American children on parents and other adults as occasional playmates isn't a bad thing. In fact it feels completely understandable given the reality of our modern lives; many children may not have playmates right in the neighborhood or siblings at home.

It's easy to understand parents who feel giving their children a chance to try something is a gift: a chance to find something they might love to do in their life. For our family, structured activities provide the kids with opportunities that no amount of free play could ever provide: the joy of playing soccer on an organized team, the thrill of making music on the violin or piano, and the ability to maintain their bilingualism so they can always talk with their friends in Japan. Like any other parent, I'm not immune to anxiety about my kids' futures, or the desire to enroll them in activities that are structured and guided and seem productive or stimulating in some way. In fact, I'm very much vulnerable to the desire to do the best I can for my kids. We, like all parents I know, give our children the opportunities we can out of love for them and concern for their futures.

I also know how fortunate we are. Not every family has the time, money, or other resources needed for enrichment. For all the nostalgic memories I might have of the childhood days I was left to my own devices, I know for many kids free time is not a choice, but a necessity due to a lack of other options.

But the evidence is clear: there are undeniable and irreplaceable benefits in play with multi-age peers, frequent physical breaks, and ample unstructured time. Now that I know how unusual American parents are among the world's parents in caring so much about cultivating our young kids' cognitive development and talents, and have learned where that idea came from, it has lost some of the power it once had over me.

The time children spend "off task"—time that might seem idle and wasted—is often full of interior richness. Children are doing exactly what they should be doing. Play, downtime, and daydreaming help them reach their innate potential. The benefits of play seem, to me, to be as crucial for our kids' futures as anything we enroll them in, because through play they internalize a valuable lifelong attitude: the idea that they have the power to make something of their own lives, and that they can create so much out of so little.

With four kids and only so many hours in the day, we are still working on creating a balanced life, and know that it will probably always be a work in progress. But I keep this in mind: play may be something children naturally do, but playing well is a skill that can be lost. If parents treat downtime and play with the same reverence our culture gives to more structured activities, kids won't lose the skill of playing well. What I've learned is that kids need a lot of time to do this. They need a lot of time to play.

PART 3

# The Teaching
# of Children

# SEVEN

# HIGH PRESSURE?
## What Asian Learning Looks Like

Xiangchen, a high school senior in Beijing, wakes up at 5:30 a.m. He scrambles himself an egg, heats a steamed bun, pours hot soybean milk into a glass, and quickly eats his breakfast. By 6:00 a.m., Xiangchen is working on his daily morning recitations (sometimes he recites Chinese classical poems, sometimes English news articles). He knows that becoming proficient at both Chinese and English takes repetition and hard work. By 6:45 a.m. it's time to leave for school. School is six kilometers (almost four miles) from home, and he usually commutes by bicycle. Classes begin at 7:40 a.m. Xiangchen and his classmates take five morning classes, eat lunch for thirty minutes, have a brief rest, and then take afternoon classes. School finishes by 5:20 p.m., but today they have an exam after class.

This is a crucial year for Xiangchen and his classmates. This year they take the *gaokao*, or college entrance exam. Their score on this exam will determine the tier of the college they may attend. Including weekends, university-bound Chinese high school seniors study up to ninety hours a week. Today Xiangchen returns home at 7:00 p.m. After a quick supper made by his mom, he clocks in several hours of homework. At midnight the tired teenager stumbles off to bed.

Is Xiangchen's life a model of how children should pursue their studies or an example of how Asian culture puts too much pressure on children? Do Asian children receive a better education than Americans? Every few years, we hear that East Asian countries like South Korea, Singapore, and China have achieved top marks on international achievement tests of math, reading, and science, while American scores typically hover around the middle. You may have heard that Asian children go to school for longer, take learning very seriously, and have an astounding work ethic. It's hard not to compare, and some parents and educators fret about what the future holds for America's children, as well as for the nation.

Although my children are still years away from college (Benjamin, my eldest, is just entering middle school), as an American mom of South Korean descent who spends a lot of time in Asia, I wanted to understand what Chinese and South Korean education are really like, and explore whether American parents can learn from these Asian nations to improve our own children's opportunities for educational success, or if the price Asian children have to pay really is too high. So on a sunny June morning in 2011, I boarded a plane for China with year-old Anna and my friend Kumi, who came along to help babysit. Several weeks later, I flew to South Korea (this time, my whole family and my mom joined me). My mission: to talk to parents and teachers to see what lessons about education we American parents could learn.

## THE TIGER NATION

Our plane to China touched down in a vast expanse of lush green fields on the outskirts of Shenyang, an industrial city in the northeast region of China (BMW and Michelin are among the corporations that have factories here). We were there to visit Northeast Yucai School, a highly regarded K–12 public school with some seven thousand students, which had been recommended to me by an expert on education in China and America.

As soon as Anna, Kumi, and I passed through customs, we were met by a group of the school's high school students and their young teacher Lois. They instantly gravitated toward Anna, exclaiming over her and bending down to engage her with kind smiles. Throughout our stay, every time we came to the slightest obstacle—a sidewalk, a short flight of stairs—which I had usually navigated by bumping Anna down in her stroller—nearby students rushed to my side to lift her stroller in the air like a palanquin.

China is a vast country. There are huge gaps between rural and urban, educated and less educated, wealthy and poor populations. Even so, several generalizations hold true. Confucian ideas about family and learning permeate society and have a strong influence on child-rearing. Learning is both a moral endeavor and a family obligation. In China and in many other Confucian-influenced Asian societies, parenting and education are closely entwined, and learning isn't just for the purpose of becoming smart and informed—it's a form of self-cultivation.

The evening of our arrival, after an afternoon of sightseeing, we met with Lois and her husband, as well as with Madame Wang, the head of the international program at Northeast Yucai and my liaison at the school, and her fifteen-year-old daughter, Angela. Angela spoke four languages, Wang told me proudly, and has helped raise money for charity.

Over sizzling plates of Korean barbecue, our conversation soon turned toward Amy Chua's memoir, *Battle Hymn of the Tiger Mother*, which had received a lot of attention in China since being published in early 2011. Chua's story of raising her two daughters to excellence in America through strict, exacting child-rearing methods she dubbed "Chinese parenting" had provoked heated discussion and controversy. While few American readers initially questioned that her book reflected what parenting was like in China, it turned out that dubbing her methods "Chinese parenting" was what made her book controversial to Chinese readers. "The Tiger Mother method is backwards and out of date," Wang insisted in fluent and capable English. "Today, parents are more concerned about how to educate children to find their own ideas, to find their own path. I have my own life, and my daughter has her life. We are trying to raise children in a more Western way. I cannot say one thing is really correct."

I was surprised. Wang had a more nuanced, if flexible, view of education and child-rearing than I'd expected to encounter. But I soon learned that many Chinese parents like her—urban and well educated and with one child to lavish their attentions on—are juggling traditional ideals about learning with the influx of progressive ideas from the West that have become popular in recent years, ideas that have an appealing cachet of cosmopolitan modernity. "Parents can't impose their beliefs on their children. What is good for parents isn't necessarily what is right for children," Wang continued, as she gazed affectionately at her daughter. The others at the table nodded their heads in agreement. "The Tiger Mother method is outdated, old-fashioned—no one here aspires to do that anymore," Lois's husband agreed.

But in spite of this new surge of fascination with Western ideas, a fierce devotion to education runs deep in China. In one study, Chinese mothers regarded high expectations, academics, and family sacrifice as important factors for their preschoolers' education, while Euro-American mothers emphasized wanting their children to experience social development, have fun while learning, and build self-esteem during their preschool years. It's likely that many of us hold stereotypes about Asian parents that dovetail with the findings of this study. To Western eyes, lots of Asian parents can seem single-mindedly focused upon their children's academic achievement. As comfortable as I am with a lot of aspects of Asian culture that feel foreign to many American parents, even I had a hard time understanding the mentality behind one mom I know of, a Chinese immigrant in the United States who drilled her son on the upcoming year's math throughout his summer break so that he could go into the new school year well ahead of his peers.

# DEDICATION TO LEARNING IS AN EXPRESSION OF PARENTAL LOVE

The cultural differences between China and the United States can sometimes look especially glaring because they often go hand in hand with different parenting styles. In the United States, authoritative parents—those who parent with warmth but also with high expectations and clear structure, taking the child's wishes and opinions into account—are thought to embody the style that best promotes children's well-being. In other words, a parent who is neither too strict, nor too lenient, is the ideal parent. The stereotypical Asian parent may appear too strict if she uses more overtly controlling strategies, gives more directives, offers less obvious warmth, and provides children fewer choices. Her children may begin academics at a younger age and learn through flash cards and rote memorization. Euro-American parents who prize the idea of developing the "whole child" worry that so much intense academic training and focus is inappropriate and potentially harmful, and also worry about the detrimental effects of controlling parenting.

But both views come from our specific worldviews about the proper role of a parent in raising her child. Ruth Chao, a psychology professor at UC Riverside, questioned how valid the typical terms to describe parenting (that is, "authoritarian," "authoritative," and "permissive") were when looking at non-Western cultures. She focused on the central child-rearing concepts of the Chinese words *guan* and *chiao shun*, concepts that are best understood within their cultural context, not through a Western lens, and help explain the paradoxical finding that strict, authoritarian parenting predicts poorer school achievement in Euro-American children but higher school achievement among Chinese immigrant children. The ideas of *Chiao shun* (training) and *guan* (to love, govern, or care for) emphasize that it is a parent's responsibility to make sure the child does not fall short of standards. In China a parent's main responsibility to her child is to monitor his learning, because learning itself *is* how you de-

velop the "whole child." It's through learning that you foster perseverance, self-regulation, and constant self-improvement, traits considered
important in all spheres of life.

To us the price of *guan* might seem too high. Intrusive parents
aren't viewed positively: we worry they inhibit their children's growing
independence or that their child isn't being allowed to live life for himself. But authoritarian parenting in the West is negatively associated with
Puritan child-rearing influences, stern or harsh domination, and "breaking a child's will," notions that have no innate roots in Chinese or Asian
culture. In China, authoritarian parenting springs from a completely different view of children, one that's rooted in Confucianism and is cen-
tered on harmony and care, teaching and inculcating. Seen through the
lens of *guan*, parental authoritarianism (or parental control) can be a
sign of parental love, simply expressed differently. Taking care of and
responding to your child means being extremely devoted to supporting
and looking out for him and his education. Even though the way parental warmth is shown is different from culture to culture, what really matters is how it's felt by the child. In a cultural system where social hierarchy
is thought to promote harmonious relationships rather than domination,
a Chinese child can feel his parents' deep care for him expressed through
their attentiveness to his education.

Consider a set of studies conducted by Sheena Iyengar, at the time
of the research a social psychology graduate student at Stanford and now
a professor of business at Columbia, and Mark Lepper, a psychologist at
Stanford. In their studies, seven-to-nine-year-old children were presented
with puzzles and markers. Half the children were Asian-American of
Japanese or Chinese heritage who spoke their native language at home,
and half were Anglo-American. They were presented with six different
markers and six different piles of anagram puzzles. One group was given
a choice of puzzle as well as color of the marker to write their answers. A
second group was assigned an anagram and marker by the researcher.
A third group was told that their *mother* had chosen which anagram to
work on and which marker to use. The Anglo-American children who
were given their own choice worked longer and completed more ana-

grams. When they were told what to do, "their performance and subsequent motivation dropped dramatically." They even looked embarrassed by the idea that their mother might have chosen for them. The Asian-American children, on the other hand, performed best and were most motivated when they believed their mothers had chosen for them. One of them even asked the researcher to make sure she told her mother that she'd done as she had asked.

For the Asian-American children, motivation came from their mothers' involvement because "their relationships with their mothers represented a large part of their identities," Iyengar explained. "Letting their mothers choose the anagrams didn't threaten their sense of control" in the same way that it did for the Anglo-American children. The Anglo-American children valued a different sort of autonomy, one that let them dictate their own preferences. They saw themselves as separate from their mothers. For the Asian-American children, forming a healthy self-identity is not at odds with being accountable to their parents. If you believe that your mother's goals are a logical extension of your own, you aren't doing something "just to please your mother," as Westerners might consider it.

Northeast Yucai School is an elite public boarding school whose students come from all over the region and must pass a competitive entrance exam to be admitted. The education is rigorous, but here students also take many electives, as in Western education. As I toured the campus with four student guides, Jessie, Stephanie, Dickens, and David (Chinese kids like to adopt English names), and met over a dozen teachers, I came to understand that this school was a hybrid model of West and East. My student guides showed me outfitted art rooms, a serene tea ceremony room, a craft room where freshly silkscreened T-shirts were drying, a debate center, the music auditorium, a robotics workshop, and a performance room with a stage.

The life of a student at Yucai is regimented. Every morning, the high school students eat breakfast at 6:00 a.m. Then they clean their dormitory room and make their beds. From 6:50 a.m. to 7:30 a.m. they study, and then from 7:40 a.m. until noon they are in classes. They have classes in the morning with a ten-minute break in between: math, Chinese, English, science, and history, politics, or geography. After lunch, there is time for a nap or studying, and then more classes in the afternoon. They get another little break between 4:30 and 6:00—some kids swim, some play badminton or table tennis, others study. After dinner they study again and then they go to sleep. Jessie and Stephanie laughed about how much they talk after lights are out.

In Chinese schools the smart kids, not the class clowns or athletic stars, are usually most popular. The middle and high school students I met were self-contained and earnest, their passion for learning and desire to talk about sophisticated issues evident. During my visit, I met with a group of middle-school students, who filed into the classroom with shy curiosity, wearing the school's signature sky-blue polo shirts. They soon warmed up, peppering me with questions in imperfect but enthusiastic English: How much do American students study? How much do Japanese students study? Do they *like* to study? They shared their dreams for the future: One boy told me he wants to be a basketball player, but laughed at himself good-naturedly because he was very short and wore glasses. Another told me she wanted to be a doctor, but now she has decided she wants to be a writer like J. K. Rowling. Her father told her that studying is so important because it is the key to having a "colorful" life (*colorful* is a Chinese-English word for vibrant, rich, and fulfilling).

The oldest one in the group, an earnest fourteen-year-old boy who loves to practice English, dominated the conversation, telling me that the secret to learning was to find out what you loved. "I always said to myself, 'Just do what you're interested in. Learn about what you like,'" he said enthusiastically, "'and then improve upon those things.'"

"How do you find out what you're interested in?" I asked.

"I tried different things. Some of them made me feel exhausted, so I felt like I didn't want to do those things anymore. Like science. It makes me have to think harder, and I feel tired. But I love English and I always speak after class to my teachers."

Another boy, who calls himself Ted, piped up. "My mother always said, 'Habit is the best teacher.' My father doesn't think so. What do you think?" he asked me eagerly.

"What do *you* think?" I deflected.

"I think habit *is* the best teacher. I like biology very much. I always read biology books, and my biology became very good."

I was confused—were we talking about habit, or interest? "How does habit help you to learn?"

"Well, I have a little book about physics, and when I was small, I hated it. But then my mother told me a lot about physics. And she told me, 'You must try to read the book often. Then it will become habit.'"

I heard a twist on Ted's mom's phrase often during the trip to Shenyang: *Interest is the best teacher.* When someone discovers what he is interested in, his passion will take him to great heights. But what remained unspoken was this: Passion isn't something you just stumble upon. The parent puts these opportunities in the child's path, and believes such passion must go hand in hand with intensively and deliberately honing basic skills. I learned that at this school in China, skill-based knowledge was nonnegotiable. Everyone had to become good at Chinese, at math, and science. Why? Because their thinking was that you can't do much with your interests if you don't have skills. This approach to life is shared in many of the Confucian nations and covers far more than mere academics. One of my friends, an American woman who lived in East Asia for over twenty years, never forgot what her Japanese calligraphy teacher once said: "No one thinks it's interesting if a calligrapher breaks rules of calligraphy that he has not totally, and utterly, mastered. Once he has mastered the rules, that's when thinking outside the box is interesting."

American teachers sometimes have a hard time convincing parents of the merits of drills or other rote learning that are the hallmark of Asian education (and, some argue, one secret to their success on examinations). American parents and even some teachers believe drill practice (sometimes referred to as "drill and kill") and rote memorization can impede creativity and take the fun out of learning. But this point of view is problematic, and not only because it leads to lower test scores. "Being smart in math is actually the combination of knowledge, skills, and creativity," Jen, a high school math teacher in Pennsylvania with twenty years of experience, explained to me. "All of these can be fostered in a good education system. Truly good mathematical problem solvers combine a mastery of knowledge and skills with creativity to solve new problems, or to solve old problems in a new way." But you can't find creative or interesting solutions to problems without the basic skills, like multiplication, which take time to cultivate to the point of automaticity. Learning any skill (playing an instrument, riding a bike, or math) takes sheer practice, and the kids who understand this often experience greater success. One study of National Spelling Bee finalists found that the quality that best predicted performance wasn't innate smarts or creative preparation so much as dogged perseverance—or grit, which is, as we saw in Chapter 4, a crucial factor in success. The children who did better engaged in more deliberate solitary practice (which has been shown to be more effective than strategies such as being quizzed by others, a more enjoyable technique that takes less effort) in pursuit of the end goal—in this case, becoming champion spellers. While lessons about perseverance and deliberate practice are important for any child (not just spelling-bee winners), our bias toward believing that learning should always be fun and engaging isn't in our kids' best interests. "The problem is that this kind of deliberate skill-learning for math has been maligned," Jen told me.

The kids I met with in Shenyang—an admittedly handpicked group—were refreshingly motivated and hardworking. They were also sweet, polite, and totally engaged and earnest. I was favorably impressed. How did their parents and teachers keep them working so hard and feeling so enthusiastic about their studies? I wondered. How did they keep them motivated?

Wang shared her favorite strategy with me through a story, famous among teachers and parents, about jumping for an apple.

"A skillful teacher balances skill and persistence in children," Wang, a short woman with a thoughtful response to all of my questions, began. "We always want to know, how high can they jump? What level can we ask them to reach without discouraging them? It's like we're holding an apple this high," she said, holding an imaginary apple up above her head. "And we're asking them to jump to get it. There's *always* a period when they think they can't do it and they just don't want to jump. But then, if it's just out of reach, they'll touch it. And when they touch it, they want to touch it again. So then we move it up again, just a little out of reach. As they jump, their ability improves, and they feel successful. We encourage them, by saying, 'You can do it.' Or we'll say, 'You really surprised me, you were able to do it, you jumped this high. You made it.' And if they fail, we say, 'Don't worry, I'm sure next time you can think about it and do it.' We really encourage them so they won't doubt their ability. But at the same time we don't overly praise them, because if you praise what doesn't deserve praise, you'll actually be encouraging *that* behavior.

"It's a little like a mountain climb," she continued earnestly as she stood up to make her point. "Just let them climb up that mountain. When they've made it partway, have them look back and see how far they already came, and then they can keep on moving." They should make enough progress that it feels like a genuine accomplishment, Wang added. "It's no fun to just move from here, to here," she explained, holding her hands apart just a bit. "Let them feel the success. Pressure is a good thing; it pushes us. We push them to jump for that apple."

As impressed as I was by the students I met at the school, at times the Chinese way feels uncompromising despite the veneer of Western progressive thought overlaying it. Yong Zhao, a professor of education at the University of Oregon and author of *World Class Learners: Educating Creative and Entrepreneurial Students*, agrees. "Asian parents typically really believe anything can come from effort," he told me on the phone. "And if you don't do something right, we won't make excuses for you." Zhao spoke slowly and with deliberation. "Americans accept individuals as we get them. In fact, we tend to make excuses for them, and that may not always be as healthy. But it's a double-edged sword." He paused. "It is true that all children can use more effort, but at the same time if you don't accept that there are individual differences, that's a mistake as well."

Zhao considers the Asian tendency for parents to prescribe the path a child will take problematic, because in his view it deprives kids of self-responsibility. In China, he told me, if anything goes wrong, people blame parents or the government: they say it is because they weren't given freedom to choose. In the United States, we give our kids freedom and choice and responsibility. But if something is their choice, they can't complain about it. Zhao, a father of young children himself, told me, "I tell my children, if it's your choice, you have to take responsibility for it. When you learn to negotiate, you learn to accept the consequences of your decisions."

More and more middle-class Chinese parents are attracted to the idea of taking a step back so their children can develop without overt parental interference. Yin Jianli's 2009 *A Good Mom Is Better Than a Good Teacher*, a memoir that questions traditional Chinese education and parenting practices, quickly became a runaway best seller. Yin, a former Beijing public schoolteacher, advocates "listening to your child," rather than imposing your own view, and allowing children independence and freedom by not overprotecting them, as well as allowing for opportunities for character growth (in one part, she relates how her own nine-year-old daughter took a seventeen-hour train ride alone).

Chinese parents are eager to learn how to achieve the right balance and they are actively looking to Western culture, particularly American culture, to help them figure out how to let their children be more creative. They want to help their children find their interests, find themselves, and thrive in a competitive society. Amy Chua's memoir hit a nerve (and was published in China with a picture of Chua standing confidently in front of an American flag) in part because it was the story of being a mom in America. When I met with a group of teachers who are also mothers, the conversation quickly shifted to questions aimed at me. (One young teacher was desperate to know how to get her son to obey her, because he won't wake up on time in the morning.) They were eager to learn more about Western parenting and how to raise the talented, creative, innovative children that they want for China's future.

It's not as though they have abandoned a traditional approach. The Confucian mindset favoring constant learning, self-cultivation, and life-long self-improvement over achievement is clearly evident at the school. It is this very emphasis on learning rather than achievement that leads to high achievement, according to Jin Li, an associate professor of education at Brown University. Focusing on learning means emphasizing things like the value of hard work and incremental progress, unglamorous but effective strategies that help lead to the kind of high achievement we often associate with Asian students.

But lots of Chinese educators are fascinated by the concept of the whole child. Northeast Yucai has the appearance of cultivating the whole child—the generous facilities allocated for extracurricular classes, the language of personal choice and Western liberal thought. Teachers at Northeast Yucai also aspire to become more Western—trying to give children more electives, helping them be more outgoing and verbal (as American children tend to be) by encouraging them to engage in debates, sending them on school trips abroad, and leading them toward innovation and creativity. In some ways this is a collective endeavor shared by the nation as a whole.

On our last day in China, I met with Gao Chen, head of the entire school, with two teachers and two interpreters. After our conversation, something happened that really surprised me. Gao Chen asked *my* advice, *my* thoughts, on learning, on how to raise children to become successful in life. The moment I began to cobble together a hesitant answer, every person in the room bent her head down to the table and began writing down every word I said. No one, not even the illustrious head of one of the most elite schools in China, was going to let a potential opportunity for learning and self-improvement pass by.

# SOUTH KOREA: TOO MUCH STRESS FOR SUCCESS?

A few weeks after visiting China, I packed our bags to go to Seoul. I've visited Seoul many times and lived there for a year on a college exchange program. My parents spoke Korean in our home and I am close to the many relatives we have in South Korea. Over the years I have seen the country transform: on my first visit to the country at age nine, the area below the Han River in Seoul (Gangnam) was rural, remote countryside; now, it is one of the most fashionable, upscale, and populated districts in the city. As a college student, I was chastised by a taxi driver for wearing a skirt that hovered above my knees—too short in that conservative country. Today I see women in fashionable tops and miniskirts and young men sporting long layered bangs or spiky hair: dress codes, and social mores in general, have loosened.

Like China, Korea is heavily influenced by Confucianism. Traditionally, learning has been about cultivating both intelligence and character, and was seen as a building block for a good society. Today, South Korea continues to be a country that prioritizes learning, but it has new notions of success that hinge on economic stability and prestige. Education is a crucial way—the only way—for parents to help their children succeed.

South Korea's famously zealous stance toward education comes from the country's drive to modernization. The nation achieved stunning success in a short period of time, pulling itself up from post–Korean War devastation to the world's fifteenth largest economy within just a few decades. South Korea has one of the highest college graduation rates in the world, amazing when you consider that just a generation ago only about a quarter graduated from high school (today 98 percent of young people do, more than in any other industrialized nation). The South Korean government invests heavily in educating its children, and parents do too, spending 16 percent of their income on a "shadow system" of after-school *hagwon*s, or private cram schools.

Many South Korean parents believe that a college education is the only way to guarantee that their children will have a comfortable middle-class life. But not just any college will do: only a degree from one of very few elite universities and colleges clustered in Seoul is considered prestigious and desirable. To get into one of these highly competitive elite schools, you need a high score on the national college entrance exam. On the day of the nine-hour test, held in November, the nation holds its breath: planes are forbidden from taking off or landing during the listening portion of the test, offices and the stock market open later, and mothers flock to churches and temples to pray for their children's success.

The cost of this pressure from a one-shot exam system to children's and parents' health and happiness is high. To prepare for the exam, children study for years late into the night, going from school to *hagwon*s and arriving home late at night. Suicides from bullying are on the rise because of increased competitiveness among middle and high schoolers. The government has instituted an educational curfew of 10:00 p.m. and conducts raids on *hagwon*s to ensure that they comply. In lots of cases there's little reward for the late nights of studying and the high pressure children feel during their childhood and teen years. South Korea now has a glut of unemployed college graduates.

On the whole, though, South Korea's passion for education hasn't gone unnoticed. President Barack Obama frequently praised South Korea's educational system because of their top-ranking scores on international achievement tests such as the Program for International Student Assessment. Yet within South Korea itself, the education system has been called "the nation's biggest problem." I traveled to South Korea to investigate what American parents and educators could learn from my parents' country of origin: Is South Korea an educational success story we should emulate, or is the price of their success too high?

O n our first day in Seoul, I met a few mothers in a café at a hotel in downtown Seoul. The hotel, Lotte World in Jamsil, is part of a family-friendly hub, housing an indoor amusement park. Visiting at the start of South Korea's summer break (which, as in Japan, begins toward the end of July), we saw lots of vacationing families, most of which were small. The birth rate in South Korea has dropped dramatically to an average of 1.23 children, in large part because of the psychological and financial cost of raising a child. As in China, having only one child makes the fate of each child feel more weighty. The women I met represented the most ferocious type of Korean education-obsessed mother, and were highly invested in their kids' success. But as we talked, it was clear that they were just doing what any "good parent" feels she must do in a society where the gateway to middle-class aspirations is so narrow.

Their conversation was a litany of worry and resignation. One mom had decided to uproot her entire family to move to Daechi-dong, a neighborhood in the southern part of Seoul, because it has some of the best-regarded *hagwon*s in the city. Another mentioned a mother who committed suicide after her children left for college, unable to handle "empty nest syndrome" after years of working so hard for her children's education. Their stress level is high because their expectations are so high. "We want our children to be number one at everything," one of them said. "But, in a way, it's liberating if your child doesn't have ambition," she added, because it removes you from the rat race at an earlier stage. If they feel their children have a chance, these moms believe there is practically a moral obligation to push their children to continue through as far as they can.

In Korea I didn't hear talk about the importance of succeeding for one's country or having what the Chinese call a "colorful" life. The emphasis was not on personal fulfillment. In South Korea, achievement is very much a reflection of family, an expression of filial piety. Research notes that Korean mothers talk about cultivating their babies' intelligence in a close and intimate way, implying the process involves them both. One small but revealing finding in a study talked about how, in a Korean home, pictures to stimulate the baby's development were placed up high so that the baby could see them only when held up by a caregiver, a contrast to the cognitively stimulating mobiles that hang over cribs in America. When I recounted my discussion with these mothers to another Korean friend later on, she told me not to take their complaining seriously. Speaking like this about your life and your children is not unusual in Korea. In this culture, you wouldn't talk about what is going well in your life because that would be considered bragging. But when you talk about all your difficulties and the effort you make to help your children, you form bonds with others through shared suffering. "When I first came back to Korea," she told me, after having lived abroad for many years, "I thought these women I was meeting had terrible marriages. Then I realized that wasn't true at all—they had great marriages. This was just their way of talking, of letting off steam." This way of speaking about hardship demonstrates your worth, your investment, your commitment, and how much you are willing to sacrifice for a goal like your child's education.

For some South Korean parents, the sacrifice is truly mind-boggling: many are willing to separate their families and live for years apart from their children rather than put them through the educational system. Lots of mothers leave South Korea for the United States, Australia, the Philippines, or other countries with their children, fathers staying behind, to escape the unforgiving system by educating their children abroad. These days, around 18,000 Korean students live abroad. Seventy-seven percent of Korean students in the United States are in elementary or middle school. Most of the Korean students I know in the United States are school-age children, living here either with their mothers or with a relative or acquaintance. They seem remarkably unfazed by the fact that they are living so far from their home.

There are parents who are more nuanced and philosophical about the educational rat race, I discovered when I met with two researchers who are also parents, at Seoul National University, South Korea's most prestigious university. Kang-Ok Cho, a senior researcher at the Institution of Sports Science at Seoul National, is a soft-spoken woman around my age who has two daughters in their twenties who are both launched in the design business. Jung-woo Oh, another researcher in the same department, is a big, athletic man who is a generation younger than Cho. He's the father of an eight-year-old girl named Sarang (or, Love).

It wasn't easy for Cho and her husband to accept the path their daughters took. When the girls first showed interest in art and design in middle school, their parents were concerned about the stability of their careers and their futures. "I felt crazy [with worry]," Cho confided with a smile. But their daughters knew their own minds, Cho said with gentle pride, and eventually convinced their parents that they had the right to follow their own dreams. After all, they pointed out, even Cho was doing what she loved (she had decided to go back to school to get a PhD after years of working as a nutritionist).

Both parents told me that the most important part of an education is not the achievement per se. It's the character and inner strength that is cultivated through doing so much hard work. "I taught my daughters to be strong girls. I always think, if they can learn to overcome stress, they will be successful," Cho told me. Oh was a bit more protective, and displayed a curious mix of acceptance and ambition for his daughter. "If there's something she loves to do, and works hard at, I don't really care what it is—even if it's being a shoe shiner," Oh claimed. "As long as she loves it and as long as she becomes expert at it! Then it doesn't matter what she's doing." "Really?" I asked, "even a shoe shiner?" He declared, "That's how I feel, right now." He continued, "I know I don't know how I'll feel in the future."

Every day, Oh's dreams for his daughter change. Maybe she could be a world-class musician or a champion golfer. Although he was half joking, he was also serious—at a stage of parenting when all things seemed possible. But he also knew, despite the grandiose dreams he was surprisingly frank about, that Sarang will best be able to do what she feels a natural passion for. "You do well at what you love," Oh said, echoing what I heard in China: "Interest is the best teacher." Americans believe in something similar: Do what you love. Follow your bliss.

But the reality of the South Korean system means parents feel compelled to stay on a frantic treadmill to help their children succeed. Dr. Mugyeong Moon, of the Korea Institute of Child Care and Education, lived in the United States when her child was young and saw distinct differences even in early childhood education. She saw how American preschoolers play more at school, while their South Korean counterparts are taught academics more explicitly. "Children now are under such pressure," she told me with a sigh when I met her at her office. "They are not even aware of the situation; they've become desensitized to their lives. They are physically very tired, but don't know that they are tired, so they keep on going." When they grow up, they should have good memories, she added. "They shouldn't just have memories of going to *hagwon*. I don't think children are happy. They are accustomed to this situation, they feel it's their destiny, but they are never given a real opportunity to explore what's good for them."

Not all South Korean parents are happy to play along with the system or to wait for things to change. My cousin Dongjoo is one of these parents who effectively opted out, leaving high-pressure Seoul (where it seemed everyone was enrolling their two-year-olds in English school) for the provinces. She, her husband, and their six-year-old daughter, Yumin, now live in Chuncheon, the capital city of Kangwon Province, with her mother-in-law. Life in Chuncheon is different from Seoul; it's slower paced, and there is less academic striving. Now Yumin goes to a school that Dongjoo chose carefully, one nestled at the foot of the mountains. The air is fresh there. Yumin spends her days at the school, playing with toys and the other children, taking swimming or badminton, catching bugs outside. Dongjoo and her husband work, so Dongjoo's mother-in-law has dinner ready when they come back home. After dinner they go to a playground, then they come home and take a bath. Dongjoo reads to Yumin before the three of them fall asleep together. "I almost feel guilty," she admitted to me, "because my life is easy." Most of Dongjoo's friends feel the same way about wanting their children to enjoy a childhood that is less pressurized, but Dongjoo's family back in Seoul worried openly about Yumin's future when the family decided to make this move. Still, Dongjoo and her husband are hopeful, even though they say they are not sure what will happen in the future.

When we leave Seoul, I have mixed feelings. I appreciate the South

Korean emphasis on education (it was that ethos from my parents that led me to push myself as a student and eventually earn a doctorate), and I know what drives the dreams of those who aspire to a better life, whether they are like the moms I interviewed who want their kids to attain middle-class status in a highly competitive society, or immigrant families like ours alone in a new land. But the modern-day incarnation of this respect for learning is so over-the-top that even South Koreans themselves are in search of a solution.

What can Americans learn from these different Asian models? How can parents be involved without impeding their children's emotional development, intrinsic motivation, or the parent-child relationship?

Eva Pomerantz, a professor of psychology at the University of Illinois at Urbana–Champaign, has long been interested in these questions. Pomerantz, who has researched the role of parents in children's motivation and achievement for more than seventeen years, has conducted a number of studies comparing Chinese and American parenting during early adolescence, a time when children across cultures commonly experience decreased interest in school. "Compared to Americans, East Asians have higher motivation when it comes to school and they do better on achievement tests. I was interested in the role that parents play in that difference," she told me on the phone.

In the United States, it's typical for a child's sense of responsibility and obligation to the family to decrease during adolescence. Americans see this distancing as developmentally appropriate and even positive: "American adolescents [typically] don't feel that they need to hang out with their family, respect their family, or do what their family wants," Pomerantz explained. "There's this pull away from parents." Parents may often go along with this distancing because we receive so many cultural messages that this is normal, healthy adolescent behavior.

But while this may be normal (in that everyone around us seems to do it), this doesn't mean it's best, nor is it universal. As American children move through adolescence and experience less closeness and more conflict with their parents, they also experience a decline in school performance. In China—where social harmony is more highly valued—these things don't happen. Pomerantz explained that in China, adolescents "actually maintain" their connection with family, or even increase it, and remaining close to their parents like this helps their achievement. In China, Pomerantz told me, "Children's independence may be accomplished not by pulling away from parents, but rather by fulfilling duties to parents—paying them back for their efforts, bringing honor to them. That keeps children on track a bit more." School becomes one area they can show their parents they are living up to expectations and becoming responsible.

Research shows that feeling responsible to their parents helps children chart their way through many of the challenges of early adolescence, not just the challenges of school. But as American parents, we're likely to worry that an adolescent's obligation to parents is stifling. Perhaps the key here is to distinguish between parental control that is intrusive and parental expectations that foster feelings of responsibility. Children in both countries find frequent controlling behaviors such as withdrawing love, inducing guilt, shaming, or rules about what to wear and who to be friends with to be extreme and intrusive. American adolescents, in particular, feel positive about being given appropriate kinds of autonomy that reflect their growing independence and separate identity in ways that our culture values.

But the most important thing for us to understand is that children in both the East and the West benefit from feeling responsible to, committed to, and close to their parents. Contrary to our cultural idea of needing to let our children go so they can develop independence and intrinsic motivation, we can feel confident that when a young adolescent feels close to his parents and knows how important school is to them, this is likely to increase his engagement and ultimately his achievement in school. "The kids who have that sense of responsibility to family in our study are more motivated and engaged whether they are in the U.S. or in China," Pomerantz assured me. They may be motivated by wanting to please their parents because they see how highly their parents value their learning and care how they do in school. It may give them a feeling of purpose to fulfill the expectations of people so important to them. But over time, adolescents internalize their parents' goals and expectations, become engaged in their work, develop skills, and achieve more. They eventually experience this motivation as not just coming from their parents *but from themselves as well*, especially if their deeper engagement in school leads them to develop skills that make schoolwork more enjoyable.

Our teens care about their parents' high regard for them more than we are led to believe, and the cultural idea that kids rebel against high parental expectations is not borne out by evidence: for example, research on American adolescents' drug and alcohol use shows that teens who are emotionally close to their parents and know they disapprove of substance use are more likely to abstain. It's our high expectations, not friendly permissiveness or monitoring, controlling behavior, that motivate kids in a positive direction. In a similar way, our children are motivated in their schoolwork when they want to live up to the expectations of parents they feel close to. Nurturing a sense of responsibility and commitment toward family in our young adolescents helps put them on a path toward academic achievement.

Ultimately, perhaps what we need is a hybrid of Eastern and Western methods: keeping kids feeling connected during adolescence while also knowing how and when to let go. Pomerantz noted that research does not yet show what happens *after* early adolescence, and whether those feelings of responsibility to family members end up stifling creativity and innovation. "I think we could use a little Chinese parenting, and they could use a little American," she said with a laugh.

On a sunny fall morning after I returned to the United States from Asia, I met with Charlotte, a student from Shanghai, who is completing her junior year at Harvard. Charlotte told me she was really surprised when she was accepted to Harvard. But when she talked about how hard she has worked from such a young age, and how her parents kept her close while supporting her autonomy, I realized it's not surprising at all. When Charlotte walks across the stage at graduation next year, her Harvard degree will be the logical end to a journey she began when she was very little.

Though her life was highly scheduled as a kid, Charlotte explained how her parents differed from her friends' parents in several ways. "My parents gave me a lot of flexibility. That's something a lot of Chinese parents are hesitant to do," Charlotte explained as we sat in a café in Harvard Square. "They think that if they let their children do whatever they want, they won't have a future." Even at quite a young age, Charlotte's parents let her drop out of activities that didn't interest her—such as violin, which she tried out for a month—though they kept offering her new things to try. Eventually she settled on Chinese dance as the activity she wanted to focus on. She was five years old.

Charlotte was a disciplined child, and dance exposed her to a wider world, literally: she was able to go to Australia, Singapore, France, and South Korea with her dance troupe. Her time abroad whetted her appetite for more international experiences, and eventually Charlotte convinced her parents to let her go to the United States to study abroad during her junior year of high school, even though it was rare for someone on the academic track in her school to take such a chance. Leaving the narrow path toward a Chinese elite university was definitely a risk, and her teachers weren't very supportive of the idea. To be truthful, at first her parents weren't crazy about it either. Going to America as a high school exchange student wasn't something that extremely high-achieving students like Charlotte usually did, but she was determined. The gamble paid off—not only did she grow to love America and polish her English during her junior year abroad, but it was perhaps a determining factor that made her such an attractive applicant at one of America's top universities.

When the word got out about her acceptance to Harvard, her father became a media darling in China. Everyone wanted to know the secrets of raising such an accomplished daughter. He soon was dubbed the Cat

Father and was held up as a shining example of a Chinese father who raised his daughter "the American way." Charlotte's father became an inspiration due to his balanced child-rearing philosophy, perfectly in tune with the changing tenor of parenting beliefs among progressive Chinese urbanites.

While I left my meeting with Charlotte feeling impressed by this articulate, confident young woman, her family is far more the exception than the rule. Evidence shows that students in nations that score highest on standardized tests tend to do the worst on measures of entrepreneurship and innovation. For the vast majority of Chinese students at this point, creativity and innovation are mostly just popular buzzwords.

Perhaps that is the problem with looking to Asian education in its modern incarnation. What we perceive as an "Asian" approach to learning is actually more a manifestation of the contemporary examination system: a system that has taken essentially constructive cultural ideals about perseverance and learning to an unhealthy extreme. In this system, skewed today toward a very narrow notion of achievement and success, children aren't encouraged to think independently and voice their opinions in the way that our culture values. To be a creative and flexible thinker, you need to be able to challenge the status quo.

But we should take care not to confuse this recent focus on the modern examination system with the values themselves, which, as we have seen, emphasize constant learning, self-cultivation, and lifelong self-improvement. The Asian approach to learning confirms the value of encouraging our children to work hard and persist, to place a high value on learning, and to hone their intellectual skills through hard work and even struggle. In its original manifestation, the Asian approach to learning holds that it is only from a place of mastery that a person can spring "outside the box."

There is a lesson for us to heed here as well: as a nation we, too, are at risk of focusing too much on short-term outcomes that stifle longer-term blossoming and potentially subvert the values that we actually care most about. In short, we need to build upon the important methods developed in both Asia and the United States, while avoiding the current focus on visible performance and immediate achievement that mark both these systems. How do we incorporate skill building and high standards into a broader approach? To get a perspective on how rigor, innovation, and individualism can all be fostered, I turned to Finland, where high achievement doesn't come at the cost of creativity.

# EIGHT

# EVERY CHILD COUNTS:
## High Achieving, the Finnish Way

When Benjamin was four years old, he started playing the violin. My mother was a violin teacher. I'd played the violin as a child and so did my brothers. One eventually even became a symphony conductor. But for our family, Benjamin's violin playing was one of those things we stumbled into—we lived right next to a music school and were intrigued by the little kids we saw carrying tiny violins in our neighborhood. Benjamin wanted to try and I was happy to let him as long as he enjoyed it. But David and I didn't want the pressure of making him practice daily.

Benjamin continued violin when we moved to Japan the following year, first with a Japanese Suzuki teacher whose combination of high standards and vague instruction confused him as well as me and left us both feeling inadequate, and then with a French violinist teaching in Tokyo whose studio smelled of cigarettes. There never seemed to be enough time to practice; the less he practiced, the less motivated he became.

But before Benjamin completely gave up the violin, he had a lesson with Kirsi, a violin teacher from Finland, soon after we arrived back in the United States. She was exacting but encouraging. She never praised Benjamin effusively—that wasn't her style.

Instead, Kirsi took a practical approach. She explained to him just how he'd benefit from practicing. "See," she earnestly told him one day as she expertly sketched out a diagram. It showed him how practicing a certain passage with concentration ten times on Monday meant that on Tuesday, he would have to practice, say, only eight times to maintain that same result and even move a bit ahead. She drew another diagram showing him how his proficiency would go down if he skipped a day. It wasn't just that day's worth of practice but cumulative gains that he'd lose. "Mistakes aren't something to fear," she told us. *They are information.* If a lot of mistakes were happening, that didn't mean you weren't good at what you were doing. It meant you had to be more strategic and purposeful about how you were practicing. Mistakes were often a sign you were taking on too much at once and should reduce your goals to mastering only two or three new skills at a time, concentrating on shorter chunks of music. Targeted bursts of practice would increase proficiency incrementally, but more effectively than going through a whole piece a few times in a row.

"Never underestimate children," Kirsi liked to say. Have faith in a child's ability to rise to expectations. But at the same time, make sure you are setting him up for success. Kirsi was attentive and tweaked goals and strategies as needed. But ultimately she was interested in giving Benjamin the tools—information, hints, and guidance—to take responsibility for the violin and motivate himself. Today Benjamin loves to practice.

When I went to Finland a few months after meeting Kirsi, I recognized an underlying ethos like hers that guides education there. The Finns believe that children learn best when they are motivated and when they're given tools to make responsible and effective choices. Teachers and other adults strive to help kids reach their potential by connecting with them, respecting them, and creating optimal conditions for learning that set kids up for success. In Finland children are regarded as the nation's most precious resource.

# FINLAND'S EDUCATIONAL SUCCESS STORY

Finnish education appears paradoxical to outside observers because it seems to break a lot of the rules. In Finland, "less is more." Children don't start academics until the year they turn seven. They have a lot of recess (ten to fifteen minutes every forty-five minutes, even through high school), *shorter* school hours than we do in the United States (Finnish children spend nearly three hundred fewer hours in elementary school per year than Americans), and the lightest homework load of any industrialized nation. There are no gifted programs, no private schools, and no high-stakes national standardized tests.

Yet over the past decade, Finland has consistently performed at the top on the Program for International Student Assessment (PISA), a standardized test given to fifteen-year-olds in nations around the world. While American children usually hover around the middle of the pack on this test, Finland's excel. But Finland's children didn't always do so well. Finland built its quality, efficient, and equitable educational system in just a few decades practically from scratch.

In order to reform itself, the Finnish educational system has gone in nearly the opposite direction of our own. While the United States has emphasized centralization, external standardized tests, and penalizing poorly performing schools, Finland deliberately moved away from a highly centralized system and extensive tracking and testing. Instead, they have implemented a system that relies on hiring highly qualified teachers who are given a lot of autonomy. In addition, the Finnish government provides more funds to schools that face challenges, rather than penalizing them. Finally, it doesn't use external tests to evaluate how schools are doing.

In America, the pressure on teachers and schools for their students to do well on standardized testing compels many educators to focus narrowly on "teaching to the test." In Finland, core subjects such as math and reading are important, but so are other subjects such as home economics, music, art, woodworking, physical education, and foreign languages. While we hear about the need to increase school hours, the Finnish model focuses more on the quality of each hour a child is in school. In Finland, teachers teach between six hundred and seven hundred hours annually (on average, four lessons a day); in the United States, teachers teach more than a thousand hours annually—an average of six classroom hours a day. Although Finnish teachers work an overall number of hours similar to what their American counterparts work, they spend less time teaching, which means they have more time to spend on other things crucial to excellence in education, such as planning curricula, collaborating with colleagues, or assessing students' overall progress.

Today, over 99 percent of Finnish students complete a basic compulsory education (the first nine years of school), and more than 90 percent graduate from upper secondary school (ages sixteen to nineteen). It's not just that achievement is high—it is more equal across schools than in other nations. Despite rising rates of immigration from the developing world, Finland has steadily closed its achievement gap: almost all students in almost all the country's schools do well. It is for this reason that educators from all over the world have flocked to Finland in recent years to discover what makes Finnish education work so well. I too joined them, flying to Helsinki with Mia, Anna, and my friend Laura and her teenage daughter Pippa, who came along to help me watch the girls.

## FINNISH KIDS ARE LESS STRESSED

Iris and Nadja, teenagers in their second year of upper secondary school (the equivalent of high school juniors in the United States), met me at a little coffee shop in Hakaniemi Square near our hotel on the evening of our arrival in Helsinki, the pristine, orderly capital city renowned for its incredible architecture and for being home to design icons such as Arabia and Marimekko. Like other young people in Finland, what Iris and Nadja know about America came from watching undubbed American television shows (one reason why so many Finns are good at English). They had heard that teachers are stricter in the United States, and they told me that they had "American week" once for lunch at school, where they ate hamburgers and macaroni and cheese.

"Teenagers have lots of rights here," Iris explained, adding that she felt that her life was pretty good. At school, she said, adults "try to listen to us. They respect our opinions." Students are given a lot of freedom to make their own decisions. They decide upon their own class schedules and are encouraged to vary their schedules to keep things interesting. They can even choose when to take their exams during exam period.

In Finland, kids don't get any homework or grades until age eleven. The school day is staggered even in primary school: students told me that some days they came to school at ten, and stayed for just four hours. A recent study shows that only 7 percent of Finnish kids feel anxiety over mathematics problems (compared to 52 to 53 percent in Japan and France). To the foreign visitor, Finnish schools are noticeably relaxed places. After school, Iris and Nadja told me, they like to hang out with their friends. Although they want to do well in school, they don't feel a lot of achievement pressure from their parents.

There is less anxiety about the future, which makes for less pressure. University is free and of broadly high quality. Vocational education is not stigmatized; on the contrary, so many hands-on activities in school send kids a clear message: they respect these professions. Less pressure about getting into the "right" university or having the right career makes for a more relaxed childhood in Finland. High school students don't fill their résumés with carefully chosen extracurriculars and community service hours to get into college, as they do in the United States. They also don't struggle to stay ahead of the pack with hours of after-school tutoring and extra lessons, which characterize life for kids in other high-performing nations such as South Korea, Singapore, and China.

# SECRET NUMBER ONE: CULTIVATING HIGH-QUALITY TEACHING

It's not easy to become a teacher in Finland. Starting in the 1970s, the government began to require all teachers to have master's degrees, not a teaching requirement in the United States. Only the very best and most qualified candidates are able to get into Finland's competitive teaching programs: every year, thousands of applicants apply to the nation's eight programs and only one in ten of them is accepted. To become a primary school teacher, applicants not only have to take an exam, but are also screened (through personal interviews) for high commitment and personal qualities such as a positive attitude and strong interpersonal skills. Finland stands out from other nations for the uniquely high qualifications of every one of their new teachers year after year.

Teachers in Finland are as highly respected as medical doctors in the United States. Finnish teachers are also given far more support than teachers in America. They have more freedom to devise their own curricula and use their own classroom strategies. It takes five to seven years to become a teacher. In Finland there is no concept of paying teachers according to their performance, because it's widely believed that teaching is an art that you can't analyze through quantitative measures such as student test scores. Instead, the Finnish government allocates the equivalent of $30 million a year to spend on teachers' professional development. Teachers don't just teach; they are also expected to remain active as researchers in the field of education.

Sarah Applegate, an American teacher and school librarian from Washington State, spent several months in Finland on a Fulbright Distinguished Awards in Education grant in 2011, visiting schools around the country. Sarah told me how surprised she was to see so much teacher observation for new teachers. "I was in one first-grade class and there were literally seven adults in the back of the room, watching," Sarah told me animatedly when I interviewed her by phone, "the master teacher, the specialty subject teacher from the university, the supervisor from the university, and then a couple of other student teachers. Right after that lesson, they all got together and talked about how the lesson went." Sarah asked the master teacher if she planned on staying in the room for the whole lesson. "I can't leave the room—how would I know how she's doing?" the teacher exclaimed, aghast at the thought.

In the United States, student or rookie teachers are usually sent to schools on their own, with less mentoring, and it's not typical for their university teachers to watch them in their new jobs to further their teaching skills. But in Finland, Sarah saw that this is a crucial part of what a teaching professor does to launch her students. Teaching professors read the class lesson plans in advance, observe the actual class, and then debrief with their students afterward. "It's a very supervised program," Sarah said to me with amazement. This sort of investment in intensive training early on and continuous professional development is what allows teachers to be trusted with greater responsibility and autonomy throughout their careers.

## SECRET NUMBER TWO: A VARIETY OF CLASSES ENHANCES CREATIVITY

While in Finland I visited a primary school, secondary school, and upper secondary school in Kauniainen, a satellite suburb of Helsinki, as well as a primary school in Lahti, a small city about an hour from the capital.

As I entered the secondary school in Kauniainen, nicknamed the Dream School, Liisa, a Finnish language teacher, came out to greet me. Liisa was friendly and approachable, wore tidy, comfortable clothing, and exuded confidence. We walked through the bright, clean hallway to the teachers' room, navigating around students on break between classes. Many of them were sitting and talking with one another, or checking their cell phones. Some students stopped Liisa to greet her or ask her a question. Though they were eager to talk to her, they were polite and careful not to interrupt. Liisa listened to each teenager with her full attention.

Eventually we arrived at the teachers' office, and Liisa introduced me to her colleague, Marjo, a smiling young, energetic woman. "We need to educate students to be the kind of people who can handle different kinds of situations in their future lives," Marjo told me in flawless English. "The aim is to give them the means to have a good future, a good life."

Each year the school picks a theme to concentrate on: the theme for 2011 was creativity. "We have lots of special events aiming to get students to become more creative," Marjo explained to me. "We need people who can come up with new ideas and technology in the future. We want to encourage kids to think more openly." Marjo and other Finnish teachers told me that they want their kids to become good at *learning how to learn*.

At the Dream School, just as at any other secondary school in Finland, compulsory subjects are Finnish, Swedish, English, math, chemistry, physics, biology, geography, history, social studies, handcrafts, arts, home economics, music, and sports (additional foreign languages are optional). In Finland, all these subjects are considered absolutely necessary to fully educate a human being broadly and deeply. The less rigorous academic subjects—like crafts and music—are just as indispensable because teachers believe that creative study transfers to a child's performance in all subjects.

Dr. Linda Darling-Hammond, a professor of education at Stanford University and a widely renowned author and expert on American education, agrees. In a 2012 television interview, Darling-Hammond compared our educational system to Finland's. In Finland the curriculum is designed around twenty-first-century skills to prepare its young citizens for the knowledge economy. Subjects like art, music, and foreign language are a fundamental part of creating a future-oriented learner who is building his "cognitive muscle." Music patterns translate over to math; foreign language builds mental flexibility that benefits one's own native tongue. "These things that we think of as frills are at the core of building an active, able mind that not only can enjoy other people, and communicate, and have artistic abilities, but also can do the core subjects in more flexible ways," she declared. While countries such as Finland are "focusing on the future," Darling-Hammond lamented that we Americans are focusing on the past.

F innish teachers believe good learning happens when kids do a variety of different things during the day. Katrina, another English teacher, walked me over to the home economics classroom. This class was for fifteen-year-olds, and most of them were boys. Today they were making sausages, pancakes, and eggs. A radio was playing and the students were quietly talking as they cooked. Some of the kids had finished and were wiping up the counters. Others had sat down and were eating together. "This is relaxing," the teacher mentioned. "They need this kind of time, to talk to one another and enjoy themselves."

In this class, kids also learn how to grocery shop, make healthy food choices, and clean up after themselves. They even learn how to do laundry. I thumbed through the class textbook, filled with photos of ethnic foods, instructions for how to plan a party, how to introduce people to one another, how to buy clothing, and how to manage finances. One fresh-faced girl, Marina, shyly showed me her notebook, filled with neatly handwritten notes and recipes. She said she's happy that she can learn how to cook (baking cakes is her favorite) and gain practical skills, but the best thing about the class is that it's fun.

In Japan, Finland, and other countries, table manners, cooking, sewing, and grocery shopping are subjects taught at school. In these nations there's a societal mandate to make sure everyone has a certain base level of know-how about everyday life and independent living. Home economics used to be part of the American school curriculum too, primarily taught to girls. Its popularity peaked at the turn of the twentieth century, at the height of the trend to recast all sorts of pursuits, including cooking and housekeeping, through a scientific lens.

Nowadays, it's much less common for home economics (now dubbed "family and consumer sciences") to be part of most American students' lives. Not only do we associate home economics with a time when gender roles were tightly circumscribed, but cooking, cleaning, mending clothes, and grocery shopping are considered the kind of commonsense wisdom individual families should be in charge of teaching their kids. Finnish educators recognize that parents don't always have the time to do this, so it's part of their job to make sure all kids get that basic know-how that will help them lead healthy lives.

Finnish children also learn hands-on skills that, in the words of one teacher, *help open up their minds.* In a handwork class I visited, the kids had just made bathing suits and duffel bags, and now they were needle felting. At a woodworking class, a group of thirteen-year-olds were making chairs. Not only do students "need to do relaxing things *every day,*" as another teacher told me, but these creative pursuits enable students to experience learning that balances out the more cerebral pursuits of academic schooling. They get a break; school feels enjoyable because of the varied routine; and they gain a sense of accomplishment from creating something tangible with their own hands.

## SECRET NUMBER THREE: THE IMPORTANCE OF SETTING UP EVERY KID FOR SUCCESS

In Finland I heard a saying: "We can't afford to waste a brain." Teachers make every effort to ensure no one slips through the cracks. All students have the right to personalized support by trained professional specialists, not just those who are struggling academically. During lower secondary school (ages thirteen to sixteen), all students are entitled to two hours per week of educational guidance and counseling. In Finland, "school readiness" has a different meaning than it does in the United States: it's not about kids being ready for school, it's about schools being ready to meet the needs of each child. Milja, a Finnish mother who raised her two kids in both America and Finland, told me that in the United States, she felt as though she had to constantly advocate for her daughter to help her do well at school. She had to recognize there was an issue, take the initiative to get her IEPs (individualized education plans), and do the legwork to convince teachers she needed more time to take tests. In Finland it was different, she explained: there is plenty of time to take tests, so there's no need to apply for exceptions. "It's almost like we're rewarding the wrong behavior with kids," Milja suggested, when the point becomes to finish things quickly rather than to make sure a child has internalized the knowledge. Exams in Finland are more forgiving because the point is to make sure you understand and consolidate the material. For some kids that means just taking more time, something teachers strive to give them. "Here, you learn by punishment—by getting a lower grade. Isn't it more sensitive to try to figure out a way the child can turn in his work on time? Do they really learn from that D?" Milja asked rhetorically.

"Here in the United States I feel like I spend all my time fighting for a situation that can work for her. They try to fit her into a box. In Finland, they fit the box around her." In Finland her learning style was not a problem. In America it became a disability.


The primary school classrooms I visited in Finland were noticeably boisterous. The sunny and spacious primary school in Lahti had wide corridors to accommodate groups of children running out the door for recess (in Finland, children average seventy-five minutes of recess per day). As he guided me around the primary school, Pekka, the school's English teacher, told me he believed students needed to be able to let off steam frequently. An enthusiastic, open man, he talked to me in bursts between engaging with his students or urging them to practice their English with me. His students regarded him with respectful affection.

The Finnish way of setting kids up for success means trusting them with many responsibilities even in primary school, so they feel ownership over their own lives and their own education. Not all of these responsibilities are academic ones, but giving children responsibility in a variety of areas conveyed the message that they were to be taken seriously. They, in turn, returned that trust by acting responsibly. I sat with Daniella, a thoughtful fifth-grader, at lunchtime (lunch was a homemade meat and vegetable soup, rye bread, and salad), and she explained to me that if there was food left over they ate it the next day "to economize." As a member of the school government, Daniella was well versed in matters of the school budget.

I met Hanna, a teacher at Sipoonjoen School, about an hour from Helsinki, for coffee during our stay. A positive and warm woman about my age, Hanna teaches German and Swedish, and is also part of a team of teachers who help at-risk and struggling students: kids who have tough family lives, are unmotivated, and are at risk of dropping out. The school's response is to reach out to them and integrate them into school life as much as possible. "After all, these are our pupils," Hanna said earnestly. "They are the collective responsibility of all the teachers."

Sipoonjoen School is participating in a new national program called JOPO to keep high-risk students on track. Teachers invite students they feel are at risk to apply to the program, which is funded by the government. Five teachers take responsibility for each student's case. "We stay in tight contact with our pupils," said Hanna. If the students don't show up by 8:05 a.m., teachers call them, their homes, or their social workers. They want the children to know that there are adults who consistently care about them and what they are doing. They have the students form individualized education plans with goals that they're accountable for. They form connections with them by spending nonacademic time together. Sometimes they'll do what Hanna calls "food pedagogy," sharing a snack or a meal (which the kids are asked to take the responsibility of purchasing and preparing).

The kids also get a lot of meaningful real-life experience to buttress their academics and keep them engaged—they might spend forty to fifty days a year in different workplaces, such as a car repair shop or a beauty salon, apprenticing at different trades so they can learn how people in various professions actually spend their time every day. This sort of hands-on experience "has been highly motivating for our students, who generally lack any motivation," Hanna told me.

Since the program began four years ago, all the students in the JOPO program at Sipoonjoen have successfully graduated. Before that, Hanna said, about one fourth of at-risk students had been dropping out. She is elated by how one-on-one, concerted attention to the students at greatest risk is clearly working. She told me, "If we can save any one of these pupils, then it will be worth it. Paying a little bit extra now—time and money—can make a huge difference for the future. You see, in Finland we feel that everyone is entitled to a very good education. It shouldn't matter what your background is."

By focusing on the bigger picture for all, Finnish educators have succeeded at fostering the individual potential of every child. That is the Finnish paradox. Instead of emphasizing global competitiveness, or high individual achievement, the concept guiding almost every educational reform and decision has been equity. For American parents who feel such pressure to oversee their children's educational futures and make sure each of their own kids gets what he deserves, it's eye-opening to see what can happen when *all* kids get the best opportunities.

Many American policy makers dismiss Finland as too small or too homogeneous to offer lessons to our country. But Stanford's professor Linda Darling-Hammond disagrees; Finland has the same population as an American state such as Minnesota. We should be able to apply Finland's principles to each state's education program, especially since education reform often happens at the state level. Pasi Sahlberg, director general of the Centre for International Mobility and Cooperation (CIMO) in Finland's Ministry of Education and author of *Finnish Lessons: What the World Can Learn from Educational Change in Finland*, writes that those who talk of the challenges of diversity in our nation should take note of how well Finland educates its immigrant students, who "seem to perform significantly better than immigrant students in many other countries in PISA"—on average about fifty points higher.

The more relevant difference between Finland and America is not ethnic diversity. It's poverty. In the United States, 23.1 percent of children live in poverty, according to UNICEF; in Finland, only 5.3 percent of children do. In Finland, there is a strong belief that students cannot be well educated if their basic needs aren't taken care of; as more than one teacher told me, "You can't learn if you're hungry." In the United States, without fundamental and comprehensive support for all students, many kids are stymied in their effort to become productive adults.

he basic secrets of Finnish educational success are surprisingly simple. They are practically mirrored in the words of John Dewey, the turn-of-the-century American intellectual and founder of the progressive schooling movement, whose philosophy helped shape the most salient characteristics of Finnish education:

> Education . . . is a process of living and not a preparation for future living. School must represent present life. . . . The school life should grow gradually out of the home life. . . . The teacher is not in the school to impose certain ideas or to form certain habits in the child, but is there as a member of the community to select the influences which shall affect the child and to assist him in properly responding to these influences.

Even though Dewey was writing in 1897, his words feel just as relevant today. Education is about more than academics, more than achievement, and more than who we will become later on. It's by preparing our kids for the lives they're living today that we can help them be well prepared for tomorrow. Even more striking, Dewey served as inspiration not just for Finnish education, but Japanese as well. It turns out we don't have to look outside our borders for an educational ethos that would work for American children.

The most significant difference between Finland and the United States is that Finnish kids have more time to *just be*. Päivi, a mother of three children (ages eleven, nine, and five) who walk through a little for-est, which is pitch-dark in the winters, every morning to catch the public bus to their school in a suburb of Helsinki, remembers a life free of pres-sure when she was growing up; she felt trusted to make her own wise decisions about school, hobbies, friends, boyfriends. She strives to be the same kind of relaxed parent to her own kids. After coming home, her kids often play with friends. Even her five-year-old tells her, "Mum, I'm going to see if my friend is home," and runs off. Päivi doesn't always know where she is, but she doesn't worry. The kids do sports (soccer, ice hockey, skiing), but, Päivi told me, "We don't like the sports to get too serious. At such a young age it should just be fun, and we like to give them a chance to try many things." Fluent in English, Päivi was sur-prised to read on an online parenting forum that when a mother was asking at what age you would leave your kids alone at a skating rink, the American parents answered: at least fourteen years old. No parent in Finland would follow their child around, or drive them around and su-pervise at that age, Päivi told me. In Finland they believe that a child's life should be his own.

Everyone I talked to—parents, educators, and children—emphasized that what characterizes the Finnish way is to give children as much responsibility for their own lives as they can handle. At the sec-ondary school in Kauniainen, kids talked to me about how much they valued having space to figure out what they wanted to do in their own lives. "In Finland, our parents don't say what we have to do," Bille, six-teen, explained. "They suggest things and they give us models, and then we decide with our own minds what we should do." Bille's soft-spoken classmate agreed: "It's a problem if parents lecture their own children. It's a problem if parents want their child to be an engineer or something because they couldn't be one themselves."

Many American parents, on the other hand, like Chinese or South Korean parents or other parents living in highly competitive societies, feel anxiety that our kids won't have the good lives we hope for them to have if we don't help shape the path that will get them there: make sure they are involved in activities that are good for them; manage their free time; ensure they are consuming the right material. Whenever Sarah Applegate, the American Fulbright Fellow in Finland, visited school libraries around the country, she asked them about book selection, Internet filtering, book choice: the things that American parents and teachers are used to thinking about in our role as our children's gatekeepers. "They looked at me very bewildered," she recalled. "They did not understand. What's a filter? That's not even a concept." In Finland, there was less talk about censorship and control, and less concern about the content kids were consuming; there was a more lighthearted and accepting approach with fewer rules about how children should behave.

"It's interesting because there's so much important supervision of kids early," Sarah told me, remembering the reflective vests that every preschooler wears throughout Finland when playing outdoors at a park, so they'd be easily spotted and recognized. There is so much attentiveness and social support for a child's basic needs for food, housing, shelter, clothing, health care, and a quality education, she continued. "In the early grades at school, the lower student–teacher ratio [than in the United States] reflects the idea that they need to 'catch' learning challenges early on rather than trying to play catch-up later," Sarah said. This is then followed by a lot of autonomy in myriad ways afterward, in a "gradual release of responsibility," which seemed to her to typify how Finland approaches child-rearing. "In the U.S., we would be afraid of giving kids so much choice. We'd be afraid they would make the wrong choice."

When Sarah returned to her American classroom after a semester away, her perspective had changed. She realized that America's teachers needed more support early in their careers and America's children needed more time outside. "We should send kids outside every forty-five minutes. When I first went to Finland, I asked, 'How does that work?' And teachers would tell me, 'I could not teach unless they went outside every forty-five minutes!' Now, after Finland, I say, 'Look. It's not twenty-five degrees below. You're going outside.'"

. . .

I too changed after my visit to Finland, after being around so many adults who gave children a combination of support and respect. There were individual practices that really appealed to me, such as their wholesome and healthy school lunches, and all that recess. But for me the bigger takeaway lay in seeing the benefits of a mindset that embraces equality, freedom, and creativity.

The visit to Finland made me more aware of how important it is for all children to have the basic necessities: good food, emotional support, resources, plenty of outdoor time, and a reassuring but varied routine. I understand now that fostering the ability to "learn how to learn" is equally, if not more, important than focusing on facts and knowledge or blind obedience. I'm more convinced that giving children the time to pursue their experiences and interests will help them to become nimble and creative thinkers, so important for the twenty-first century.

As Benjamin's violin teacher Kirsi first modeled for us, and as I'm continuing to learn as I make my way through parenting, I don't help my children when I try to coerce or compel them to do what I think is good for them. Although it's hard to resist the cultural norms that convince anxious parents that we must help our children prepare for their future, the way my kids dig in their heels when I'm tempted to be too overbearing has proved to me that this approach is not how engaged learning happens. But when we take the time to explain why a certain method works, help them set achievable goals so they can feel successful, and have high expectations that they are capable of great things, not only does this help children learn best, but it also makes them enjoy the process and want to learn more. It's not *what* kids know that is important: what they'll need most and what we should foster is an eagerness to gain that knowledge in the first place and a feeling of engagement as they apply it to their own lives.

# PART 4

# The Character
# of Children

# NINE

# RAISING KINDNESS:
## Cultural Notions About Raising
## Kids Who Care

An experienced summer camp counselor, Ellen thought she had seen it all. Among the children in her charge there were kids who interrupted, spoke rudely, and even some who grabbed her. There was a girl who shouted, "I want to do it myself!" as she ripped off the name tag her mother had just put on her dress and plastered it back on askew. Of course, the campers were only five and six years old. They were all still learning how to be kind, how to share, how to take turns and how to listen when someone else was talking. But today was especially trying because of a new boy, Harry, who talked over the other children, interrupted, and grabbed things out of the counselors' hands. During circle time he told the other kids they were boring and bragged he knew more. When Ellen opened a picture book to read to the group, Harry stood in front of it so no one else could see the book. He brought a bag of chips to the counselor and demanded, "Open it!" Harry's behavior to the counselors and to other campers was so off-putting that no one wanted to be with him.

At the end of the day, Ellen had a conversation with Harry's mother,

Bridget. "Oh, I know, he's got no impulse control," Bridget said, laughing. "But he's like a puppy! You know, he has a very high IQ!" Ellen had met many parents like Bridget who were proud of their kids' smarts, but seemed unconcerned about their child's impact on those around them. These parents got defensive with Ellen or shrugged off their child's inappropriate behavior, insisting that fostering individuality in their child was more important than fostering kindness. But Ellen knew from experience that unless Bridget recognized that Harry's unkind and disrespectful behavior was bothering others and hurting his ability to make friends, nothing would change.

Most of us care deeply about raising our children to be kind and compassionate toward others. Though we may have different tolerance levels for what we deem appropriate behavior (Harry's mom tolerates more than most of the rest of us would be comfortable with), no one wants to be the parent who is called out by the teacher because our child was rude, disruptive, or disrespectful. But as parents, we feel unsure or even disagree about the best way to foster kindness in our children. For some parents, manners are the priority: we prompt our children to be polite (with "What do you say?" after getting a gift or "Say you're sorry!" when they knock another child down), we insist they say please when they want a second helping at the table, and we try to teach them other social courtesies, such as saying, "Nice to meet you," making eye contact, and shaking hands. We teach kids manners because we believe that social niceties pave the way toward kindness, giving children the opportunity to show appreciation and respect.

For other parents, like Bridget, insisting children have good manners feels antithetical to the goal of raising a spirited and independent child with a mind of his own.

Teaching children kindness and respectfulness by holding them to manners and other social conventions can feel too old-fashioned or traditional, or misses the point. Indeed, Heather Shumaker, author of *It's OK Not to Share*, points out that just saying "sorry" can let kids off the hook without giving them a chance to learn about real compassion.

In the 1960s and 1970s, traditional values—including having good manners—came to simply seem too conventional, and the personal growth and self-esteem movements in the decades after encouraged people to put their happiness first rather than subjugating themselves to others. By then, more parents, educators, and social scientists were arguing that it was more respectful to and healthier for children to express themselves however they wanted without our imposing societal standards on them. The idea sounds like a good one: figure out why a child was behaving the way he was and work with him instead of demanding he comply with external rules of social conduct. There was even a handy acronym, adapted from the addiction recovery movement as a way to help adults get in touch with their feelings, which was useful to help us understand where our own kids' less-than-stellar behavior was coming from: HALT—was our child *hungry, angry, lonely,* or *tired*?

Nowadays many American parents—especially those who identify themselves as open-minded, modern, and progressive—associate too much emphasis on manners and respect with traditional and hierarchical parenting, which holds little appeal. Shumaker suggests that instead of forcing an unfelt apology, adults could help preschoolers realize what they did and take action (like grabbing a tissue or bringing over a Band-Aid) to help fix it. This is good advice and is an important way to build compassion. At the same time, when we look at parenting practices and child behavior across a variety of cultures, we find that the pendulum in America has swung too far in the direction of devaluing social conventions.

In 1970, the primary goal stated by most college freshmen was to develop a meaningful life philosophy; in 2005 it was to become comfortably rich. Empathy has declined over the past thirty years among U.S. college students while narcissism has risen, and more Americans than ever believe we have a "major civility problem."

Richard Weissbourd, a child and family psychologist teaching at the Harvard Graduate School of Education and author of *The Parents We Mean to Be*, surveyed high school students from five different U.S.

schools and asked them to rank what they wanted in life. Did they want to be happy? Did they want to be good, caring for others?

Two-thirds of the students ranked happiness above goodness, and said they believed their parents held the same goal for them. Through interviews and discussions with parents, Weissbourd told me, he found this generally held true. Unlike parents of past generations, these modern parents were giving their kids the message that they cared more about their happiness than their kindness.

How did such a change come about in the span of a few decades? We can all agree that it is a good thing that in America we are raising kids to be independent thinkers who have a strong sense of their own individual right to happiness. We'd also agree that it's a problem that somewhere along the line, caring for each other gave way to caring mostly for the self. By ignoring manners and prioritizing individuality over community awareness, we risk failing to teach our children to be kind at all.

## THE IMPORTANCE OF OLD-FASHIONED MANNERS

Growing up in a Korean immigrant family, I learned that greetings and respect were extremely important. This was how you made people around you feel good and welcome. In Korean culture, you show respect to others, especially people who are older than you, by doing things for them such as greeting them properly, serving them food first, never talking back, and seeing them to the door when they leave your home.

My own parents were not insistent: they understood I was a very shy child, and that greeting people I hardly knew was sometimes beyond my capabilities. Being polite and kind meant noticing people's presence and doing considerate acts of service for them, and this made sense to me as long as these things did not feel like weighty obligations. As I grew older, though, I started to feel that the expectations of less-assimilated

Korean relatives or family friends were just too much. There was such emphasis on form, on saying the right things, on using the right body language: things I couldn't see the value of. So much hierarchy went against my grain as a teen being raised in America.

Yet when I finally had a child of my own, I realized that I wanted to raise him to be kind and was at a loss about the best way to do so. It wasn't just that I'd been raised in two different cultural worlds. Most American parents today hear conflicting and confusing messages about how to teach kindness.

For me, kindness meant being polite in social situations, thinking about other people, performing thoughtful acts, feeling compassion for others' misfortunes and remorse at your own mistakes. But when I quietly nudged my son to say hello, or reminded him to say "Thank you" or "I'm sorry," more experienced moms told me to relax; my little boy was too little to understand. "I don't see any point in apologizing when you can't understand what you're sorry for yet," one friend told me. She explained that not only did rote words have nothing to do with bringing out innate kindness, but she believed asking my toddler to apologize was disrespectful of him. The best way for him to learn how to be empathetic would be by modeling kindness myself, she assured me, not requiring anything of him until he made the choice himself to behave kindly. Instead, I should concentrate on raising his awareness of his own feelings and emotions by talking to him a lot about how he felt. Another friend said I should teach him to assertively say, "I need space," if another child was crowding him. And one day, I observed another mom friend rushing to her three-year-old and comforting him, holding him close in her arms and murmuring to him, after *he* threw a wooden toy at my two-year-old son, hitting him squarely in the head, because for her raising a compassionate child meant walking him through all the feelings that compelled him to strike out like that.

I was a new mom and open to rethinking my assumptions and my upbringing, but even I could see that this kind of focus on the self and inattention to basic social kindness didn't always work very well. Instead of being compassionate and having good manners, the children around me who were being raised in this sort of self-affirming way acted self-centered and unkind:

- Ten-year-old Gracie, a nimble, athletic girl, ignored her grandmother and gazed off in the other direction when the elderly woman asked if she wouldn't mind picking something up that she'd just dropped on the floor.
- Six-year-old Kayleigh demanded something to eat *right now*.
- Nine-year-old John and his seven-year old brother, Nicholas, constantly interrupted people's conversations, bragged while putting other kids down, and thoughtlessly left their trash on the floor or shoved it in someone else's hands demanding it be thrown away.
- Ten-year-old Kevin yelled, "I want the first piece of cake!!" at another child's birthday party, creating such a racket that he became the center of attention.

Molly, a seven-year-old, suddenly declared to her friend Lila, "I got tired of playing with you today." Later, Lila's mother brought it up to Molly's mother, Eve, who told her that Molly was "just being honest." Eve saw nothing wrong with Molly's hurtful words; after all, she was raising her daughter to know that it was important to recognize and express her own feelings.

When we treat our kids like friends, talk to them like peers, and allow their behavior toward others to slide beyond casually friendly into thoughtlessness—when we allow them to be consistently disrespectful to others (including ourselves), to take people for granted, and to treat people civilly only when they feel like it—we are not teaching them positive lessons about being authentic and true to themselves. We are teaching them to feel self-important and entitled instead of compassionate and kind, showing them that it's totally okay to put their happiness and their needs above others'. Then we compound the problem by justifying their rudeness as we explain that today they are just having a bad day, that they are "hungry, angry, lonely, or tired," or that they're just being honest.

If we look at what research shows actually promotes kindness—as well as expectations of kindness in other cultures—we can see that my well-meaning friends were a bit misguided: allowing children to behave as they want to until they feel like acting differently actually makes our children more miserable and less compassionate. Children who have too few boundaries often flail around for a solid surface to ground them. It is we parents, as well as other adults in our children's lives, who are best equipped to provide them with structure, guidelines, and practice in social interactions as we initiate them into the fine art of keeping everyone's needs, including their own, in balance. It will even help us in our goal of raising happy kids: there is evidence that people who are compassionate to others experience lasting happiness, that being generous and helpful leads to better relationships, in turn leading to more happiness. In order for our children to be happy and feel good about themselves, they need also to be kind.

## BABIES ARE BORN KIND

Babies are born to bond. Babies learn to empathize with others through their utter connectedness to us. As we know from numerous research studies (and our own personal experience), babies imitate us. They respond with distress to the cries of other infants. They become distressed when our own faces are blank and unmoving. We instinctively do things that help them to connect to us: we mirror their expressions, respond to their cues. This connection is a building block for altruism. UC Berkeley psychologist Alison Gopnik tells us in her book *The Philosophical Baby*, "It's possible that babies literally don't see a difference between their own pain and the pain of others. . . . Moral thinkers from Buddha to David Hume to Martin Buber have suggested that *erasing the boundaries between yourself and others in this way can underpin morality*" (emphasis added).

More and more research shows that there is an innate basis for morality that all babies share. At the same time, babies take what they are learning about the world and apply that information to their own growing knowledge of how the world works. Infants are born with their own theories about the world—what researchers call "skeletal expectations"—but they are also born with tremendous abilities to change those theories as they interact with the environment, and integrate this information in a way that makes sense to them. These ideas can be changed for better, or they can be changed for worse.

In one recent study, nineteen- to twenty-one-month-old babies were shown two giraffe puppets dancing. Soon after, a person arrived with two toys on a tray, announced they had toys, and distributed them to the giraffes. Three-quarters of the babies stared longer when one giraffe got both toys than when each giraffe got one toy. (Babies stare longer at things that surprise them or go against their expectations.) In a second, related experiment, babies watched two women with an empty box and a number of toys. In the first scenario, one woman didn't put toys away while the other did, and both were rewarded. In the other scenario, both women put toys away and both received a reward. The babies stared longer at the scene where the woman didn't do her share, yet still got a reward. Both scenarios show us that even babies apparently have an understanding of what is fair and can recognize unfairness.

But it is not enough that babies have this innate sense; it is only a start. Lead author of the study, Stephanie M. Sloane of the University of Illinois at Urbana–Champaign, told me, "Yes, my study suggests that babies are born with a basic sense of fairness. But it's also really important for parents to teach and reinforce the ideals that are important to them, because it's not always easy for a child to act on this basic sense of fairness that he was born with, especially if it goes against what is in his own self-interest. For instance, it's fair to give each person a cookie, but it's not easy to do if you want more than one cookie for yourself.

"In other words, having those expectations, and being able to act on them, are two different things. Behaving in a way that reflects what you know is fair is a much more complex and difficult achievement for a child."

Sloane told me that parents can help their children develop this ability to act on what they know is right by modeling the values they want their children to internalize. How parents model what is important to their family or their culture shapes how an infant comes to incorporate those values in his own worldview. How parents stick to and reinforce the values that are important to them varies both across and within cultures. One family might value helping those in need over all else, and spend much of their time and energy working in homeless shelters and soup kitchens. Another family might also value helping others, but they do this by donating money to a charity once a year. "These differences can make a difference in how compassionate and empathetic a child becomes toward other people," said Sloane.

In other words, our children learn, from watching and doing things with us, what matters to us: they see whether we as a family value putting in our money or our time toward being generous to others. The family that puts in time, not just money, is teaching kids that doing something for others is worth their time too.

Even very young children want to be kind to others and *are happier* when they are. One recent study at the University of British Columbia showed that toddlers were happier after giving treats to others, even more than when they received them themselves. In fact, they were even happier when this giving came at a price to themselves: when it meant that they wouldn't get anything at all. Even toddlers apparently feel a "warm glow" after doing something kind for someone else. (But don't reward your kids for sharing. Other research has shown that rewards undermine these generous tendencies in both toddlers and in older children.)

What happens as our kids grow older? Cross-cultural research highlights the link between a child's innate, prosocial tendencies to kindness, and cultural context: the attitudes we teach our children or that they pick up from the world around them. One study compared three- and five-year-olds' sense of fairness and sharing candies and other desirable items in seven different cultures: China, Peru, Fiji, the United States, and three distinct urban sites in Brazil. The study showed that while many traits were consistent across cultures (by five years old, all children tended to show more fairness in sharing), they differed in the degree of self-interest that children showed. More fairness was evident among the children growing up in societies promoting more collective values, where they saw people around them building houses, farming, cooking, and eating together. Two groups of children displayed the highest and most similar degree of self-interest: impoverished, unschooled, unsupervised Brazilian street children and the middle-class suburban American children.

## BALANCING ASSERTIVENESS AND KINDNESS

Many American parents correctly believe in the importance of teaching their children to stand up for themselves. Being able to say what you think without being fettered gives children power over their lives. Children become aware that they don't always have to go along with things for the simple sake of manners. This is really important if they witness or experience a situation that violates larger ethical issues, such as bullying or child abuse. The independent thinker is the one who can stand up against group solidarity, peer pressure, or adult coercion at moments that range from merely uncomfortable to absolutely immoral.

Although as parents we must teach our children to speak up when they are in danger in order to keep them safe, we have an equal responsibility to teach them to be conscientious and kind on a daily basis. If we dismiss all manners as unauthentic or potentially dangerous, or teach kids that being true to their own genuine feelings is always the only important thing, we are inadvertently teaching our children another lesson too: that empathy and consideration of others is a choice, not a basic expectation of human decency.

Parents who teach their children to speak with authenticity and honesty but do not simultaneously teach them the art of being considerate send their children the message that it is always better to be honest to your true self even if it means hurting someone. Natalie, a ten-year-old girl, walked right past a teacher who asked her a friendly question, self-absorbed, her eyes blank, barely mumbling a reply. We're teaching children like Natalie that they have the right to choose to regard others around us as they like, or even to ignore their existence. It's important not to raise a potential victim, and to help guard our kids against the rare dangerous situation that might pop up, yes. But it's also important not to raise habitual perpetrators of insensitive, unkind acts.

## THE IMPORTANCE OF SAYING HELLO

Japan is a famously polite country. There isn't any confusion about whether to teach children manners, or how to do it without making them feel too deferential, or worrying about authenticity or trampling on their sense of self. In Japan, we quickly learned after we began living there, raising a polite child is important to everyone.

Greetings are the glue of Japanese society and are a really important socialization ritual for children there. Starting when they are the tiniest of toddlers, Japanese children learn the importance of a considerate greeting. The parents and teachers I knew weren't insistent: everyone knows this isn't something that all kids will feel comfortable doing at first. But they made sure their children had plenty of opportunities to practice, and the expectation was clear; people don't wait for kids to decide to greet people on their own, or not, as they wish. In Japan the mind-body connection goes two ways; there is a folk belief that "the body learns first and then the mind and heart come to understand." Teachers took a concerted role in this, guiding and modeling and role-playing kind interactions. Classes began formally with a greeting exercise, as two children in the front of the room called the class to attention with a greeting and a bow.

Before eating, Japanese people say, *itadakimasu* ("I am about to feast"). After eating. they say, *gochisousama deshita* ("Thank you for this meal"). Before entering someone's house, they say *Ojama shimasu* ("Excuse me"), and they say *ojama shimashita* ("Thank you for having me") before leaving. Kids at our elementary school rotated duties on the "greeting committee," a group of kids and teachers who joined the principal in the morning to stand at the entranceway and greet each child as he came to school.

As an American, I was used to things being a bit more hurried and more casual. For encounters to be formal and deliberate seemed silly. All the rote phrases honestly made me a little uncomfortable. I wondered why there were so many of them and what kind of lesson my kids would learn by repeating formulaic phrases they might not authentically mean. I wondered if it wasn't better to speak one's original, sincere thoughts, thus conveying how we *really* felt about something.

It took time for me to realize that greetings and other ritual phrases were considered so important in Japan because of how tied they were to awareness of others. I began to understand that repeatedly giving thanks and always being polite was a social glue. It helped keep kids and adults from sliding into the all-too-easy habit of ignoring and overlooking others. Naoko, a Japanese mother of two boys, first helped me make sense of this. Active in the PTA, Naoko served on a parent committee that oversaw the safety patrol, the children's commute to school, and the greeting exercise at her elementary school. Naoko explained that safety, commuting, and greetings were covered by the same committee for a reason.

For the first two weeks of each term, the four schools in her neighborhood promote greetings together. PTA committee members stand on the roads and greet all the people who pass that corner: the businessman, the young woman rushing to work, the mother with two kids on her bicycle. "The main idea is to promote greetings among children," Naoko told me, "but it's also about promoting greetings in the neighborhood, so that we can check out strangers and so that criminals will avoid conducting crimes in our neighborhood because they know there are 'eyes' on them—the eyes of parents and neighbors." The Japanese increased the focus on greetings after the devastating March 2011 earthquake, tsunami, and ensuing nuclear disaster, to help people to recognize and know others in their communities in case of other disasters. After the earthquake, television stations stopped their regular commercial advertising and instead went on a blitz of public service messages, reminding viewers, "Let's greet each other."

Not only do greetings help create feelings of community solidarity; they even help reduce crime. One industry analysis showed that in 2009 bank robberies in the United States were reduced almost by half after banks began to consistently use "greeters" who would look every customer in the face and greet them as they came in.

What I understand now that I didn't understand when I first lived in Japan is that a greeting is one of those small things, like having a moment of silence before a meal or taking the time to really listen when someone tells you how they're doing, that reminds us that we are not alone, and compels us to see and notice others. This is one way we remain *aware*. This small practice helps encourage children to be more kind and attentive, because it asks children to recognize the world beyond themselves. I came to see how daily greetings could almost become like a form of daily meditation to train each of us to be mindful and focus our attention outside ourselves, even if just for a moment.

While American mothers often orient their babies to things apart from themselves, such as objects (telling them to look at the big boat, quizzing them on what color that toy is, or describing what that lion at the zoo is doing), in order to encourage exploration, Japanese mothers more often orient their babies to themselves, encouraging a constant awareness of relationships and the impact of one's actions on other people. This general difference continues as infants grow older as well. Other research shows that while young American children often ignore what others are saying to them (even when they clearly can understand what is being said), Japanese parents concertedly work on teaching their children to be responsive because it's so socially important that they respond as soon as they're spoken to. Orie, a mom I knew, told me that she had always tried to teach her daughters, Kanna and Kotone, one basic, easy-to-remember principle: *Always stand in the other person's position and imagine things from his or her point of view.* For her *this* was the key to developing compassion and empathy.

As Japanese kids get older, they are reminded that constant awareness of others helps you live in balance with people. In disagreements that warrant adult intervention, kids are asked what they think the other person felt or what motivated him. Discipline in schools takes on the form of asking children to think about their impact on others around them, an indirect way of coaxing them toward kinder behavior. "Character class" was part of the elementary school curriculum where every week children discussed and reflected upon different compassionate ways to deal with moral dilemmas, such as bullying on the playground.

"To have compassion for others by being polite helps us to realize we're not the only ones who live in this world," Eriko, a mom of two, told me. Modeling kindness to one's own children and to others was a really important way to lead kids to empathetic behavior too. But these strategies don't cancel each other out. They work well in tandem. "It makes me keep an eye on my own behavior so I will be a good example to my children," Eriko said with a smile.

All this focus on cultivating awareness of someone else's perspective makes it second nature to consider others as well as yourself, to look at things from a nuanced, multifaceted point of view, and to be more understanding. Anticipating the needs of others, in contrast to the American goal of assertively stating one's own needs, becomes a positive thing—the sign of a socially skilled person. As Anna, a young woman raised in Japan and now attending college in the United States, told me, "In Japan, mind reading is the pinnacle of politeness."

## HOW RITUALS HELP CHILDREN TO BE KIND

"I don't like you," eight-year-old Eliza told Lily, the third-grader sitting next to her, out of the blue. When Lily started crying and the teacher reprimanded Eliza, Eliza protested, "But it's true!" She was being raised to believe that honesty mattered more than kindness or fake manners.

Shawn Smith, a Colorado-based psychologist and author of *The User's Guide to the Human Mind,* has no patience with this sort of thinking. He has heard parents say, "My child doesn't respect adults unless adults respect my child," but in his mind this is entirely backward. He strongly believes that it's not compassion that precedes manners but manners that create feelings of compassion. "Contemplating manners requires empathy and compassion," he told me. "Children aren't born understanding manners and respect—they learn it from the adults around them. It is unfair to make children take the lead on respect when they don't understand how it works. That's setting them up for failure." (And, one might note, setting us grown-ups up to be disrespected.)

Shawn and his wife emphasize courtesy with their little girl and discuss it often. Recently they were talking about a kid who refused to let their daughter play on a piece of playground equipment. She wanted to know the best way to respond to that kind of situation. "These are not easy questions, but they are important ones. Without a foundation of manners and respect, she would not be pondering the best way to get what she wants without harming someone else," Shawn told me. "She would have simply pushed past him without another thought, or she might have submitted to his bullying behavior. Neither response is compassionate to herself or the other child."

As a psychologist, Shawn regularly works with the counterintuitive idea that *actions can come before feelings.* "In fact, it can really exacerbate problems like anxiety and depression to wait until we feel like doing something before we actually do it. It's natural to believe that feelings must come before actions. But it's just not true." It's true that children don't understand what's happening when they apologize, for example, and may not feel remorse at first. "But when they see and experience that things work out better when they use social skills, they will understand. We should not deny them that experience because it violates their 'authenticity' to require words like 'I'm sorry' when they don't truly feel remorse yet. They are still learning."

Richard Sennett, a professor at New York University and author of *Together: The Rituals, Pleasures, and Politics of Cooperation*, declares that people who learn to live together harmoniously reap the rewards of enjoying each other's company. The more rituals and formulas are practiced, the more deeply ingrained and automatic they become. Sennett explains, "Rituals . . . transform objects, bodily movements or bland words into symbols." Those symbols, which have such rich common meaning that everyone can understand, allow people to express far more than may appear on the surface.

When Natalie ignored her teacher, she probably wasn't trying to be rude. She may not have had any idea how to respond. Without enough practice, kids feel unclear about what to say or do in particular settings or situations. But in cultures with more scripted rituals and clearer expectations, there is less confusion and anxiety about expressing yourself socially. Set phrases aren't confining. They're freeing. They let children know what to say and do that will be mutually understandable in situations, in the way that an actor who has practiced his lines to automaticity can then concentrate on letting his genuine self emerge.

These phrases also give children, still working on learning and practicing acceptable behaviors, a safety net. An impulsive child who might easily put a foot in his mouth can learn the socially appropriate thing to say at the correct time, while a shy and guarded child has the comfort of knowing what is expected of her in each situation without the pressure of having to come up with spontaneous things to say.

It's okay that these polite words are "formulas." It's not the actual words we say that matter so much as showing that we are thinking of the other person. Through the act of speaking a polite, albeit formulaic sentence ("Pleased to meet you," "Won't you come in?" "Thank you for coming over"), we convey a much deeper meaning, in shorthand both parties know: "I see you, and you are important to me." When formulas like this are embedded in daily life, they give children the chance several times a day to feel valued within a web of social relationships. If we let this slide, we are actually actively reinforcing, multiple times a day, the opposite message.

When we encourage our children to use manners, greet people or see them off, and acknowledge their presence, we inscribe in children's hearts the idea that we live together on this earth with other people, and must care for each other. We show them that when we notice someone else, we make them happy, and that we should not take our nearest and dearest for granted, but take a moment to actively notice and appreciate them.

## LIVING IN A GROUP IS A SKILL

Courtesy looks different around the world. In America, children get used to a casual hand wave or handshake while their French and Italian peers learn to give a kiss on each cheek. In Korea, children are taught the extensive, complicated forms of address for everyone in their extended family (older sister of mother, older brother of father, father's younger female cousin), because knowing the social hierarchy—how people are related to one another—is the mark of a socially competent child in that world. In France, interruptions in conversation (among adults) add sparkle and vitality to the discussion. In Germany, I'm told, one sincere "Thank you" is enough, though it may seem curt and inadequate to those used to American interactions.

In most countries, a child who can greet others properly and has good manners has a social advantage, because the well-mannered child is so highly regarded. Pamela Druckerman, in her memoir of raising American children in France, *Bringing Up Bébé*, talks about how much emphasis French parents put on raising a child who is able to greet people, be with adults without interrupting their conversations, and generally get along with others.

What's most important is for a child to learn the customs of her culture and become fluent in social skills that will be widely understood. These skills don't always translate well between cultures. Alice Sedar, a professor of French culture at Northeastern University and former cultural reporter for the French newspaper *Le Figaro*, explained to me over coffee that *living in a group is a skill*, and one that's "particularly important in France." Sedar declared that American parents seem to have gone woefully astray to French eyes: it doesn't seem to matter as much to us that our children have good manners. Raising a child who is able to experiment, to ask questions, and to flourish in a competitive, individualistic society (with a weaker safety net than in France), is a more important goal here than raising an impeccably polite child.

In Korea, a lot has changed since my parents were growing up there, but one thing is still the same: children are encouraged to display good manners from the time they are very young, in order to show that they are fully aware of those around them. "I feel that when you're raising a child, the most important part of it is 'character cultivation,' or shaping a child's personality," one Korean mother explained to me. "We do this by continuously teaching them all the time, repeating your expectations consistently and giving them positive reinforcement so children know what they are doing well and can be proud of themselves."

In Germany, a nation known for striving for a healthy work-life balance, being considerate to others comes from being able to take the time to slowly foster genuine, deep, and sincere human connections. Jane, an American mother of three young children living in southwest Germany with her German-born husband, observed, "I think that raising kids to live in a society is the biggest difference between Germany and America." In Germany, kids have plenty of practice being in a group. Jane, who has parented in Germany for more than five years, noted how the fact that preschools typically have mixed ages gives kids repeated opportunities to learn how to be kind to younger ones, or how to emulate the self-control of older ones. "Older kids learn to be more patient or more gentle because of the smaller kids: they might take the time to teach them how to use a slightly more complicated toy instead of pushing them aside or just doing it for them," she told me.

Britta, a German mother of two boys living in the United States, noticed that the ways people spent their free time differed quite a bit between the two cultures she knew. In Germany, it was common for families to drop in on each other spontaneously and spend time together.

Weekends were often spent visiting relatives or friends for coffee and cake, or helping others to celebrate a birthday or christening, or going on a walk or a bike ride. In Britta's neighborhood in a town near Boston, when she tried dropping by her neighbors' homes with a cake on the weekend, most people were just rushing out the door to an activity. Britta thought it might be easier back home to spend time cultivating relationships because of the built-in cultural expectation that people take ample time to relax together, fostering deep relationships that form the basis for kindness and consideration.

## HOW WE CAN ALL RAISE KINDNESS

Amanda, a mom I know, regularly prompted her shy children to greet the crossing guard, Kathy, who helped them every morning and afternoon. It didn't feel natural to them at first, but they grew to love seeing how happy they made Kathy every day. Melinda, a mother of three who had spent most summers as a teenager living abroad in France, brought home one custom from her host family: greeting her children every morning with a kiss and the same question, "Did you sleep well?" because she remembered how good it felt when her host mother recognized each child this way every morning.

Research shows that kids are motivated to be kind when we combine high expectations and explanations with modeling and lots of practice. We can tell our kids what the benefits are, and explain why it's good to be courteous. This makes their choice to be kind an informed one; they are more motivated when it feels like something they've chosen to do. We can also make our expectations clear before we put them in a situation where they need to behave a certain way ("I expect you to be patient at the restaurant, not to bang your silverware on the table, and say thank you to the waitress after she brings us our food") and buttress them through polite (albeit discreet) reminders. If we take the time to remind our children *before* an interaction that it is courteous to look someone in the eyes, shake their hand, or offer a simple greeting, then they know what's expected of them. Sometimes what looks like rudeness in children is actually just social awkwardness. Children are inexperienced in the ways of the world. They can't magically know how they're expected to behave if no one has told them in advance.

Most of us have had the frustration of asking a child to do something—clear the table, put away toys, pick clothes up off the floor—to have them answer, "I didn't do it," assuming that since they didn't make the mess in the first place they should not be responsible for cleaning it up. But the more children see that they are part of something larger than themselves—a family, a school, a community—the more readily they perform acts of kindness that benefit everyone, not just themselves, and remember that other people have needs too. We can think of raising kindness as one way to cultivate this attunement to other people.

In our family we talk a lot about manners and kindness because it's sometimes confusing to navigate between cultures with different ways of expressing care. I realize now that it's okay to remind the kids that each "Please" and "Thank you"—and each greeting to our neighborhood crossing guard, to their teachers, to relatives and friends, and to people in stores and restaurants—has a positive impact on a person's day. At the same time, I try to be patient and kind with my children (and with myself): I don't expect them to master social courtesies overnight. We try to be consistent—we try not to let rude behavior slide—but not overly insistent. It isn't easy, but I try to remember that learning good behavior is a lifelong project, even for me. I know I'm guilty of rudeness too. Just last night I snapped at the kids for not responding to something I said, while I was on the computer not paying attention to them. But what we're learning is this: though manners and courtesies may look different all over the world, being aware and considerate is the foundation for compassionate behavior everywhere.

Researchers tell us that three-month-olds prefer faces of the same race as those they know, eleven-month-olds prefer people who eat the same food as they, and twelve-month-olds prefer to learn from those who speak the same language they do. Many cultures, like Japan, cement this natural bias to be kindest to those we know best through social courtesies to ensure harmonious relationships with those they know and interact with daily. But we know Japanese culture can also have the unfortunate tendency to encourage people to put up boundaries that foster intolerance between themselves and others who are different. It can be difficult for some people living in Japan, especially if they don't speak Japanese, to master the social conventions and feel warmly accepted into Japanese society. In the United States we strive to raise children who are able to see, appreciate, and understand the perspectives of people who are different from themselves. Our social ideal is to strive for inclusiveness, encouraging our children to befriend people who are different and to be curious about, not afraid of, difference. In America we try to foster tolerance in a way practically no other culture does as well. This gift to our children is one that cultures around the world can benefit from.

Alice Sedar noted that despite how well-mannered French children seemed in comparison to many American kids, she has always been touched and impressed by the friendliness and warmth of American adults. "It's a pleasure to hear young people say, 'Can I help you?'" Sedar told me. "I've witnessed more courtesy in the Boston subways than in the Paris Métro. A young American seems more likely to get up and let an older person sit down in the subway."

The foundation is there: because our kids are skillful at expressing themselves, they have the strength to express compassion to a stranger. We can aim higher than this, and encourage them (and ourselves) to extend this kindness to all, including those who are so close that it's easy to take them for granted. We give a gift to our children when we teach them to advocate for themselves without being disrespectful, and to express their feelings graciously without sharing every thought that springs to mind. They benefit from the positive responses people have to well-mannered kids and from the good feelings that come from acting considerately toward others. It's a kindness to our children to help them become thoughtful people who make the world a little brighter for everyone, even themselves.

# TEN

# RAISING RESPONSIBILITY:
## Avoiding the Helplessness Trap

enny, a busy single mother of four, got a frantic phone call on her cell phone while out doing the groceries. It was her second son, Tom, crying. He had football practice in five minutes and demanded to know where she was. He yelled, "You didn't feed me lunch! Now I'm going to have to do two hours of practice with no food in my stomach!"

Jenny raced home to drive Tom to practice, even though football was within walking distance. Even after she picked him up, Tom continued to rant and yell. She suggested he grab some fruit from the grocery bags to eat on the way. "That will just make me late," he cried. Getting out of the car, he called her stupid. Furious, Jenny told him he wasn't allowed to speak to her that way, and that he could walk home. She drove off.

After Jenny returned home, she mulled over what had happened. Tom was eleven. He could easily have made himself something to eat. He could have respectfully reminded her about practice. He shouldn't have called her stupid, But Jenny also felt guilty for angrily telling him to walk. He was hungry already—after a long practice in the heat, wouldn't making him walk home when he was starving be too much? In the end she went to practice at pickup time and told him she'd drive him home if he wrote down three alternative ways he could have handled the situation. He agreed and they drove home together.

A gentle and thoughtful mom, Jenny strives to respect each of her children and believes they have rights too. She tries not to be too controlling of their time. Yet all too often she notices that she's the only one doing chores when they are whiling away hours on the computer, and she is the person they blame when things go wrong. Jenny's dilemma is one every American parent faces: How do we help our children without spoiling or babying them? How do we raise children who will become responsible, competent adults?

## LOWERED EXPECTATIONS

Chances are most of us have found ourselves in a similar situation as Jenny's at one time or another. Instead of doing it themselves, our children get angry at us for not making them something to eat when they are hungry, become sullen when we're not being available to help with homework, and whine because we can't drive them somewhere when they could perfectly well walk on their own. We may feel bewildered that our kids aren't acting as capable as we suspect they are, or as we remember being when we were young. Yet it starts to seem normal to see a six-year-old hand her coat to her mom to hang up in her cubby, third-graders toss their backpacks at their parents to carry as they walk home from school, or eleven- and twelve-year-olds sit down and wait for dinner to magically appear at the table. It's nothing unusual when kids leave their plates on the table after they're done eating, leave their wet towels on the floor, or hand their trash to an adult to throw away. Parents in other countries, where even small children are expected to clean up after themselves, help prepare meals, and take responsibility for getting themselves to and from school and other activities every day, would gape at this American trend toward helpless children. But to many American parents, though it frustrates and annoys us, it has become unremarkable.

American children haven't always been so needy. Philip, an eleven-year-old growing up in a one-bedroom apartment in Brooklyn in the 1950s, was responsible for waking up on time, making his own breakfast, and getting himself out the door. After school, he would accompany his little sister Penny and her friends home, helping them cross busy Ocean Parkway, avoiding the whizzing cars. They came home for lunch, which he would make because his mother was often out working. He'd complete his homework and take care of his bike and his fishing equipment. He also did the family shopping: going to a corner grocer to buy bread or rolls (three for a dime), or to pick up milk. He often commuted into Manhattan by subway by himself to visit his father, or took the trolley to his own doctor's appointments. In college he met Laurie, who had also been raised to take care of herself, her belongings, to help out with dinner (and to make it as she got older), and to watch over her little brother while growing up in upstate New York. They eventually married and had four children, one of whom is my husband, David.

It was the same for my parents growing up in postwar Korea half a world away. As kids, my parents were responsible for washing and folding their own clothes, running to the marketplace to buy tofu or bean sprouts, watching their younger siblings, shining their father's shoes, taking meticulous care of their things, and being responsible for getting themselves from place to place.

For my brothers and me, growing up in the 1970s, life was cushy in comparison to our parents'. Still, it was common for most kids to have regular chores. Some of these chores, depending on the family, could be quite extensive. I was expected to set the table every day, help clear the table, and clean my room. My brothers had to clean their rooms and toys, fold and put away their clothes, vacuum, and when they were old enough, do the snow shoveling and lawn mowing. Beth, a mother of three, who grew up in Pennsylvania, washed the bathroom and polished the kitchen floor every Friday. She also polished the woodwork with Murphy Oil Soap, dusted the mirrors, vacuumed the whole house, and did the family's laundry.

For those of us who remember things being different in the past, it's not our imagination: historians tell us that American children's chores declined steadily over the twentieth century. (The amount of time spent on chores has dropped 25 percent since 1981 alone.) This change is due mostly to the very same thing that has influenced so many aspects of modern parenting: our changing view of our children from being economic assets to "economically worthless but emotionally priceless," in the words of Princeton economist Viviana A. Zelizer.

Not only did this view of our children's preciousness and vulnerability become more entrenched, our lives became more automated thanks to time-saving devices like the laundry machine, dishwasher, and vacuum cleaners. There was less kids could do to really contribute, and chores began to seem optional rather than necessary to help the family function. Parents worried about overburdening children. They worried about things like accidents (lawn mowing) or germs (bathroom cleaning). Child-rearing experts continued to vigorously debate which chores were best for kids, but one pattern remained consistent: the range of expected chores dramatically decreased over the course of the century.

In America today it is less common for children to be as responsible as they were in the past. Beth asks far less of her own children now, two boys, age nine and twelve, and a girl, age eleven. "I pretty much do all the chores in the house," she told me on the phone. The kids will do things like strip the beds when she asks them to, but there's no set routine. "I'm hoping they'll do more chores as they get older," she admitted. "I think my kids need more chores, but I can't say I'm that great at giving them." Right before we spoke, she had just asked two of the kids to clean their flip-flops downstairs. Throughout our conversation she was half distracted wondering why the water was running for so long.

Cross-cultural research shows children in many different communities helping out the family in tangible ways: gardening, running errands, doing child care, doing housework, caring for animals. In fact, there are practically no cultures where children don't help out. David Lancy, a professor of anthropology at Utah State University and author of *The Anthropology of Childhood* and other books on childhood and culture, told me it's "absolutely universal" for children to want to help adults in their communities. Though we aren't used to thinking of kids as developmentally capable of helping, their helpfulness kicks in early: a child's capacity to cooperate begins by fifteen months, and his desire to start willingly pitching in starts at around eighteen months. In many cultures parents begin to hone their children's helpfulness especially between the ages of five and seven, and children this young competently assist in many domestic tasks. Some cultures actually define intelligence as being socially aware of what needs to be done and doing it, and adults cultivate this form of intelligence just as adults in our own culture might cultivate verbal precocity or learning the ABCs.

Carolina Izquierdo, a medical anthropologist at UCLA, noticed how much work Yanira, a community member, did when she was doing anthropological fieldwork with the Matsigenka of the Peruvian Amazon. Yanira fished for shellfish, cleaned, boiled, and served them; she stacked and carried leaves to use for roofing; she swept sand off the sleeping mats twice a day. She was six years old. Other children in her community skillfully used knives and machetes and heated their own food in the fire. At age six or seven, boys started hunting, fishing, and planting gardens, while girls helped with chores around the home: child care, food preparation, tidying up, or taking care of the gardens. The societal goal was for children to do things quickly. What's more, children anticipated what needed to be done and just did it. Adults weren't telling them what to do. Since adults in the Peruvian Amazon value self-sufficiency and autonomy, they consider directing others in what to do to be disrespectful.

I f young children across diverse cultures show a common desire to help out, why are some cultures so much more successful at harnessing and channeling this desire than others?

No one would argue that children in the United States should be doing as many chores as Yanira and her peers. But it's not the amount of work that matters. It's the fact that in Yanira's community, children help in concrete ways that contribute to their own well-being, as well as the well-being of the family and the community. While American children do some chores, it's not uncommon for American family members to help their children—even older children—with the most mundane tasks such as brushing their hair or teeth, picking up their belongings, making their beds, and toasting their bread, even after asking them to do these things on their own.

Today, chores aren't typically a way for most kids to contribute to their family's livelihood and economy. The twenty-first-century priorities for young people, especially upper-middle-class young people, is for them to do well at school, cultivate themselves so they can fulfill their potential, and keep up with the many activities that we think will make them successful in the future. We feel ambivalent about requiring anything more of our children, given all that's already on their plates, and it feels reasonable to lighten our kids' burden by helping them out: bringing forgotten homework to school in the middle of the day, carrying their bags, picking up after their messes, or doing their laundry.

Even with younger children who aren't under the same academic pressure as a middle or high school student, chores have become optional and our instinct is often to protect our kids from work. What's more, Lancy explained to me, we tend to ignore a child's early desire to fit in by helping out, often in the name of being protective of our kids. We also overlook it because we are short on time, or we know we can do a better job (of brushing their teeth, for instance), or we want them to have a carefree childhood. But when we ignore our children's eagerness to participate when they are younger, they internalize the idea that contributing is unimportant and that they are helpless. They also begin to expect that things will be done for them.

Karen, a third-grade teacher in California, is still astonished by an incident that happened over the class jobs the kids rotated, from dusting with the feather duster to taking out the trash or compost. One of her students, Eliza, tended to complain a lot in class, and Karen had a hard time getting her to do anything that was the least bit challenging. Then one day, Eliza's father came to see Karen. "He was hoping she wouldn't have to do her 'job' for the day since she was 'composter' and she really didn't like it," Karen remembered. Eliza had been whining and complaining about it all week at home and thought it wasn't fair that she had to do a job she didn't enjoy. Her father had agreed to come in and talk to the teacher to get her out of the duty, and was surprised when Karen told him that community jobs were important for everyone. (Karen didn't let Eliza off the hook.)

Even when our children have jobs and responsibilities, researchers have noticed that parents help them to carry out their duties, often after a great deal of cajoling, negotiating, and stalling, even when it comes to self-care duties such as brushing their hair, taking a shower, picking up their belongings, or tying their shoes. An illuminating study led by researchers affiliated with UCLA's Center on Everyday Lives of Families captured the daily lives of Los Angeles middle-class families on hours of videotape. None of the thirty families the researchers observed had children who spontaneously did chores or household help on their own. In twenty-two families, the children outright resisted or refused to help. Sometimes parents backtracked and did a chore they'd just asked a child to do. Parents didn't seem to think their children were capable of competently doing things on their own in some cases, not a surprise in a culture where children are sometimes praised for failed efforts ("good try") and parents are used to assisting their children with their schoolwork.

The legendary and beloved pediatrician Dr. Benjamin Spock pointed out that chores (even if not perfectly done) help children gain good self-esteem and make them feel that they are contributing to the family. But sometimes it is easier for parents to just take over the jobs themselves. It can be hard to wait for the slower pace of a child. Parents and adults in other cultures foster their children's willingness to do chores by actively noticing and quietly recognizing their children's contributions, expecting them to do chores and providing them with enough guidance and practice that they become really capable. They offer positive attention to their children only when they see them helping out, and discipline kids who are not acting responsibly. But in our country, it's more typical for parents to be a lot less deliberate about fostering these skills. We want our kids to help out, but we're ambivalent about it, especially since we tend to view young children as not yet developmentally capable of being effective.

Not only are we ambivalent, we value the idea of having an equal relationship with our kids and respecting them as individuals, so we often ask our kids to do things in polite and respectful language. This is respectful, but it also gives children the impression that it's *their choice* whether to help out or not, especially if we don't use clear directives or (as is common) we add reasons and options, rewards or veiled threats. Parents in other cultures whose children are more helpful and willing are extremely consistent in their expectations and remain present to follow through until the task is done.

It's worth it to rethink how we raise responsibility: Doing household chores (particularly from a young age, around three to four) is a strong predictor of success later on in life, including abstaining from drugs, graduating from college, and getting a job. Other research indicates that children who are more hardworking in tangible ways are more "nurturant" and "sociable," and even have a more developed moral sense and awareness of other people's needs. In other words, when children are used to helping out regularly and being depended upon to concretely and usefully help others around them, they show more strength of character and kinder social behavior.

## CREATING CLEAR EXPECTATIONS

In Japan, there's no ambivalence about kids pulling their own weight. Children are expected to be responsible for themselves at a very young age, as well as to help out their families.

Daniel's friend Taka, ten years old, cleans the family bathroom every week. His mother asked him to choose a chore when he was in second grade, because she knew it would be one way to help him to feel more self-responsible. In a country like Japan where people depend upon one another so much, independence—in the form of self-sufficiency—is highly valued. "In Japan we have the firm idea that you shouldn't be a burden on others in society, and family is the basic unit of society," she told me. "We have a saying, *Jibun no koto wa jibun de.*" "Each person should take care of himself and his own things."

For Taka this means cleaning the bathroom (after all, he uses it too) as well as riding his bicycle by himself to the optician to replace a pair of glasses that he'd carelessly left somewhere to be stepped upon and broken. According to his mom, the family is a safe place for children to learn how to feel responsible for themselves and help out so they can be even more self-reliant as they get older.

"I like to help my family," Taka told me matter-of-factly. His five-year-old sister, Mari, picks up a few items for the family occasionally at the corner store (it's not uncommon in Japan for children to run small errands like this), helps wash vegetables while her mom is cooking dinner, brings trash to the basement, and folds clothes. She even likes to imitate her brother cleaning the bathroom.

One reason children like Taka and Mari know what they are expected to do, and don't mind, is that these clear expectations are reinforced by everyone—teachers, other parents, other friends—and aren't just left up to parents swimming against a societal tide. In the United States, our kids lounged on the couch while I tidied up (even as I write this I see dirty socks left on the bathroom floor and know I'll need to remind the boys to put their pajamas away when they wake up). But in Japan it was much easier for us to get our kids to pitch in or want to do things for themselves. I was surprised in the United States when a nine-year-old asked me to butter his bread because he wasn't "allowed to use a knife," even a butter knife. Our *yochien* in Japan taught the five-year-olds to prepare an entire meal for their parents at school and had them do everything by themselves, from paring the potatoes to cutting the meat and carrots for the stew with chef's knives. Because the social expectation in Japan was that children were capable of acting responsibly and doing chores, the kids had daily practice in helping out at school. Our kids were getting clear and frequent messages about how highly valued it was to be helpful, self-reliant, and responsible from just about everyone—teachers, friends' parents, and even from their own friends.

We know from social science research that in families where children have more household responsibilities coupled with more time on their own to do them, children are more responsible, independent, and autonomous. They grow "more," according to researchers. The reverse is also true: fewer responsibilities and less unsupervised, independent time result in children growing "less." Household responsibilities are one pathway for children to mature and feel equal to other members of the family. Anne, a twelve-year-old girl depicted in a Norwegian study, lived in a family that had made an effort to create an atmosphere of equal rights and duties for each family member. "Like her mother, father, and older sister, Anne decides how to spend her own time and takes on a quarter of the housework," wrote Anne Solberg, the author of the study. "She cleans the whole house every fourth week, and prepares the family dinner twice a week. Anne regards this equality between the sexes and ages as both practical and reasonable."

And the benefits of chores aren't confined to the family. Research on a group of more than three thousand adults showed that those who pitched in at home as children were more likely to volunteer or do community service when they grew up.

I n Japan, when children are babies and toddlers, they can appear highly indulged. They sleep with their parents, they're worn on their mother's bodies and rarely separated from them, and they often get their own way without being disciplined. But as Japanese children get older and enter *yochien*, Japanese preschool/kindergarten, they are expected to be able to care for themselves in a number of ways that encourage independence.

One clear expectation of three-year-olds is that they walk to school (with a parent) and carry their own belongings (and for a child in *yochien* there are a lot of belongings: different bags for their lunch box, cup, a school bag, a book bag, an indoor slipper bag, a reusable water bottle). Each child is responsible for all his things. It took time for me to realize I was the only one holding my children's school bags and coats (sometimes I even offered to take them for them), burdened down with their stuff while they ran free. Other kids around us kept track of and carried their own water thermos and all those bags by themselves, on their tiny bodies.

*My First Errand*, a popular Japanese television show, features a young child in each episode taking the brave step of going on his first errand all by himself—to bring lunch to his father at work, purchase something at the corner store, or bring a gift to a neighbor. In some of the episodes I've seen, the child has been as young as two or three years old! But the young age isn't for shock value—it's for inspiration. (And it turns out it's common around the world for little errands to be among the first chores children do.) Our Japanese friends believed certain challenges for preschoolers, such as going to overnight camp or on a sleepover, or getting up the courage to run an errand for the first time, really transformed their children and gave them confidence.

Such expectations of responsibility for such tiny people seemed unnecessary, potentially dangerous, even harsh, to David and me at first. What we didn't realize was that strong expectations for social responsibility and self-care began kicking in early so that by the time a child was in elementary school, where children really need to be autonomous and self-reliant, being able to care for yourself and your things was second nature. The flip side of this was that if you didn't start teaching kids to take care of their things and help out early on, it was so much harder to change these patterns later.

I was very skeptical at first. Still, I couldn't help noticing how carefully, automatically, and consistently a lot of Japanese children we knew would take care of each of their own belongings, such as folding their own clothes, while our kids tossed their clothes on the floor and forgot about them unless reminded. In our house, stray bits of toys, containers, or other things got lost or separated and we found ourselves having to buy replacements or keep extras on hand. But most of our kids' friends didn't have the same problem. When the boys' friends came over, they carefully hung their jackets and put their shoes away before coming in to play. Before they left, they searched all over to make sure they had everything they'd come with. These kids had internalized standards of self-care that were new to me, that I didn't even realize such young children were capable of.

As I thought about the different things that parents wanted to cultivate in their kids and marveled at how proficient so many Japanese children were in caring for their things while I struggled to get my kids to clean up their toys (even when I helped them), I realized this: It wasn't that the Japanese were naturally neater. It was that care and competence were values their parents had consistently prioritized. Teaching kids to take care of their belongings instead of being careless with them was a social dictum, expected by schools and the society at large. Parents paid attention to this specific skill because they knew that throughout their lives, kids would be expected to be neat, organized, and self-reliant. Parents like Atsuko, a mom of three kids, took time to teach their children to learn how to fold clothes, for instance, and consistently made sure that their children looked out for their things and hadn't forgotten anything. She wasn't the one scurrying around before they left our house, looking for her kids' belongings. She had her kids do this, which kept them more conscious and aware. Atsuko consistently reminded and guided her children until it became second nature.

Eriko, mother of nine-year-old Mai and five-year-old Kazuya, told me that in the past, kids' chores at home were really necessary, to help reduce adult labor. These days, when almost all chores at home can be done with the aid of machines like washers and vacuum cleaners (though most families in Japan don't have dryers or dishwashers, so hanging laundry out to dry or doing dishes by hand are daily chores that kids see adults doing), it can be more hindrance than help for kids to pitch in, especially at first. "It requires a lot of patience from us. But I believe chores are important for kids' growth," Eriko declared.

"Kids love to help their parents, as the people they love the most," Eriko continued. "It makes them feel they are welcomed and important. I think this is a kind of genuine good feeling they can get through their own work. And also, chores are basic skills which will surely make it easier for kids to manage their own lives later."

. . .

s Japanese children grow older, expectations and responsibilities increase even more: children walk to elementary school on their own, serve each other lunch, and clean up their schools together. Each child brings his own cleaning rag to school and uses it to clean the classrooms and hallways every day for fifteen minutes after midday recess. They get brooms out of the closet, sweep the floors, get down on the floor and wipe it, and clean the bathrooms. "It's fun, because we can chat. We race down the hallway with our rags," Daniel and his friend Leon explained to me. They also wipe off the tables in the library and throw out the classroom trash. When I heard this, it didn't make me feel so bad about expecting them to help out at home.

Children also regularly help clean the local park, raking leaves, clearing brush, and picking up trash. Cleaning isn't considered a menial task in Japan. Influenced as Japan is by Buddhist thinking, cleaning is thought to help train the mind and lead to spiritual awakening.

We sometimes thought Japanese parents and teachers were surprisingly relaxed about children's social behaviors, like talking out of turn or being rambunctious. They trusted that interpersonal maturity would develop over time. But when it came to practical daily matters, most people we knew were actually very concerned about guiding kids from a young age to pull their own weight.

## RESPONSIBILITY THROUGH CAREGIVING

In most societies, older children take care of younger ones. Anthropologists have noticed that in some places, young children don't even play house or play with dolls so much, because they have their own real babies to care for: their younger siblings. It's common for five- to ten-year-old children to care for their younger siblings or cousins, carrying them, entertaining them, disciplining them, bringing them to mother to nurse if they get hungry, and also sleeping with them. A mother's role is to oversee what's going on in the family.

In twenty-first-century America, though, we typically assume that the mother, father, or another adult caregiver is the person in charge, the one who will take care of all the children, with older ones occasionally helping out if and as they wish. One study of Kenyan graduate students at Harvard showed that they were surprised that American children sought out their parents rather than their siblings to play with, and in a study of working-class Mexican families, siblings and mixed-age play-mates, not parents, provided tolerant, nurturing, and cooperative play support for toddlers.

Most of us try to treat our children with equal attention and equal respect. We try to avoid privileging one sibling over the others. A study by Christine Mosier, then at the University of Utah, and Barbara Rogoff, a professor of psychology at the University of California, Santa Cruz, compared Guatemalan Mayan and middle-class American mothers of toddlers and found, not surprisingly, that the American eighteen-month-olds in the study had the same status in the family as their three- to five-year-old older siblings, and were held to similar standards. American mothers more often viewed their toddlers as willful and knowing but also capable of learning how to share by giving up a coveted toy to the older sibling so they could learn to "take turns." In contrast, the Guate-malan Mayan toddlers were seen as not yet able to understand how to cooperate. They were never asked to give up a toy. Their wishes always came first. And the researchers found that their older siblings accommo-dated them even when their mothers were not around. In stark contrast, the middle-class American older siblings claimed equal right to the toy three times as often as their Guatemalan Mayan counterparts did.

American parents might look at Guatemalan Mayan toddlers as spoiled and overindulged. But this is a misperception caused by our cul-tural belief that we must correct a toddler's behavior. The other view, the one held by the Guatemalan Mayan mothers, is that respecting toddlers' "freedom of choice" actually shows them a consistently generous way of treating others. By seeing their toddlers' whims and desires as age-

246 • CHRISTINE GROSS-LOH

appropriate instead of "hurrying them" to follow rules, by viewing them as incapable of intentionally mistreating others, and by patiently giving them their way and fully trusting that their behavior will change as they get older, Guatemalan Mayan culture does not experience the terrible twos. Their siblings—having had their own turn being treated with kindness and patience in an age-appropriate way (that is, "indulged" as toddlers)—are now able to graciously and voluntarily step into the role of cooperative, indulgent brother or sister.

In the Guatemalan Mayan community, "community-wide expectations of responsible behavior appear to be a very strong guide for children's actions and are quite different [from] requiring or compelling children to behave according to adults' will," the study's authors explain. Conventional parenting wisdom in our country encourages us to teach our littlest ones to share and cooperate (often against their wishes), using what researchers call "power assertive" strategies—strategies rooted in our Puritan past, where a child's will is broken in order to mold him for good. We use whatever methods we know of to compel children to comply with our wish that they take equal turns and share: giving them time-outs, taking toys away from them to give to another child, offering extensive explanations about why sharing is important, punishing them, or even bribing them to make them conform to our will. Yet what is this kind of insistence teaching our toddlers? As a culture, we tend to underestimate what our littlest ones are capable of doing physically (as in helping out with chores), but overestimate what they may be capable of comprehending intellectually. By expecting our children to behave in a way that they may not be developmentally capable of, we may actually, though unwittingly, be socializing them to misbehave. We may be stunting our children's capacity to be spontaneously cooperative and kind as they grow more mature, paving the way for them to be defiant and less adept at learning how to balance their needs with the needs of others.

Lorenz, a sixteen-year-old from Gothenburg, Sweden, loves math and hopes to be an engineer one day. He has a little sister, Helena, who just turned thirteen. Lorenz has taken care of his sister every day after school since he was ten years old. When he was still in elementary school, he would pick her up, bring her home on the public bus, give her a snack (waffles were a favorite), and then make sure that she completed her homework and piano practice. Lorenz also manages his own schedule. He completes his own homework, piano, and drum practice with time to spare to play video games. Lorenz does chores around the house— regular ones as well as intermittent tasks such as mowing the lawn or decorating the house for Christmas.

Lorenz's mother, Laura, told me that in Sweden it's expected that older siblings care for younger ones. She likes how older children seem good at taking care of younger ones, like the ten-year-old boys she saw gently and ably assist a little one-year-old at a park recently. Like him, Lorenz's friends took care of their younger siblings. There's no other option, really, in a country where most parents work. "I have a theory that when you start putting responsibility on the kids when they are young— saying, 'Okay, pick up your little sister from day care and feed her a snack,' then you are helping them be both capable and responsible," said Laura.

For many families, sibling caregiving and child work are necessary for the household to function. Sibling caregiving was common in our own country during the colonial age, before the era of age-segregated schooling; when families were large, generations mixed freely, and children played a crucial role in the household economy in this and so many other ways. But even in societies where sibling caregiving isn't economically necessary, it is considered an important way for children to learn self-reliance from interacting with people of all ages, unmediated by protective parents.

There are other European countries where the cultural assumption is the same: older siblings are expected to care for younger siblings. The reasons for this go beyond the practical. The act of caring for others literally becomes a pathway to responsible and nurturing behavior. Cathy, a French mother of three, told me, "In French families, which I think are very much influenced by Latin cultural beliefs about families, older siblings help raise the younger ones almost as much as parents do. We believe it makes kids more autonomous when they learn what these responsibilities are—home is a safe place to provide real-life training to do things like look after the baby. And for the little ones it's also a great experience, because the big sister or brother might be a little tougher on them than parents, so they learn to speak for themselves." Cathy has her oldest son help his younger siblings with homework and tie their shoes because, she told me, "I think it's important to learn to help people who need it."

Though American parents expect and welcome older siblings playing with younger ones, it's not as typical to depend heavily on our older children to actually be in charge of taking care of their siblings. We might even worry that obligation would foster resentment. Instead we are told how healthy it is to hone each sibling's distinct sense of identity in the family by giving them individual attention (sometimes reinforced by giving them separate rooms, duplicate toys, separate playdates, and one-on-one time). Yet we now know that older siblings benefit in a lot of ways from nurturing their younger sisters and brothers. Researchers have observed that children who are required to care for siblings have shown more "prosocial" tendencies: they appear more socially responsible and more nurturing.

Eighteen months older than my brother, I was expected to help care for him and the brother who followed one and a half years later. I loved to dress them, play with them, and teach them how to read. I liked feeling that I was important to my family. (Though I didn't know it at the time, it's common for some immigrant subgroups, including Asian-American, to hold strong expectations of sibling caretaking.) After I became a mom, I had friends who worried that I was imposing a burden on my boys, as I expected them to help with their younger sisters, but in Japan I never ran into this notion. In Japan, sibling caretaking is not an unusual expectation; it is admired. If anything, parents I know do not worry that it burdens older children; they worry their older kids should be helping even more.

As an elementary school student in Japan, Benjamin brought home weekly homework assignments to write down what he did to help his family at home. One of the more popular duties for him and his classmates was "taking care of the baby" (along with related tasks, such as "reading to the baby," "bathing the baby," and "feeding the baby"). Benjamin and his classmates saw that other kids did this in addition to their other jobs at home, such as cleaning the bathtub or the entranceway. They saw that sibling care and household chores were valued, admired contributions, and that this was the sort of behavior that they'd be recognized and praised for.

## IN THE WORLD ON THEIR OWN

During the peak of Japan's rainy season a few years ago, I peered anxiously out the window, wondering whether I should get the car out of the garage to meet the boys on their way back from school, a twenty-minute walk away. It had been sunny in the morning and I'd forgotten to check the forecast. Wasn't having to walk a mile every day to and from school, even in a downpour, a little too much? Just then, the buzzer rang; they were home. Seven-year-old Daniel was dry underneath a large raincoat he always kept tucked inside his backpack "just in case," and nine-year-old Benjamin had borrowed an umbrella before leaving school. Their feet were soaked, but they were fine.

In Japan, kids begin to walk to school on their own starting in first grade. Almost every child walks to school (or uses public transportation if the school is very far away) without a parent. At 7:30 a.m., and again in the afternoon, groups of young children are everywhere, walking together or alone, with their school hats and leather backpacks.

You see this in other parts of the world too. In countries such as Germany, Switzerland, Finland, Sweden, Norway, and many others it's a common sight to see young children walk to school on their own.

These kids aren't just let loose on the street. Safety skills are taught and honed. In Japan, our children took a free safety course at school several times a year where kids role-played how to assess and respond to potentially dangerous situations, such as being approached by a stranger. Kids usually walk to school together in groups and help watch out for one another. They're taught how to use their hard leather backpacks to protect their heads in case an earthquake happens while they're out. Katrin, a mother living in Basel, Switzerland, told me that in her city they prepare young children to walk about on their own, starting at age four or five, through free training courses and public-safety awareness campaigns near the beginning of the school year. "There's a general consensus that the public sphere is there for everyone, including children, even small ones, even on their own," she explained.

Swedish schools similarly expect kids to get where they need to go by themselves. Parents told me that Swedish children don't gather at school first and then take a private school bus if they're going on a field trip. Instead, they assume the kids will use public transportation to meet up at their destination. Schools can assume this because they know the kids know how to get around by themselves.

When the boys were still little, before I ever let them walk out of my sight, another mother told me about her six-year-old daughter taking a bus and then a train on her daily commute to a private school in Tokyo. Six years old! I gasped in disbelief, thinking this would never happen with my kids until they were teenagers, at least. She looked at me, slightly amused, and said, *Christine, kids can do more than you think they can.* Those words have stayed with me ever since, making me wonder if my overprotective attitude was wrong and if children in fact learn responsibility, gain self-esteem, and become competent through the actual experience of getting themselves where they need to go.

Mary, a mother of two in Minnesota, was convinced her child should never walk on his own. Justin, seven, was always doing dangerous things, like darting into the street, and he couldn't be trusted. A firm grasp on his hand at all times was the only way to prevent him from endangering himself. So Mary always walked Justin and his little sister, who was six, right to their school bus stop, one block and a street crossing away. Mary was right to be cautious of Justin's impulsivity: it would be dangerous for him to walk a short distance alone.

But Justin had also never had the chance to practice street safety. He lived in a neighborhood where he was usually driven in a car. Children in Japan are no different from kids like Justin—lots of them are impulsive too. But the reason you don't tend to see them darting into the street is that they've practiced and been taught to do otherwise. That daily practice over and over makes things like turning their head to check both ways before crossing the street so ingrained as to be automatic. Road safety is something that Japanese adults teach kids to protect them, in the same proactive way we teach our kids to swim so they'll be safe in the water.

This practice starts early. In Japan you don't usually see a child over the age of two in a stroller. Risa, a Japanese mother, told me that when her daughter turned two, she stopped using the stroller and insisted she walk. I was confused. What was the merit in making a two-year-old walk, especially in an urban environment? It seemed unnecessary and cruel. Most of my memories of raising young children in the United States revolved around planning how to transport them safely and quickly from one place to another. In the end, my solution was a single stroller with a ride-on board so my four-year-old could ride on it as I strolled his two-year-old brother around the city. It was definitely a little cumbersome (I had to walk with my arms stretched out to accommodate the board) but it had never occurred to me that a four-year-old, let alone a two-year-old could, or should, walk the long distances I needed to go.

We found out later that many Japanese parents encourage their children to walk. This helps them see the world from the vantage point of a pedestrian, rather than through being passively strolled. That freedom of movement is key to their independence and competence as they get older. As they walk, they see the interconnectedness of the world all around them: adults sweeping their entranceways, grandmothers tending their plants, people heading off to work, other children commuting to school.

One of Benjamin and Daniel's best memories of a trip to Korea was walking fifteen minutes or so home in the dark with my friend's son, through the streets of Seoul—a huge urban center with a population of more than ten million—while their nine-year-old guide showed them his favorite spots—a park with a small stream and a little swing set, the view from a low pedestrian bridge—that you could see only if you were on foot. They have a different memory of Seoul now, one of an adventure that was theirs alone.

We moved back to the United States when the boys were ten and eight, and they missed the kind of freedom of movement kids have in Japan and the adventures they'd had. They even missed what it felt like to be completely responsible for yourself when out on your own. But back in the United States, one American friend told me she saw absolutely no benefit to letting her boys walk or ride their bikes a few blocks down the street, because she simply could not accept the possibility that something could happen to one of them. This gave me pause, until another friend mused, "When people talk only about what they're protecting their kids from, they're not thinking about what they're depriving them of."

Parents in Japan are not careless or complacent about their kids' safety. They know life is full of risk and bad things sometimes happen. But here's the thing: communities work actively to give their children skills and support and maintain the safest conditions they can. Children pass the same people every day. There are designated homes along the path to school that they could go to if they needed help. Children wear hats that identify them as schoolchildren on their commutes, and each carries a safety buzzer to alert passersby in case of a dangerous situation. Parents convey clear expectations: children can do this and we all will work together to do our best to keep them safe. And that *practice* is how kids form the *judgment* they need.

It isn't just because it is convenient for adults (though it's undeniable that parents experience less stress when kids are able to get themselves around on their own). As we've seen in previous chapters, being outside and getting exercise are essential for children; when we keep them indoors or in cars in order to keep them safe, there are measurable and worrisome consequences on their health and well-being. When children are in the habit of being active, they are far more likely to become active adults. The confidence that comes from knowing how capable you are resonates in so many areas of a child's life. That day in early summer when they trekked home in the rain is among my boys' happiest memories.

## RAISING RESPONSIBLE OLDER KIDS

In our country, it's hard to be a teenager. They are sometimes treated as adults and sometimes as children. College students often live independently in dorms or off-campus housing, but they are not considered trustworthy enough to be allowed to drink alcohol. We permit eighteen-year-olds to vote in political elections and to enlist in the United States military without parental consent, but simultaneously assume adolescents will be irresponsible and that their behavior must be limited or controlled. These inconsistencies make it hard to know where you stand. "When you're in that liminal state, you're neither here nor there, neither a child nor an adult," explained Nancy Darling, a professor at Oberlin College who specializes in adolescence, when I interviewed her. "You're getting a lot of mixed messages about what's appropriate. This can make things stressful."

When we do not expect our children to do chores, look after their own things, or feel responsible for themselves when they are younger, it is that much more difficult to start giving them the right kind of freedom as they get older. The stress American teenagers feel trying to understand what's expected of them often leads to fraught relationships between adolescents and their parents. Jeffrey Arnett, a researcher and psychology professor at Clark University, told me, "What makes the U.S. unusual is that we often expect very little out of our teens. We don't expect them to make meals, or clean up, or take care of younger siblings—though most minority parents expect more, especially Latinos and Asian-Americans." While good at promoting tolerance for others and self-esteem, Arnett continued, "we are perhaps not so good at cultivating in them a sense that they should contribute to the family in return for all that they receive."

As a culture we dread the adolescent years. Arnett points to the unusually high level of disrespect American, middle-class white parents tolerate from their children. "It's not unusual for teens in these families to refuse to do what their parents ask, and to curse them or call them names, or insult the way they talk and dress," Arnett explained to me. "It's a cultural cliché that American teens are embarrassed to be seen with their parents in public."

While we consider rudeness from teens and friction between teens and their parents to be normal, even acceptable, it turns out it is not. Arnett has done research in many countries around the world, and has not found another country where rudeness is quite as common. He noted, "I think American parents in this generation are so eager to be friendly and emotionally close to their teens that they tolerate more disrespect and plain rudeness than they should."

One American mom living in Sweden remembered how a Swedish colleague who lived in the United States as a teenager was shocked by the automatic assumption that she should be at odds with her parents. "She didn't understand it. It wasn't part of her experience," she told me. In Sweden teens of any age may legally drink in private moderation, the voting age is eighteen, and spanking a child is a criminal offense. Japanese adolescents spend more time at home, have more harmonious relationships with their parents, and don't seem to feel an expectation that they separate from their parents, partly because the values of their home and their peer group are more aligned, and living at home is not considered incompatible with being independent in Japan. On the other hand, American parents see noncompliance as normal and appropriate, but at the same time try to exert more authority over their teens; their teenagers tend to see freedom as something they experience outside the home, not within it.

The problem is that we well-meaning parents want to shield our teens from the very experiences they really need. A different response on our part—one that offers children more, rather than less, concrete responsibility and meaningful work that actually impacts others—is what researchers are finding makes for a healthier adolescence than the one that so many American teenagers experience, where doing well at school is their most (and often only) meaningful work and adults are fre-quently monitoring their behavior and activities. The kind of teenage problems Americans have grown to think of as normal are not necessar-ily inevitable.

Cultures that are better able to promote a healthy transition to adulthood are ones where parents maintain close ties to their teens while also expecting and providing them with opportunities to act like compe-tent young adults. Nancy Darling thinks that Sweden does particularly well ushering children into adulthood. "One of the norms is that in Swe-den, for instance, parents really see their job as providing advice and support for the kids to become autonomous. That seems to be a fairly healthy transition. That [attitude] seems to help kids be able to use their parents as a support into moving autonomously and making adult deci-sions." An open give-and-take among parents and teens is common in Sweden. In a study of more than one thousand sixteen-year-olds in Swe-den, 72 percent said their parents used a "democratic style" of negotiat-ing at home.

Catarina, a Swedish mother of three boys who are now nineteen, seventeen, and twelve, explained to me in a phone interview from her home in Linköping how their family has cultivated an atmosphere of trust and self-control, which she thinks is representative of the wider Swedish culture. That mutual trust didn't start all of a sudden when the kids became teenagers, Catarina explained. It started when they were small.

From the time her children were able to speak, their relationship with Catarina and her husband, Johan, was characterized by abundant communication. "We talked to our kids from very early on. But we didn't tell them what to do. We'd discuss, and negotiate, with them. But we don't want them to *obey*. We want them to really understand why they should consider this or that." She experienced that when her chil-dren knew that she trusted them and respected them, they wanted to live up to that trust.

Catarina and Johan didn't see their role as being the ones who made the right decisions for their kids. The role of a good parent was to help one's *children* become good at making smart decisions for themselves. Catarina explained, "My goal was for them to have with them an inner voice they can listen to so they can know for themselves why they should do this or that. If you're too controlling, you might get kids who say what they know you want to hear, and they'd say 'Yes, Mum, yes, Dad,' but actually do the opposite. But if you trust in them, and show that you trust that they will make the best decision for themselves, there's no reason why they should sneak around behind your back."

Of course, some things are nonnegotiable to them, like seat belts, bike helmets, and curfews. Their style isn't permissive and their standards are clear. Their guiding principle is this: It's most important for children to hone their inner judgment. After all, you can't always be there for them. So Catarina asks lots of questions, to model what it's like to question yourself and your own motivations in order to make a good choice.

If she knows her son will be going somewhere where there's likely to be alcohol, she'll talk to him about drinking, asking if he will want to drink and why. "Is it because you feel nervous? Is it because you feel insecure about girls? Ask yourself what your inner voice is saying." She explains that she wants him to know that drinking, especially in the winter in Sweden, can be extremely dangerous, even fatal, if you get drunk and fall asleep outside. There are boundaries, but as her children grow older the limits get wider and wider, because there is mutual trust and her children show that they can handle more.

Part of raising a self-responsible child is giving him a genuine sense of ownership over his own choices and his own life, something that can begin when he's young and the stakes are low: whether it's a choice of what T-shirt to wear to school (even if you think the shirt just doesn't match the outfit) or choosing which foreign language to study in school (as Johan and Catarina experienced recently with their youngest son). Even though they didn't always agree with their children's choices, they wholeheartedly supported their right to choose.

## RESPONSIBILITY MATTERS

Most parents would concur: it would be nice to have a child who does helpful things around the house without being asked, is able to care for himself reliably, and can be counted on to watch over his siblings. But this seems to come at such a high cost: to our time and convenience, to our children, to family harmony. In fact, it can seem impossible, or maybe just a matter of luck or personality, to raise a child who is helpful around the house. Yet I've come to understand that it's possible, and that there is an urgent reason why it matters: in cultures where children are expected to competently help out, take care of others, and be responsible for themselves, parents benefit *because these practices mutually reinforce one another.* Instead of merely talking to children about why they should be empathetic, responsible, aware, and considerate (something that we know doesn't always work) while giving them a contradictory message when we let their obligations slide, parents in other cultures benefit from consistently expecting their kids to help out.

In other words, raising responsible children isn't just nice for practical reasons, because it eases family life, or helps us get chores done. Acts of responsibility cultivate awareness of others—they provide daily training in seeing and anticipating the needs of those around us. They are how we can give kids an opportunity to remain aware, sociable, and empathetic in ways that transcend feeling and become actual practice. As Elinor Ochs and Carolina Izquierdo of UCLA write in their paper on childhood responsibility, "moral responsibility is an active turning towards the other" that begins through meaningful physical responsibilities in early childhood, and "develops as a capacity for compassion." The physical acts required to become competent and responsible, they contend, may help a child to become morally conscious—something that's not just good for him, but for the community he's a part of. Parents in cultures where children are expected to competently help out, take care of others, and be responsible for themselves and their younger siblings benefit from the ways these expectations *consistently reinforce one another*.

But where do you begin? Most of us know it would be good for our kids if we gave them more to do. We struggle with chore charts, buy toy-size brooms, and nag our kids to make their beds. It works. Sometimes. But the problem is that kids really aren't capable of doing tasks without our assistance when they're not used to doing them. Cultivating these skills requires consistent guidance and training and attention, and what parent has the time for that?

Marjorie Goodwin, a linguistic anthropologist at UCLA, has found that the way we ask our children to do something matters. When parents themselves were involved in something else while asking their children to do something (what parent hasn't called out to his children in the next room that it's time to take a shower, while he himself is finishing up the dishes or reading e-mail on the computer?) and weren't face-to-face with the child, they encountered more resistance and less success in getting their children to do what they were expected to do. Mutual distraction, where a parent doesn't show he's aware that a child might be doing something else, feels disrespectful. But a parent who goes over to his child and puts his hand on her shoulder, gives her a brief, clear direction, and walks with her together to get ready for bed will have more success. Even better is if a parent has already been warmly engaged in some interaction with the child (sitting together reading a book) and they are already mutually oriented toward one another. "Nothing ever comes out of the blue," Goodwin told me on the phone. In successful interactions between parents and children, there is "a whole history of interaction that makes it possible" for the short directives to work.

Playfulness works too. One favorite strategy for Japanese parents is to give life to inanimate objects when they speak to their young children and attribute feelings to the things. They'll tell their toddlers that a toy is lonely and sad not to be put away with the others, or that their teeth want to be nice and sparkly clean. Rather than feeling ordered around, children are reminded that their acts of responsibility are nurturing and kind acts that affect others.

Sixteen-year-old Jackson, who lives in Massachusetts, willingly helps around the house and pitches in without being asked. Jackson told me his motivation comes from a single principle woven into his upbringing: that of awareness. "I grew up with the idea that it is important to be aware of my surroundings," to be aware of when to pitch in. "The problem for some parents is that their children aren't aware of how much their parents do for them," he told me, and how much they should do in return. His father, John, has always held high expectations of him in the community of their family. He expects him to be a respectful and considerate member of their home, but it goes both ways: pitching in and carrying his own weight also gave Jackson the kind of practice he needed to become that respectful, considerate person. When children like Jackson help out, when they carry their own weight, when they are given a chance to feel responsible, it simultaneously feeds off awareness *and* nurtures it.

Before, I might not have bothered to take the time to teach my children a skill when there was so much else to do that seemed more important and pressing. But once I learned how consistently many families around the world teach children to take care of themselves and each other at all ages, I began to incorporate these lessons into my own family. If I followed my Japanese friends' lead, two-year-old Anna probably wasn't too young to learn how to fold her own clothes. Though I was bluffing when I first tried it (sure I was setting both Anna and me up for failure), it turns out two was exactly the right age to take advantage of her toddler desire for independence by sitting down and showing her how to fold her clothes every day and encouraging her two-year-old's desire to imitate others in what she saw as meaningful work. At the same time, we knew that nine-year-old Daniel loves working with his hands, so we asked him to make lunch from time to time. Not only was he old enough, he blossomed when he was trusted to decide on a dish (like udon noodles or egg rolls), cut up the vegetables, and turn on the gas to make things the whole family could enjoy

Our kids have a long way to go—they still need lots of reminders, and we're far from where I wish we were. But that's okay. The difference is in my conviction: I'm now convinced why making it a priority for kids to pull their own weight is good for them, good for the household, and good for the community. *It's on my radar now*, and I can see the small opportunities every day in expecting them to carry their own bags, throw out their own trash, pour their own milk and clean up their own spills, hang up their own coats or towels, or start a load of laundry. I'm no longer ambivalent or impatient about taking two minutes to wait while I watch Anna fold her shirt, carefully patting it into place and carrying it over to her drawer. I've seen how it pays off to consistently pay attention to seemingly small things; those two minutes a day are an investment worth making. This is what we can learn from parents around the world—that in order for children to be mindful and aware, to practice nurturing, to feel proud of themselves and independent, and to want to do good for the world around them, we can start by setting our expectations for their responsibility in this realm a little higher.

# CONCLUSION:

## It Takes a Village

When my labor with Benjamin began on a muggy August night nearly thirteen years ago, I called my mother. She left her home in Pennsylvania the next morning at sunrise and drove for eight hours straight, her car packed with bags of dried seaweed, which Korean grandmothers make into a postpartum soup to help the milk come in. My mother arrived in time to meet her first grandchild when he was just minutes old, wrapped snugly in a blanket at our quiet birth center in Cambridge, the generous mop of hair on his head covered by a little cap with an embroidered yellow duck. For weeks afterward, as the summer heat gradually gave way to crisper, cooler days, I ate seaweed soup and rested at home while my mother and David, who was between jobs, helped care for the baby and me. Other relatives came and went, bringing meals, impossibly small bodysuits, and silly little rattles.

When Elenida and her husband, Obaldino, who live in a small city in southeastern Brazil, returned from the hospital with their third child, Elenida's mother had a pot of special chicken soup for new mothers bubbling on the stove. She kept a platter of assorted sweet, milky treats, which local wisdom claimed help mother's milk come in, on a table by a comfy chair so Elenida could enjoy them while nursing her two-day-old. Elenida and Obaldino appreciated having Elenida's sister and parents around (they lived in the apartment downstairs and moved freely between the two apartments, the way a lot of extended families do in Brazil), and welcomed the steady stream of relatives and neighbors who came to prepare food, talk, hold the baby, and amuse the older children.

Claire, an osteopath who lived in England for many years, returned to Kenya when she was five months pregnant to have her baby. The support she would get at home in East Africa meant more to her than England's modern birthing facilities and state-of-the-art medical technology. In Kenya every child is a precious gift—not only to the mother, but to the whole society. People greet a new mom with the words, "Thank you. Thank you, and welcome to this guest that you've brought us." In many traditional Kenyan cultures a guest is precious and honored, so the new mother has brought a gift to the world. That world, in turn, is responsible for the mother and the baby—entrusted to everyone's care.

In Finland the government ensures that new moms and dads have the support they need: women, like Michele, mom to baby Hilla, get to visit maternity clinics for free. Child health clinic visits are free too. There is generous paid parental leave including a "daddy month," which helped make it possible for Michele's husband, Janne, to spend time with their new baby; all families get generously subsidized child-care options (municipal day care, or an allowance for private day care or home care) for their babies and young children, child benefits to help support single parents, adoptive parents, or parents who must temporarily stop working to care for a child who is sick. Every new family receives a free baby box that contains over two dozen garments, including a snowsuit (for those long Finnish winters), bodysuits, leggings, and socks, and other baby supplies such as a quilt, a hairbrush, cloth diapers, and a picture book. The box itself can be used as a crib.

In cultures around the world, a baby begins his life enfolded into a larger community. Rarely would two parents be expected to care for their baby on their own. Throughout Asia, the Middle East, and Africa, just as in Korea, new mothers "lie in," resting their bodies after the momentous transition of birth, while others—often the baby's maternal grandmother or other female relatives—tend to both mother and baby. In Latin America new mothers are cared for by relatives for forty days after birth in a practice called *cuarentena*, which eases the stressful transition to motherhood during what the community recognizes as a vulnerable period. Immigrants who practice this custom in our country suffer lower rates of postpartum depression than those who don't. In some Guatemalan communities, relatives and neighbors visit the mother and newborn, bringing gifts of Mayan hot chocolate, bread, and a spicy corn drink thought to stimulate lactation. In Japan, mothers typically travel back to their childhood home to give birth and remain there for two months with their newborn to be cared for by their family.

"It's our collective responsibility to bring up the child in a nice way," Vicky, a Spanish mom from Barcelona with a close-knit family, told me in a phone conversation. Vicky helped raise her younger brother and sister, who were born when she was a preteen, and now that she has a daughter of her own her relatives drop in several times a week without calling first. Her niece comes over at night to give baby Nara a bath. Her family freely comments on how Vicky's raising her little girl, but these opinions don't make Vicky defensive. She and her partner feel her family is not being judgmental, but caring, and Vicky welcomes the feedback. "My grandmother always said to me, 'The more we look after children, the happier they'll be, the better they'll be, the better citizens they'll be later on,'" Vicky remembered. "She always said, 'We *all* have to make an effort that they be happy.'" Raised in a culture and a family that encourages people to lean on one another, not stand apart, Vicky has found the transition to becoming a mother something that has brought her more support, instead of making her more isolated.

In America a baby is seen as an individual member of one nuclear family. Though friends, family, or paid employees such as a baby nurse, postpartum doula, or babysitter help out, the cultural expectation is that the baby belongs to his family and we parents (still in shock that the hospital is even allowing us to take our helpless little newborn home) are fully responsible for his care and well-being. Which seems reasonable, given how much we value our privacy. We want to do things our own way, invent our own traditions, and make our own mistakes behind closed doors. We don't always appreciate input from family members, and we may feel judged and defensive when more experienced moms suggest we take it easy when we are frantically mopping the kitchen floor, or tell us to avoid certain foods that we want to eat. Our can-do attitude, which helps us succeed in so many other contexts, along with the contemporary conviction that women can have it all, gets in the way of our ability to relax and let others care for us after a child is born.

But if you look at the range of human societies across the globe and throughout time, you find that it is unusual for a mother and her partner to take sole responsibility for pregnancy, birth, and the rearing of an infant. Child-rearing in most societies has always involved not just two parents and a baby, but a network of people. This is something that other developed nations know and foster, through government support for social policies that will enhance every child's well-being and cultural customs that encourage togetherness. We cherish having choices in America. We are proud of our diversity and our options. But the price we pay for having choices is too high: moms and babies in America, instead of being part of a community, are too often left alone, just when they are most vulnerable. Without a community of support, without family within driving distance, and with no government-mandated paid leave or other forms of meaningful support, new moms in America often feel insecure or anxious, suffer from postpartum depression, have difficulty getting the support they need to successfully breast-feed, and find themselves overwhelmed by the shock of new motherhood.

As difficult as it is in the twenty-first century to have a baby in America, we still manage to do well at parenting, enjoying our children more as they grow up. Jennifer Lansford, a research professor at Duke University's Center for Child and Family Policy, has been working on the largest multicultural research study on parenting and children's adjustment to date. The Parenting Across Cultures Project examines parenting strategies, and how they affect child development, in China, Jordan, the United States, Sweden, Colombia, Italy, the Philippines, Kenya, and Thailand. The project's findings indicate that American parents display more warmth and are less rigid than parents in countries where parent-child relations are more hierarchical and attitudes are more traditional. In Lansford's view, American parents are doing okay.

But Lansford has also found that we could give our children more respect and autonomy, as parents do in Sweden. "Sweden is one of the countries in our sample that is often held up as an example of being a very child-centered place," Lansford told me. "It's child-centered in the right ways." Sweden is among the safest places in the world to give birth, has one of the world's most generous parental leave policies, does not allow children's television programs to be interrupted by advertising, and has comprehensive laws that protect children's rights and safety. This child-centered, pro-parent approach pays off: Swedish children rank among the best-cared-for and most fortunate children in the world.

"There's no perfect culture, no perfect way of parenting," Lansford noted, even as she extolled the virtues of a Swedish childhood. But the takeaway from a country like Sweden is that it is possible to be highly respectful of our individual children and give them the autonomy that all children need to thrive, while recognizing that raising a child is a community responsibility for all to share.

The difficulty with parenting in America, as I've tried to show in this book, is that it's too easy to lose sight of the fact that we are all in this together. In our zeal to make sure our own child has everything he needs (because if we don't look out for him, who will?), caring for one another is inevitably low on our list of priorities. Instead of finding ways to help support and encourage parents, we give them space and stay out of their way (but all too often judge each other's parenting choices, secretly believing that if someone else's child is having problems, only his parents are to blame). As a result, in our country, parents are on their own. A major report on the culture of the American family out of the University of Virginia shows that whether it's by choice or by circumstance, we parent with only the thinnest webs of support. The report states, "As much as experts might assert that it 'takes a village to raise a child,' for most American parents, the village is absent."

That's what makes American parenting unusual—and challenging. Lisa Belkin, a prominent parenting journalist and former writer for *The New York Times*, sums it up well:

> Whatever American parenting is, it's the result of the "my problems are my problems and I have to fix them" thread of the American psyche, which leads us to treat parenting as a private not a communal concern. The countries we are told are so much better don't do that. They believe that raising children, particularly very young children, is best done with generous dollops of maternity leave and health care and child care.

It's easier to be the parents we want to be when we have support. When kids are raised by supported parents, it's easier for them too. David and I noticed that family life with young children felt less stressful in Japan. People throughout the community helped by having the same expectations for children that we held too, and caring for children together, making us feel less on our own.

There's a reason why children's well-being is higher in countries like Sweden, Norway, Denmark, Finland, or Japan than it is in other places. Though we can feel critical of these countries because their social dictates seem to infringe upon personal freedom, these are all countries where it's easier for parents to impart to their children unified, widely shared notions about good ways to live. When they have been raised to be mindful of their impact on the world, and when they see other kids around them being mindful too, children are more likely to feel safer, be responsible, be considerate of others, enjoy healthier lives, and act capably without adult supervision.

· · ·

As I parent my four very different children, who are now twelve, ten, six, and three years old, I struggle to find ways to raise them to be compassionate, have strength of character and the courage to act on their convictions, and feel competent. I've been learning so much about how to do this by crossing the border into other parenting cultures.

Parents in many of the countries I've visited and learned about are doing something we (David and I included) can learn from: staying out of the way of their children's independence. Instead, they embrace it. They believe in it and foster it. They expect children to develop a different sort of independence: one born of self-reliance more than self-expression, and by pulling together, they make it possible for this to happen. Interestingly, parents in many of these same nations also expect babies to be babies, understanding that early dependence and nurturing, not separation, is how to ensure that children become independent when they are developmentally ready.

In America we are told how important it is to teach our babies to become independent, but then we help, closely monitor, and control them as they grow up. In other cultures, the dependency of very small children isn't looked upon as problematic or pathological. In other cultures children mature more slowly in many ways. Parents allow for an early childhood free of the pressures our children feel at a very young age to behave, to make choices and negotiate, to assert their individuality, to seek attention, to master formal learning. In other countries, families are focused, consistent, and clear in their guidelines for how to treat others, and then offer children increasingly substantial responsibilities and physical independence as they grow older.

They view babies as dependent—after all, they are *babies*!—but see older children and teenagers as tremendously capable, including them in society rather than segregating them, and respecting, fostering, and taking into account their growing capabilities. This view of the arc of childhood—which is in some ways the *opposite* of our own—makes it easier for parents to navigate some major transitions that we've grown to think of as inevitable and difficult, from toddler clashes to parent-teen conflict.

It's telling that first-generation immigrant children, across almost every immigrant group, fare better and have fewer health and behavioral problems than their American-born counterparts—a phenomenon known as the "immigrant paradox." Adults who work with immigrant children describe them as "sweet, engaging, open, respectful," eager to learn and optimistic, asserts Richard Weissbourd, a child and family psychologist at Harvard, in his book *The Parents We Mean to Be*. But, he points out, "The longer immigrant children live in this country, across almost all immigrant groups, the worse are the indications of their health, their school performance, and their moral functioning. . . . [A]s English proficiency grows, school performance drops: the two are *inversely* related." Immigrant families aren't, he notes, "a threat to America's moral culture." Rather, "America is a threat to immigrant children's moral development."

There are so many thriving families in this country, of course, who have found a healthy balance. The very aspect of American parenting that makes it difficult to define means that we have a variety of models to pull from even within our own culture. Our "do it yourself" attitude enables parents to follow the path they believe in once they find it, as long as their personal and material circumstances permit. But I've come to realize how growing up in an environment that prioritizes care over competition and cooperation over judgment benefits *all* children and all families.

Happiness comes not just from individual success and achievements; it also comes from stepping outside our own individual bubbles. We can benefit from best practices when we blend a more heightened awareness of those around us with what many American parents are so good at: raising individualistic, confident children who have been encouraged to know themselves and express their thoughts since they were very young. American children haven't been told over and over to keep their opinions in check, as is more common in societies where societal harmony is a greater priority. Things that are perceived as threatening in more conformist or traditional societies (Japan is notoriously insular, and conformity is valued over diversity in many of the places I visited) are celebrated and valued in America. We feel sure that our kids will benefit from this open view. In the end, David and I know that one of the best things about having come home to raise our children in the United States is that they'll have a chance to develop the breadth of mind, tolerance, and empathy that come only from living in a nation that celebrates difference. I believe this sort of tolerance is one of America's most unique and dynamic strengths.

Like many parents I know, I sometimes wondered if there could be another way to parent, but I couldn't see my way past the invisible cultural box surrounding me. In fact, I didn't even know it was there. But now that I do, I've learned that good parenting isn't so much about being more involved, or being less involved, or about how much we do. It's about *how* we're involved and what we focus on cultivating. Some things matter and have surprisingly broad effects, such as encouraging our children's awareness of others around them and facilitating their ability to do things for themselves. Other things, such as accelerated classes, a stimulating environment, or the "right" possessions, don't matter as much as our culture tells us they do. It would be a powerful combination if we taught our children that, yes, their questions, opinions, talents, and accomplishments are genuinely important, and that kindness, empathy, self-reliance, and community are important as well. When children are attuned to others and more autonomously capable, it is easier to enjoy relationships of free and mutual respect with them, instead of relationships based on constant monitoring, control, and power struggles, or, conversely, being burdened with their care long after it should be necessary.

As the world becomes smaller, our perspectives broaden. Parents everywhere can learn from each other how to raise children who thrive. We can advocate for the common good of all children as we also raise our own as best we can. We can raise free-thinking children who are concerned about other people near and far, are ready and able to act on their convictions, stand up for injustice, don't take no for an answer, and think outside the box.

· · ·

A close friend, also a mom of four, told me on the phone last week that her children are growing so fast that when her eleven-year-old daughter wakes up in the morning she looks taller than she did the day before. Now instead of opening one eye to read to an energetic toddler who is ready for action before the birds are even up, my friend finds herself going to bed before her thirteen- and eleven-year-old girls and getting up hours before they're ready to stir. It feels like just yesterday that Benjamin was a baby in my arms as I watched autumn leaves swirl to the ground the first few months of his life, my first year as a mother, but he is now nearly my height, and I know the other children aren't far behind. The relationships we have with our children change over time—as our children grow and go through different life stages and as we, too, change. But it turns out that what our children need as they become adolescents is remarkably similar to what they needed as young children: parents who maintain warm, loving relationships with them while at the same time providing them with clear and consistent boundaries, who give them the right kind of autonomy when they are ready for it, who provide them with the tools, encouragement, and practice they need to manage their own lives, and who believe in and support their ability to become competent, happy, successful, and responsible adults.

# Acknowledgments

This book simply wouldn't have come into existence without the generous help of so many people. I'm particularly indebted to my agent, Gillian MacKenzie, who tirelessly worked with me on shaping these ideas, my editor, Lucia Watson, whose exacting standards inspired me, and Gigi Campo, for help managing matters big and small. Thanks too to William Shinker and Megan Newman for their supportive belief in the message of this book.

Many researchers took the time to explain their findings to me, and I am immensely grateful. Special thanks to: Carol Dweck, Thomas Weisner, David Lancy, Gilda Morelli, Candy Goodwin, Ellen Beate Sandseter, Tony Wagner, Richard Weissbourd, Barbara Hofer, Margaret Nelson, Heidi Keller, Lauren Hale, Tim Kasser, Meret Keller, Stephanie Margaris Sloane, Barbara Welles-Nystrom, Josefine Wendel, Dawn Olcott, Eva Pomerantz, Pei-Chia Lan, Jennifer Lansford, Katherine Curhan, Yong Zhao, Ida Fadzillah, Karen Adolph, Peter Gray, Nancy Darling, Yeh Hsueh, and Jim McKenna.

Parents, teachers, and children around the world thoughtfully guided me through their own parenting cultures. Special thanks to: Sohani Crockett, Dongjoo Shin, Dongeun Shin, Jeannie Marshall, Karen Le Billon, Shawn Smith, Jennifer Keddy, Kathleen Weidenfeller, Mali

Colás, J. Claire, K. Niala, Jane Joo Park, Eriko Osugi, Chiemi Tsuji, Naomi Nagato, Makiko Yasoshima, Makito Hara, Maiko Nagata, Nancy Ota, Orie Sawa, Miho Asahi, Kerrin Scott, Becky Paulson, Drielle Nascimento, Jennifer Loh, Katherine Ozment, Melinda Rothstein, Rania Melki, Alice Sedar, Brittany Shahmehri, Vicky Mateu Simeon, Kara Porter, Naoko Belitz, Elena von Naumann, Mikaela Johannesson, Heleen, Jinah Roh, Jennifer Fink, June Sobel, Allison Walton, Jessica Lahey, Kay Lee-Fruman, Alyea Riker, Vijay Owens, Jade Eisman-Grace, Sarah Ludwig, Denise Schipani, Rachel Rose, Hena Khan, Allison Laverty Montag, Milja Poe, Jill Sanders, Mika Saarinen, Kelly Webster, Britta Panda, Gerhild de Wall, Christine Wortham, Daniella Eltvik, Jill Balzer, Akiko Endo, Ulrika Björkstén, Michele Simeon, Syra Morii, Robin Fleming, Terry Kawashima, Michaela Schonhoeft, Christa Xydaki, Hanna Graeffe, Catherine Bendl, Gloria Xu, Steven Kong, Jessica Halpern, Julia Priest, Victoria Whitney, Andrea Bernard, Kang-Ok Cho, Jung-Woo Oh, Mugyeong Moon, Johan Sievers, Catarina Gisby, Janne Hukka, Kerry Dickinson, Dawn Hubbell-Staeble, Kevin Kirsch, Els Kushner, Tonya Oya Orme, Kirsi Pertulli, Veera Gindonis, Päivi Laukkanen, Scott Barney, Charlotte Chang, Anastasya Partan, Melinda Rothstein, Anita Truong, and Elina Pöllänen.

Kanako Katsumi, Chieko Uemura, Kumi Naruse, and Yuri Hayano were much-loved babysitters.

In Finland, Michele Simeon helped me by offering contacts and information, and Erik Bäckman provided transportation and good conversation.

Kumsun Chung and Ahn Chung offered liaisons to schools and a cozy place to stay in Germany.

Xuyang Yao and Yong Zhao kindly gave me the introductions that led me to Northeast Yucai School.

Liisa Viirimäki and Pekka Niiranen set up my visits to their schools in Finland.

Special thanks to the teachers and administrators of Shibuya Douhou Yochien and Shinno Shogakko, two warmly welcoming schools that made a real difference in our children's lives.

Thanks to the other schools that opened their doors to me: Matthew Greenberg and the teachers at Growing Up Green, in New York City; Fletcher Maynard Academy, Cambridge, Massachusetts; Waldkobolde Kindergarten, Düsseldorf, Germany; the Dream School in Kauniainen, Finland; Lahti Primary School, Lahti, Finland; and Northeast Yucai School in Shenyang, China.

Anna Novick was a perfect research assistant and cross-cultural guide. Pippa Marple was a lovely babysitter in Finland and Germany.

Others who helped in numerous, indispensable ways: Laura Fraser, Aliyah Baruchin, Gish Jen, Djamila Fitzgerald, Akiko Sugaya, Martha Collins, Claire Messud, Michael Puett, Eve Bridburg, Leanne Ogasawara, Brandy King, Dianne Bilyak, Orion Jong Haeng Lee, Suzy Feinberg, Marie Colantoni Pechet, Mark and Victoria Oliva, Alisa Bowman, Alexandra Grabbe, Brette Sember, Debbie Koenig, Melanie McMinn, and Meredith Resnick.

I'm thankful beyond words for my special tribe: Laura Simeon—a beloved friend who truly helped research and shape so many of these ideas and connected me with many parents and teachers; Jennifer Margulis, for unerringly expert editorial instincts and cheerleading throughout; and Melissa Chianta, for dedicated fact-checking and quiet encouragement. This book would not have come to be without the three of you, and I cannot thank you enough.

My patient and loving husband, David Gross-Loh, deserves a medal for so many things but especially for tirelessly watching all four children weekend after weekend so I could write.

Our families, the Loh and Gross clans, were there for me as always: the web of support I'm so lucky to have. I'm especially grateful to my parents, Charles and Hwasun Loh, who have offered a lifetime of wise lessons in parenting between cultures.

# Notes

## Introduction

**Page xi Robert LeVine, an eminent Harvard anthropologist:** Robert A. LeVine, "Parental Goals: A Cross-Cultural View," *Teachers College Record* 76, no. 2 (1974), 226–239.

**Page 5 There are many different childhoods in America:** Two books capture some of these differences: Annette Lareau, *Unequal Childhoods: Class, Race, and Family Life* (Berkeley: University of California Press, 2003); and Adrie Kusserow, *American Individualisms: Child Rearing and Social Class in Three Neighborhoods* (New York: Palgrave Macmillan, 2004). My book focuses its discussion of American parenting primarily on the upper-middle-class "soft" individualism detailed in *American Individualisms* (as opposed to the "hard" individualism of working-class families), because this script has become so widely disseminated throughout our society as good parenting.

**Page 6 We have one of the highest child obesity rates:** Organisation for Economic Co-operation and Development (OECD), *OECD Obesity Update 2012* (Paris: OECD Publishing, 2012), 7, http://www.oecd.org/els/healthpoliciesanddata/49716427.pdf.

**Page 6 one in four American children is on medication:** Maggie Kozel, "Little Pharma: The Medication of U.S. Children," *The Huffington Post* (February 5, 2011), http://www.huffingtonpost.com/maggie-kozel-md/childrens-health-care_b_803167.html.

**Page 6 and American kids are three times more likely:** Julie M. Zito et al., "A Three-Country Comparison of Psychotropic Medication Prevalence in Youth," *Child and Adolescent Psychiatry and Mental Health* 2, no. 26 (2008).

**Page 6 even their empathy:** Jamil Zaki, "What, Me Care? Young People Are Less Empathetic," *Scientific American*, January 19, 2011, http://www.scientificamerican.com/article.cfm?id=what-me-care.

**Page 6 creativity:** Po Bronson and Ashley Merryman, "The Creativity Crisis," *Daily Beast*, July 10, 2010, http://www.thedailybeast.com/newsweek/2010/07/10/the-creativity-crisis.html.

**Page 6 According to a recent major study:** Carl Desportes Bowman et al., *Culture of American Families: Executive Report* (Charlottesville, VA: Institute for Advanced Studies in Culture, 2012), 6, http://iasc-culture.org/survey_archives/IASC_CAF_ExecReport.pdf.

**Page 6 we worry we are simply not doing enough:** Ibid., 11.

**Page 6 Parents suffer too:** Kathryn M. Rizzo, Holly H. Schiffrin, and Miriam Liss, "Insight into the Parenthood Paradox: Mental Health Outcomes of Intensive Mothering," *Journal of Child and Family Studies* (June 30, 2012), doi: 10.1007/s10826-012-9615-z.

**Page 8 seventeen times more than their American peers:** F. Thomas Juster et al., *Changing Times of American Youth: 1981–2003* (Ann Arbor, MI: Institute for Social Research, University of Michigan), 8, http://www.ns.umich.edu/Releases/2004/Nov04/teen_time_report.pdf.

## Chapter 1. Sleep Time: Keep Our Babies Close or Give Them Space?

**Page 14 Sleep disturbances have:** Émilie Fortier-Brochu et al., "Insomnia and Daytime Cognitive Performance: A Meta-Analysis," *Sleep Medicine Reviews* 16, no. 1 (February 2012), 83–94, http://www.ncbi.nlm.nih.gov/pubmed?term="Insomnia%20and%20Daytime%20Cognitive%20Performance%3A%20A%20Meta-Analysis%2C"; Jessica D. Payne and Elizabeth A. Kensinger, "Sleep's Role in the Consolidation of Emotional Episodic Memories," *Current Directions in Psychological Science* 19, no. 5 (October 2010), 290–295, http://cdp.sagepub.com/content/19/5/290; M. P. Walker et al., "Sleep-Dependent Motor Memory Plasticity in the Human Brain," *Neuroscience* 4, no. 133 (2005), 911–917, http://www.ncbi.nlm.nih.gov/pubmed/15964485; M. Kopasz et al., "Sleep and Memory in Healthy Children and Adolescents—A Critical Review," *Sleep Medicine Reviews* 14, no. 3 (June 2010): 167–177, http://www.ncbi.nlm.nih.gov/pubmed?term="Sleep%20and%20Memory%20in%20Healthy%20Children%20and%20Adolescents—A%20Critical%20Review%2C"; S. Cortese et al., "Sleep in Children with Attention-Deficit/Hyperactivity Disorder: Meta-analysis of Subjective and Objective Studies," *Journal of the American Academy of Child and Adolescent Psychiatry* 48, no. 9 (September 2009), 894–908, accessed at http://www.ncbi.nlm.nih.gov/pubmed/19625983; Dag Neckelmann et al.,"Chronic Insomnia as a Risk Factor for Developing Anxiety and Depression," *Sleep* 30, no. 7 (July 1, 2007); 873–880, accessed at http://www.ncbi.nlm.nih.gov/pmc/articles/PMC1978360/; Kristen L. Knutson, "Does Inadequate Sleep Play a Role in Vulnerability to Obesity?" *American Journal of Human Biology* 24, no. 3 (May–June 2012), 361–371, accessed at http://www.ncbi.nlm.nih.gov/pubmed/22275135.

**Page 15 Sleep is highly valued in America:** Laura Vanderkam, *168 Hours: You Have More Time Than You Think* (New York: Portfolio, 2010), 13.

**Page 16 In most cultures around the world:** Meredith F. Small, *Our Babies, Ourselves: How Biology and Culture Shape the Way We Parent* (New York: Anchor Books, 1998), 184.

**Page 16 Out of one hundred countries in another survey:** Ibid., 111.

**Page 16 "Resisting the intense desire of young children for close proximity with caregivers at night":** Sara Latz, MD, JD, Abraham W. Wolf, PhD, and Betsy Lozoff, MD, "Cosleeping in Context: Sleep Practices and Problems in Young Children in Japan and the United States," *Archives of Pediatrics and Adolescent Medicine* 153, no. 4 (April 1999), 339–346, http://archpedi.jamanetwork.com/article.aspx?articleid=346276.

**Page 17 A human baby is hardwired:** Peter Gray, "Why Young Children Protest Bedtime: A Story of Evolutionary Mismatch," *Psychology Today*, October 11, 2011, http://www.psychologytoday.com/blog/freedom-learn/201110/why-young-children-protest-bedtime-story-evolutionary-mismatch.

**Page 17 A 2011 advertisement from Milwaukee's health department:** Dana Macario, "Babies with Knives? Co-sleeping Ad Angers Some Parents," *Today Moms*, November 16, 2011, http://moms.today.msnbc.msn.com/_news/2011/11/16/8836623-babies-with-knives-co-sleeping-ad-angers-some-parents.

**Page 17 In a survey of fifteen countries:** Fern R. Hauck, MD, MS, and Kawai Tanabe, MPH, "International Trends in Sudden Infant Death Syndrome and Other Sudden Unexpected Deaths in Infancy: Need for Better Diagnostic Standardization," *Current Pediatric Reviews* 6, no. 1 (February 2010), 95–101, http://www.ispid.org/fileadmin/user_upload/textfiles/articles/CPR17_Hauck_SIDS_Trends.pdf.

**Page 17 But SIDS is notably low in countries like Japan:** Ibid.

**Page 17 Although the American Academy of Pediatrics:** American Academy of Pediatrics Task Force on Sudden Infant Death Syndrome, "The Changing Concept of Sudden Infant Death Syndrome: Diagnostic Coding Shifts, Controversies Regarding the Sleeping Environment, and New Variables to Consider in Reducing Risk," *Pediatrics* 116, no. 5 (November 1, 2005), 1245–1255, http://pediatrics.aappublications.org/content/116/5/1245.

**Page 18 Observing mother-baby pairs in slumber:** James J. McKenna et al., "Sleep and Arousal Patterns of Co-Sleeping Human Mother/Infant Pairs: A Preliminary Physiological Study with Implications for the Study of Sudden Infant Death Syndrome (SIDS)," *American Journal of Physical Anthropology* 83 (1990), 331–347. James McKenna et al., "Parent-Infant Cosleeping: The Appropriate Context for the Study of Infant Sleep and Implications for Sudden Infant Death Syndrome (SIDS) Research," *Journal of Behavioral Medicine* 16, no. 6 (1993), 589–610.

**Page 18 And while a co-sleeping infant wakes more frequently:** James J. McKenna, *Sleeping With Your Baby: A Parent's Guide to Cosleeping* (Washington, DC: Platypus Media, 2007), 39.

**Page 18 In this way mother-child sleep may actually protect:** P. Okami, T. Weisner, and R. Olmstead, "Outcome Correlates of Parent-Child Bedsharing: An Eighteen-Year Longitudinal Study," *Journal of Developmental and Behavioral Pediatrics* 23, no. 4 (August 2002), 244–253.

**Page 18 the overwhelming majority:** J. McKenna and T. McDade, "Why Babies Should Never Sleep Alone: A Review of the Co-sleeping Controversy in Relation to SIDS, Bedsharing and Breast feeding," *Paediatric Respiratory Reviews* 6, no. 2 (June 2005), 134–152, http://www .isisonline.org.uk/hcp/where_babies_sleep/parents_bed/why_parents_bedshare/.

**Page 18 Smoking, drug or alcohol use:** Ibid. "Why Parents Bed-Share," *Infant Sleep Information Source*, July 20, 2012, http://www.isisonline.org.uk/hcp/where_babies_sleep/parents_bed /why_parents_bedshare/.

**Page 19 In one study, 99 percent of SIDS deaths had at least one:** B. D. Gessner, "Association Between Sudden Infant Death Syndrome and Prone Sleep Position, Bed Sharing, and Sleeping Outside an Infant Crib in Alaska," *Pediatrics* 108, no. 4 (October 2001), 923–927, http:// www.ncbi.nlm.nih.gov/pubmed/11581445.

**Page 19 In an analytical report of infant deaths in Milwaukee:** K. Michalski, *2010 City of Milwaukee Fetal Infant Mortality Review (FIMR) Report: Understanding and Preventing Infant Death and Stillbirth in Milwaukee* (Milwaukee: City of Milwaukee Health Department, December 2010), 17.

**Page 19 "I have thoroughly researched this common concern":** Dr. William Sears, "Ask Dr. Sears: Co-Sleeping a SIDS Danger?" *Parenting*, n.d., http://www.parenting.com/article/ask -dr-sears-co-sleeping-a-sids-danger.

**Page 19 When babies sleep:** *Information Statement: Room Sharing with a Baby* (Melbourne: SIDS and Kids National Scientific Advisory Group, 2008), http://sidsandkidswa.org/assets /info-statements/room_sharing.pdf.

**Page 19 Most parents are surprised to learn:** G. A. Smith, "Injuries Associated with Cribs, Playpens, and Bassinets Among Young Children in the U.S., 1990–2008," *Pediatrics* 127, no. 3 (March 2011), 479–486.

**Page 19 Once babies become toddlers, they may start waking up at night:** Jeffrey Jensen Arnett, *Human Development: A Cultural Approach* (Upper Saddle River, NJ: Pearson, 2012), http://www.pearsonhighered.com/showcase/arnett/assets/pdf/arnett1e_sc_020559526X_ web.pdf, 180.

**Page 19 Interestingly, studies show that co-sleeping children:** Sarah Mosko, Christopher Richard, and James McKenna, "Infant Arousals During Mother-Infant Bed Sharing: Implications for Infant Sleep and Sudden Infant Death Syndrome Research," *Pediatrics* 100, no. 5 (November 1997), 841–849; Sarah Mosko et al., "Infant Sleep Architecture During Bedsharing and Possible Implications for SIDS," *Sleep* 19, no. 9 (November 1996), 677–684.

**Page 20 The Western idea that mothers and babies should sleep separately:** Small, *Our Babies, Ourselves*, 122.

**Page 20 Still, most Western babies continued to sleep together:** Christina Hardyment, *Dream Babies: Childcare Advice from John Locke to Gina Ford* (London: Frances England, 2007), 177.

**Page 20 Communal sleep was so normal:** Peter N. Stearns, Perrin Rowland, and Lori Giarnella, "Children's Sleep: Sketching Historical Change," *Journal of Social History* (Winter 1996), 357, 362–363.

**Page 21 As historian Christina Hardyment tells us:** Hardyment, *Dream Babies,* 56–57.

**Page 21 People assumed that babies:** Stearns, 345–366.

**Page 21 that they didn't need a whole lot of nighttime sleep:** Ibid., 346–347.

**Page 21 But anxiety about children's well-being:** Ibid., 357.

**Page 21 Professional advice and rules:** Ibid.

**Page 21 Experts began to warn mothers against rocking:** Hardyment, 53.

**Page 21 Cradles were out:** Stearns et al., "Children's Sleep," 358.

**Page 21 Once a mother, and no one else:** Hardyment, *Dream Babies,* 177.

**Page 21 The accompanying surge of expert advice:** Stearns, "Children's Sleep," 348.

**Page 21 But the new view of sleep:** Ibid., 362.

**Page 21 "The goal was":** Ibid., 362–363.

**Page 23 Insomnia and sleeplessness:** Ibid., 345.

**Page 24 The Japanese don't see the early attachment:** Abraham W. Wolf et al., "Parental Theories in the Management of Young Children's Sleep in Japan, Italy, and the United States," in *Parents' Cultural Belief Systems: Their Origins, Expressions, and Consequences,* eds. Sara Harkness and Charles M. Super (New York: Guilford Press, 1996), 364–384.

**Page 25 In one of their studies, mothers of preschoolers:** Meret A. Keller and Wendy A. Goldberg, "Co-sleeping: Help or Hindrance for Young Children's Independence?" *Infant and Child Development* 13, no. 5 (December 2004), 369–388.

**Page 27 "The child is considered an individual with certain rights":** Barbara Welles-Nystrom, "Co-sleeping as a Window into Swedish Culture: Considerations of Gender and Health Care," *Scandinavian Journal of Caring Sciences* 19, no. 4 (December 2005), 357.

**Page 30 In Scandinavia, it's customary for babies:** Anna Cronin-de-Chavez, "Cultural Beliefs and Thermal Care of Infants: Protecting South Asian and White British Infants in Bradford from Heat and Cold" (doctoral thesis, Durham University, 2011), 103.stm.fi/suomi/eho /julkaisut/mamuvauva/vauva_englanti.pdf; M. Tourula et al., "Children Sleeping Outdoors in Winter: Parents' Experiences of a Culturally Bound Childcare Practice," *International Journal of Circumpolar Health* 67, no. 2–3 (June 2008), 269–278.

**Page 30 The Finnish government assures new mothers:** Ulla Hoppu et al., *Having Children in Finland* (Helsinki: Ministry of Labour, Migration Division, 1997), http://pre20031103.stm.fi /suomi/eho/julkaisut/mamuvauva/vauva_englanti.pdf. This isn't a new idea—1920s English mothers were told that keeping their babies outdoors as much as possible would assure they would sleep well and grow robust and healthy. But while the fresh-air cure fell out of fashion in Anglo-American baby care, it remains in full force throughout Scandinavia.

**Page 30 After that, her little boy Oliver:** Anastasya Partan, "Let Your Baby Sleep Outside: Surprising Parenting Wisdom from Scandinavia," *Babble,* December 27, 2010, http://www.babble .com/baby/baby-health-safety/baby-sleep-parenting-wisdom-scandinavia/.

**Page 31 Most American infants and toddlers:** Jodi A. Mindell et al., "Cross-Cultural Differences in Infant and Toddler Sleep," *Sleep Medicine* 11, no. 3 (March 2010), 274–280.

**Page 31 it's always been about thirty-seven minutes more:** Lisa Anne Matricciani et al., "Never Enough Sleep: A Brief History of Sleep Recommendations for Children," *Pediatrics* 129, no. 3 (March 2012), 548–556.

**Page 31 And that solid eight-hour sleep:** David K. Randall, *Dreamland: Adventures in the Strange Science of Sleep* (New York: W. W. Norton, 2012), 32–34.

**Page 31 Bedtime routines are more complex:** Marie J. Hayes, Shawn M. Roberts, and Rebecca Stowe, "Early Childhood Co-sleeping: Parent-Child and Parent-Infant Nighttime Interactions," *Infant Mental Health Journal* 17, no. 4 (Winter 1996), 348–357.

**Page 31 Guatemalan Mayan babies, who share a room or co-sleep:** G. A. Morelli et al., "Cultural Variation in Infants' Sleeping Arrangements: Questions of Independence," *Developmental Psychology* 28, no. 4 (1992), 604–613.

**Page 32 Children learn to sleep "at will":** C. M. Worthman and M. Melby, "Toward a Comparative Developmental Ecology of Human Sleep," in *Adolescent Sleep Patterns: Biological, Social, and Psychological Influences*, ed. M. A. Carskadon (New York: Cambridge University Press, 2002), 77–80.

**Page 32 Transitional attachment objects also aren't common in cultures:** Mieko Hobara, "Prevalence of Transitional Objects in Young Children in Tokyo and New York," *Infant Mental Health Journal* 24, no. 2 (March–April 2003), 174–191.

**Page 32 In Taiwan, picture books specifically about bedtime:** Wan-Hsiang Chou, "Co-sleeping and the Importation of Picture Books about Bedtime," *Children's Literature in Education* 40, no. 1 (March 2009), 19–32.

**Page 32 One popular American picture book:** Rosemary Wells, *McDuff's New Friend* (New York: Hyperion Books for Children, 1998), n.p.

**Page 33 best sleep happens when there is what researchers call "goodness of fit":** Oskar G. Jenni and Bonnie B. O'Connor, "Children's Sleep: An Interplay Between Culture and Biology," *Pediatrics* 115, Supplement 1 (January 1, 2005), 204–216, http://pediatrics.aappublications.org/content/115/Supplement_1/204.full.

**Page 35 Once a staunch proponent of babies' sleeping alone:** Richard Ferber, MD, "Dr. Ferber Updates His Landmark Sleep Book," *Pediatric Views* (June 2006), http://www.childrenshospital.org/views/june06/sleep.html.

## Chapter 2. Buy, Buy, Baby: Why Are We Drowning in Stuff?

**Page 37 According to one study, the average American family:** Laura Vanderkam, "How Having Too Much Stuff Wastes Your Time," *CBS MoneyWatch*, August 2, 2012, http://www.cbsnews.com/8301-505125_162-57484989/how-having-too-much-stuff-wastes-your-time/.

**Page 39 According to one study, three-quarters of American families surveyed:** Ibid.

**Page 39 Our child-centric culture:** Viviana A. Zelizer, *Pricing the Priceless Child: The Changing Social Value of Children* (Princeton, NJ: Princeton University Press, 1994), 96.

**Page 40 University of Pennsylvania sociologist Annette Lareau refers to this as "concerted cultivation":** Annette Lareau, PhD, *Unequal Childhoods: Class, Race, and Family Life, Second Edition with an Update a Decade Later* (Berkeley: University of California Press, 2011).

**Page 40 Most parents, regardless of socioeconomic class:** Allison J. Pugh, *Longing and Belonging: Parents, Children, and Consumer Culture* (Berkeley: University of California Press, 2009).

**Page 41 They tried to steer their kids away:** Ibid., 86.

**Page 41 In the United States, where we have more shopping centers:** Barry Schwartz, *The Paradox of Choice: Why More Is Less* (New York: HarperCollins, 2004), 18.

**Page 41 93 percent of teenage girls:** Ibid.

**Page 41 American children get an average:** Brad Tuttle, "Got Stuff? Typical American Home Is Cluttered with Possessions—and Stressing Us Out," *Time*, July 19, 2012, http://moneyland.time.com/2012/07/19/got-stuff-typical-american-home-cluttered-with-possessions-and-stressing-us-out/.

**Page 42 A consumer-oriented lifestyle:** Juliet Schor, *Born to Buy: The Commercialized Child and the New Consumer Culture* (New York: Scribner, 2004), 167.

**Page 42 "Less involvement in consumer culture":** Ibid.

**Page 42 There is some evidence to suggest that financial security:** See, for instance, Talya Miron-Shatz, "Am I Going to Be Happy and Financially Stable? How American Women Feel When They Think About Financial Security," *Judgment and Decision Making* 4, no. 1 (February 2009), 102–112.

**Page 42 In fact, children of affluent families:** Suniya S. Luthar, "The Culture of Affluence:

Psychological Costs of Material Wealth," *Child Development* 74, no. 6 (2003), 1581–1593; E. Diener and M. E. P. Seligman, "Beyond Money: Toward an Economy of Well-Being," *Psychological Science in the Public Interest* 5, no. 1 (2004), 1–31; Mihaly Csikszentmihalyi and Barbara Schneider, *Becoming Adult: How Teenagers Prepare for the World of Work* (New York: Basic Books, 2000). Luthar (2003) suggests that the well-being of affluent children suffers because of isolation and achievement pressure. Also see Diener and Seligman, 2004. Csikszentmihalyi and Schneider (2000) did a longitudinal study that found that adolescents from affluent suburbs were less happy and reported lower self-esteem than adolescents living in middle-class neighborhoods and inner-city slums.

**Page 42 And through what social scientists call "invidious comparison":** Richard Sennett, *Together: The Rituals, Pleasures and Politics of Co-operation* (New Haven, CT: Yale University Press, 2012), 141. But as Sennett writes, "in capitalist societies with strong family cohesion, in schools which emphasize the value of studying seriously together, the social consequences of economic inequality can be countervailed."

**Page 42 When children are highly aware that status is conveyed:** Ibid., 142–143.

**Page 47 Kids learn to get hooked on the novelty:** Susan Linn, "Commercialism in Children's Lives," *State of the World 2010* (Washington, DC: Worldwatch Institute, 2010), 63, http://commercialfreechildhood.org/resource/commercialism-childrens-lives.

**Page 48 Research shows that simpler, open-ended playthings:** "The Commercialization of Toys & Play," *Campaign for a Commercial-Free Childhood*, n.d., http://commercialfreechildhood.org/sites/default/files/toysandplay.pdf.

**Page 48 In 2009 alone, $5.4 billion:** Georg Szalai, "Toys Based on Sequels Take Center Stage," *Adweek*, February 11, 2010, http://www.adweek.com/news/advertising-branding/toys-based-sequels-take-center-stage-107036.

**Page 52 Retailers are well aware of this brain science:** Cheryl Lu-Lien Tan, "The Neuroscience of Retailing: Research Shows Shopping Can Make People Euphoric," *The Wall Street Journal*, May 15, 2008, http://online.wsj.com/article/SB121081365150393885.html.

**Page 52 extending easy credit:** Gregory Karp, "Cash vs. Credit Mindset," *Chicago Tribune*, December 15, 2011, http://articles.chicagotribune.com/2011-12-15/news/sc-cons-1215-karp-spend-20111210_1_credit-cards-card-balances-debit-cards.

**Page 52 cloaking items in "halo":** Schor, *Born to Buy*, 59.

**Page 52 The problem is that once we buy:** Schwartz, *The Paradox of Choice*, 172.

**Page 52 Though commercialism:** Linn, "Commercialism in Children's Lives," 63–64.

**Page 52 Today's children see more than 25,000 advertisements:** Debra J. Holt et al., *Children's Exposure to TV Advertising in 1977 and 2004* (Washington, DC: Federal Trade Commission, June 1, 2007), ES-5, http://www.ftc.gov/os/2007/06/cabecolor.pdf.

**Page 53 Kids are uniquely vulnerable to marketing:** "Marketing to Kids: Toy Sellers' Bonanza or Parental Danger Zone?" Knowledge@Wharton, http://knowledge.warton.upenn.edu/article.cfm?articleid=3127, accessed December 5, 2012.

**Page 53 By the age of two:** Schor, *Born to Buy*, 19.

**Page 53 Today's generation of children is the most brand-conscious:** Kenneth Hein, "Teen Talk Is, Like, Totally Branded," *BrandWeek*, August 6, 2007, http://www.kellerfay.com/news-events/teen-talk-is-like-totally-branded/.

**Page 53 teenagers talk about brands an average of 145 times per week:** Monica Corcoran, "These Days, Some Teens Covet Expensive Brand Names in Purses, Accessories," *Los Angeles Times*, September 25, 2007, http://www.commercialexploitation.org/news/teenluxury.htm.

**Page 53 In order to capture:** Susan Linn, *Consuming Kids: The Hostile Takeover of Childhood* (New York: New Press, 2004), 110–113 and 188–190.

**Page 53 "pester power":** Schor, *Born to Buy*, 61–63.

**Page 53 a major UNICEF report was released:** UNICEF, "Child Poverty in Perspective: An Overview of Child Well-being in Rich Countries," *Innocenti Report Card 7* (Florence, Italy: UNICEF Innocenti Research Centre, 2007).

## Chapter 3. Global Food Rules: How Parents Around the World Teach Their Kids to Eat

**Page 57 Nearly 40 percent of the calories:** Jill Reedy and Susan M. Krebs-Smith, "Dietary Sources of Energy, Solid Fats, and Added Sugars Among Children and Adolescents in the United States," *Journal of the American Dietetic Association* 110, no. 10 (October 2010), 1477–1484, http://www.journals.elsevierhealth.com/periodicals/yjada/article/S0002-8223(10)01189-2/abstract.

**Page 57 People in our nation eat more packaged food:** Hannah Fairfield, "Factory Food," *The New York Times,* April 3, 2010, http://www.nytimes.com/2010/04/04/business/04metrics.html.

**Page 57 Processed foods are full:** Sarah Kobylewski and Michael F. Jacobson, *Food Dyes: A Rainbow of Risks* (Washington, DC: Center for Science in the Public Interest, 2010), vi.

**Page 57 A study of nearly four thousand children:** Kate Northstone, "Are Dietary Patterns in Childhood Associated with IQ at 8 Years of Age? A Population-based Cohort Study," *Journal of Epidemiology and Community Health*, February 7, 2011, http://jech.bmj.com/content/early/2011/01/21/jech.2010.111955?q=w_jech_ahead_tab.

**Page 58 Supermarkets often put this kid-friendly food:** Leah Zerbe, "Five Ways Grocery Stores Try to Trick You," Rodale, http://www.rodale.com/supermarkets-and-healthy-food.

**Page 58 In the past thirty years, portion sizes:** Nancy Gottesman, "Generation XL: The Rise of Childhood Obesity," *Parenting*, n.d., http://www.parenting.com/article/fat-kids.

**Page 58 Our kids get used to eating more:** Barbara J. Rolls, Dianne Engell, and Leeann L. Birch, "Serving Portion Size Influences 5-Year-Old but Not 3-Year-Old Children's Food Intakes," *Journal of the American Dietetic Association* 100, no. 2 (February 2000), 232–234.

**Page 58 American children today eat almost two hundred:** Carmen Piernas and Barry M. Popkin, "Food Portion Patterns and Trends Among U.S. Children and the Relationship to Total Eating Occasion Size, 1977–2006," *The Journal of Nutrition*, April 27, 2011, http://jn.nutrition.org/content/early/2011/04/27/jn.111.138727.abstract.

**Page 58 Though the processed and unhealthy foods:** Jennifer Van Hook and Claire E. Altman, "Competitive Food Sales in Schools and Childhood Obesity: A Longitudinal Study," *Sociology of Education* 85, no. 1 (January 2012), 23–29, http://www.asanet.org/images/journals/docs/pdf/soe/Jan12SOEFeature.pdf.

**Page 58 Their diets get even worse as they get older:** Andrea Carlson et al., "Report Card on the Diet Quality of Children Ages 2 to 9," *Nutrition Insights*, September 2001, Center for Nutrition Policy and Promotion, U.S. Department of Agriculture, http://www.cnpp.usda.gov/Publications/NutritionInsights/Insight25.pdf.

**Page 58 Our children are the first in centuries:** Pam Belluck, "Children's Life Expectancy Being Cut Short by Obesity," *The New York Times*, March 17, 2005, http://www.nytimes.com/2005/03/17/health/17obese.html.

**Page 59 By offering many options:** Amy Paugh and Carolina Izquierdo, "Why Is This a Battle Every Night?: Negotiating Food and Eating in American Dinnertime Interaction," *Journal of Linguistic Anthropology* 19, no. 2 (December 2009), 185–204.

**Page 60 "These interactions point to an uneasiness":** Ibid., 200.

**Page 60 Any conscientious parent who opens a newspaper:** Harvey Levenstein, *Fear of Food: A History of Why We Worry About What We Eat* (Chicago: The University of Chicago Press, 2012).

**Page 62 Japan has the lowest obesity rate in the world:** Organisation for Economic Co-operation and Development (OECD), *OECD Obesity Update 2012* (Paris: OECD Publishing, 2012), 1, http://www.oecd.org/els/healthpoliciesanddata/49716427.pdf.

**Page 66 In the United States, it's typical:** Nanci Hellmich, "Cutting Short Lunch Time in School May Lead to Obesity," *USA Today*, August 17, 2011, http://www.usatoday.com/news/health/wellness/story/2011/08/Students-feel-rushed-at-school-lunch/50027612/1.

**Page 70 As I watched them enjoy themselves:** Benesse Educational Research and Development Center, "Basic Research on Academic Performance: International Survey of Six Cities,"

*Child Research Net*, n.d., http://www.childresearch.net/RESOURCE/DATA/SPECIAL/SIXCITIES/FIGURE1.html.

**Page 70 But overall, they have fewer hours:** Jim Hull and Mandy Newport, "Time in School: How Does the U.S. Compare?" The Center for Public Education, December 2011, http://www.centerforpubliceducation.org/Main-Menu/Organizing-a-school/Time-in-school-How-does-the-US-compare.

**Page 70 A 2012 study of fifth-grade children:** Y. L. Chu et al., "Involvement in Home Meal Preparation Is Associated with Food Preference and Self-Efficacy among Canadian Children," *Public Health Nutrition* (published online May 2012), 1–5.

**Page 71 Then they run outside to play:** Alice Gordenker, "Making Lunch a Learning Experience," *The Japan Times*, June 1, 2001, http://www.japantimes.co.jp/text/fl20010601ag.html.

**Page 73 Meals are slow, and shorter work hours:** "Work-Life Balance," Organisation for Economic Co-operation and Development, n.d., http://www.oecdbetterlifeindex.org/topics/work-life-balance/.

**Page 73 Swedes are healthy:** "Sweden," Organisation for Economic Co-operation and Development, n.d., http://www.oecdbetterlifeindex.org/countries/sweden/.

**Page 75 South Koreans tie with Japanese:** OECD, *OECD Obesity Update 2012*, 1.

**Page 77 TV snack ads appear with a banner:** Karen Le Billon, *French Kids Eat Everything* (New York: HarperCollins, 2012), 136.

**Page 78 The French workday accommodates leisurely meals:** Ibid., 93.

**Page 78 American parents are urged to space vegetables:** "Solid Foods: How to Get Your Baby Started," Infant and Toddler Health, Mayo Clinic, June 17, 2011, http://www.mayoclinic.com/health/healthy-baby/PR00029.

**Page 78 Some mothers:** Dina Mia, "Early Vegetable Variety: The French Advantage," *It's Not About Nutrition* (blog), January 31, 2012, http://itsnotaboutnutrition.squarespace.com/home/2012/1/31/early-vegetable-variety-the-french-advantage.html; A. Maier et al., "Food-related Sensory Experience from Birth Through Weaning: Contrasted Patterns in Two Nearby European Regions," *Appetite* 49, no. 2 (September 2007), 429–440, http://www.ncbi.nlm.nih.gov/pubmed/17434647.

**Page 78 This approach helps:** Le Billon, *French Kids Eat Everything*, 93–94.

**Page 79 rates of mortality from heart disease:** "Mortality from Heart Disease and Stroke: Figure 1.3.1. Ischemic Heart Disease, Mortality Rates, 2009 (or Nearest Year)," OECD iLibrary, http://www.oecd-ilibrary.org/sites/health_glance-2011-en/01/03/index.html;jsessionid=1icu970depqup.delta?contentType=&itemId=/content/chapter/health_glance-2011-6-en&containerItemId=/content/serial/19991312&accessItemIds=/content/book/health_glance-2011-en&mimeType=text/html.

**Page 79 greater longevity:** "Country Statistical Profile: France 2011–2012," OECD iLibrary, http://www.oecd-ilibrary.org/economics/country-statistical-profile-france_20752288-table-fra.

**Page 79 much lower obesity rates:** Ibid.

**Page 79 than do people in the United States:** "Country Statistical Profile: United States 2011–2012," OECD iLibrary, http://www.oecd-ilibrary.org/economics/country-statistical-profile-united-states_20752288-table-usa.

**Page 79 When gourmet school lunches:** Le Billon, *French Kids*, 47.

**Page 79 Freshly prepared three-course hot lunches:** Karen Le Billon, "French School Lunch Menus," *Karen Le Billon* (blog), n.d., http://karenlebillon.com/french-school-lunch-menus/.

**Page 79 Children get one and a half to two hours:** Ibid., 36, 93.

**Page 79 A typical menu for preschoolers:** Karen Le Billon, "Yummy French School Lunches . . . What Preschoolers Are Eating This Week in Versailles!" *Karen Le Billon* (blog), January 10, 2012, http://karenlebillon.com/2012/01/10/yummy-frenchkids-lunches-what-pre-schoolers-are-eating-this-week-in-versailles/.

**Page 80 Mealtime is a particularly important moment:** Ibid.

Page 82 **In Korea, a child at school would be served:** *What's for School Lunch?* (blog), http:// whatsforschoollunch.blogspot.com/.

Page 84 **The key component seems to be:** Suzanne Rauzon et al., "An Evaluation of the School Lunch Initiative," The Robert C. and Veronica Atkins Center for Weight and Health, University of California at Berkeley, September 2010, http://edibleschoolyard.org/sites/default/files /file/An_Evaluation_of_the_School_Lunch_Initiative_Final%20Report_9_22_10.pdf.

Page 84 **Feeling in control is important:** Brian Wansink, David R. Just, and Joe McKendry, "Lunch Line Redesign," *The New York Times*, October 21, 2010, http://ben.dyson.cornell.edu /pdfs/LunchLineREdesignGraphicRedesign.pdf.

## Chapter 4. Feeling Good: Can Self-Esteem Be Harmful?

Page 90 **In one poll, 85 percent of American parents:** Claudia M. Mueller and Carol S. Dweck, "Praise for Intelligence Can Undermine Children's Motivation and Performance," *Journal of Personality and Social Psychology* 75, no. 1 (July 1998), 33–52. Also see Carol S. Dweck, "The Secret to Raising Smart Kids," *Scientific American Mind* 18, no. 6 (December 2007/January 2008), 36–43.

Page 90 **The average American person:** Roy F. Baumeister et al., "Does High Self-Esteem Cause Better Performance, Interpersonal Success, Happiness, or Healthier Lifestyles?," *Psychological Science in the Public Interest* 4, no. 1 (May 2003), 4, http://persweb.wabash.edu/facstaff /hortonr/articles%20for%20class/Baumeister%20public%20interest%20self-esteem.pdf.

Page 90 **Resilience is so crucial:** David Brooks, "The Psych Approach," *The New York Times*, September 27, 2012, http://www.nytimes.com/2012/09/28/opinion/brooks-the-psych-approach .html.

Page 90 **But it is not something our kids are born with:** Kenneth R. Ginsburg and Susan FitzGerald, *Letting Go with Love and Confidence: Raising Responsible, Resilient, Self-Sufficient Teens in the 21st Century* (New York: Avery, 2011), 9.

Page 92 **Self-esteem was first mentioned in 1890:** William James, *The Principles of Psychology: Volume 1* (New York: Henry Holt, 1890), 310.

Page 92 **But it wasn't until decades later:** Morris Mianberg, *Society and the Adolescent Self-Image* (Princeton, NJ: Princeton University Press, 1965).

Page 93 **"We simply take it for granted":** Jean M. Twenge, PhD, *Generation Me: Why Today's Young Americans Are More Confident, Assertive, Entitled—and More Miserable Than Ever Before* (New York: Free Press, 2006), 49.

Page 93 **But the earliest proponents:** Stanley Coopersmith, *The Antecedents of Self-Esteem* (San Francisco: W. H. Freeman, 1967), 236.

Page 93 **People with high self-esteem don't always make good leaders:** Mark Greer, "Charisma Doesn't Guarantee Leadership Success," *Monitor on Psychology* 36, no. 1 (January 2005), 29, http://www.apa.org/monitor/jan05/charisma.aspx.

Page 93 **"People with unstable high self-esteem":** Baumeister et al., "Does High Self-Esteem Cause Better Performance, Interpersonal Success, Happiness, or Healthier Lifestyles?" 6, 27.

Page 93 **Addicted to feeling good:** M. Menon et al., "The Developmental Costs of High Self-Esteem for Antisocial Children," *Child Development* 78, no. 6 (November–December 2007), 1627–1639, http://www.ncbi.nlm.nih.gov/pubmed/17988311.

Page 93 **One scholar even pointed out:** Nicholas Emler (author, *Self-Esteem: The Costs and Causes of Low Self-Worth*), quoted in Lauren Slater, "The Trouble with Self-Esteem," *The New York Times Magazine*, February 3, 2002, http://www.nytimes.com/2002/02/03/magazine/the -trouble-with-self-esteem.html.

Page 93 **"After all these years":** Roy F. Baumeister, "The Lowdown on High Self-Esteem," *Los Angeles Times*, January 25, 2005, http://articles.latimes.com/2005/jan/25/opinion/oe -baumeister25.

Page 94 **Self-maximization (reaching one's potential):** Peggy J. Miller et al., "Self-Esteem as Folk

Theory: A Comparison of European American and Taiwanese Mothers' Beliefs," *Parenting: Science and Practice* 2, no. 3 (July–September 2002), 209–239.

**Page 97 In the United States, it is controversial:** Jessica Lahey, "Black and White and Red All Over," *The Core Knowledge Blog*, August 13, 2012, http://blog.coreknowledge.org/2012/08/13 /black-and-white-and-red-all-over/.

**Page 97 What we do know is this:** H. W. Stevenson and S. Y. Lee, "Contexts of Achievement: A Study of American, Chinese, and Japanese Children," *Monographs of the Society for Research in Child Development* 55, no. 1–2 (1990), 1–123, http://www.ncbi.nlm.nih.gov/pubmed/2342493.

**Page 97 Seventy percent of American freshmen:** John H. Pryor et al., "The American Freshman: National Norms Fall 2009," Higher Education Research Institute, UCLA, 2009, https://heri .ucla.edu/PDFs/pubs/TFS/Norms/Monographs/TheAmericanFreshman2009-Expanded .pdf.

**Page 97 In fact the ten countries in which students:** Tom Loveless, "How Well Are American Students Learning?" *The 2006 Brown Center Report on American Education* 2, no. 1 (2006), 14–18, http://www.brookings.edu/~/media/Files/rc/reports/2006/10education_loveless/10edu cation_loveless.pdf.

**Page 98 Overall, American students feel:** See Harold W. Stevenson and James W. Stigler, *The Learning Gap: Why Our Schools Are Failing and What We Can Learn from Japanese and Chinese Education* (New York: Touchstone, 1992), especially chapter 4, "Socialization and Achievement," and chapter 5, "Effort and Ability."

**Page 98 But "happiness is not everything":** Loveless, "How Well Are American Students Learning?" 14.

**Page 98 High self-esteem in sixth grade:** Baumeister et al., "Does High Self-Esteem Cause Better Performance, Interpersonal Success, Happiness, or Healthier Lifestyles?" 12; E. M. Skaalvik and K. A. Hagtvet, "Academic Achievement and Self-Concept: An Analysis of Causal Predominance in a Developmental Perspective," *Journal of Personality and Social Psychology* 58 (1990), 292–307.

**Page 98 Without the incentive, students might have:** Baumeister et al., "Does High Self-Esteem Cause Better Performance, Interpersonal Success, Happiness, or Healthier Lifestyles?" 13; D. R. Forsyth and N. A. Kerr, "Are Adaptive Illusions Adaptive?" (Poster presented at the annual meeting of the American Psychological Association, Boston, Massachusetts, August 1999).

**Page 98 Another truth is that successful:** Loveless, "How Well Are American Students Learning?" 17–18. According to the report: "National measures of self-confidence, enjoyment of the subject, and relevance of lessons are inversely correlated with student achievement. The evidence presented here does not mean that we should undermine students' confidence, teach math in a way sure to induce revulsion to the subject, or present math in such an abstract manner that it bears no relevance to daily life. The evidence does suggest, however, that the American infatuation with the happiness factor in education may be misplaced. The international evidence makes at least a prima facie case that self-confidence, liking the subject, and relevance are not essential for mastering mathematics at high levels."

**Page 99 "America has seen thirty years":** Martin E. P. Seligman. PhD, *The Optimistic Child: A Proven Program to Safeguard Children Against Depression and Build Lifelong Resilence* (New York: Houghton Mifflin, 2007), 36.

**Page 99 Rates of depression:** Polly Young-Eisendrath, PhD, *The Self-Esteem Trap: Raising Confident and Compassionate Kids in an Age of Self-Importance* (New York: Little, Brown, 2008); P. J. Wickramaratne et al., "Age, Period, and Cohort Effects on the Risk of Major Depression: Results from Five United States Communities," *Journal of Clinical Epidemiology* 42, no. 4 (1989), 333–343; Robert D. Putnam, *Bowling Alone: The Collapse and Revival of the American Community* (New York: Simon & Schuster, 2000), 261.

**Page 99 young people struggle in college or their first jobs:** Martha Irvine, "Age of 'Entitlement' Changes Rules: Generation of Workers Demand More from Workplace," *Grand Rapids Press*, July 3, 2005, section H.

**Page 99 and empathy among young people:** Sara H.Konrath, Edward H. O'Brien, and Courtney Hsing, "Changes in Dispositional Empathy in American College Students Over Time: A Meta-analysis," *Personality and Social Psychology Review* 15, no. 2 (2011), 180–198, http://dx .doi.org/10.1177/1088868310377395.

**Page 99 narcissism has risen:** Twenge, *Generation Me,* 69.

**Page 99 People who have been told to put themselves and their needs first:** Young-Eisendrath, *The Self-Esteem Trap,* 32–33.

**Page 102 People tell me it reflects:** Steven J. Heine, "Is There a Universal Need for Positive Self-Regard?" *Psychological Review* 106, no. 4 (1999), 771, http://faculty.washington.edu/janleu /Courses/Cultural%20Psychology/547%20Readings/Heine%201999.pdf.

**Page 102 Cultural psychologists have noted:** See, for instance, Alina Tugend's interview with Stanford cultural psychologist Hazel Markus in *Better by Mistake: The Unexpected Benefits of Being Wrong* (New York: Riverhead, 2011), 70.

**Page 103 In Japan and other Asian cultures:** Alix Spiegel, "Struggle for Smarts? How Eastern and Western Cultures Tackle Learning," NPR, November 12, 2012, http://m.npr.org/news/front /164793058.

**Page 104 While American teachers tend to believe:** James W. Stigler and James Hiebert, *The Teaching Gap* (New York: Free Press, 1999), 94.

**Page 104 It would be considered wrong in Japan:** Ibid., 94.

**Page 104 not only do Japanese children report being happier:** Organisation for Economic Co-operation and Development (OECD), *Lessons from PISA for the United States: Strong Performers and Successful Reformers in Education* (Paris: OECD Publishing, 2011), 147, http://www .oecd.org/pisa/46623978.pdf.

**Page 105 Japanese kids tended to hold:** Kristi L. Lockhart et al., "From Ugly Duckling to Swan? Japanese and American Beliefs about the Stability and Origins of Traits," *Cognitive Development* 23, no. 1 (January 2008), 155–179.

**Page 105 As a society we are attracted:** Carol S. Dweck, PhD, *Mindset: The New Psychology of Success* (New York: Ballantine, 2008), 41.

**Page 106 It's not surprising that American:** Alina Tugend, *Better by Mistake: The Unexpected Benefits of Being Wrong* (New York: Riverhead, 2011), 54.

**Page 106 In one study:** Angela L. Duckworth et al., "Grit: Perseverance and Passion for Long-Term Goals," *Journal of Personality and Social Psychology* 92, no. 6 (2007), 1087–1101, http:// www.sas.upenn.edu/~duckwort/images/Grit%20JPSP.pdf.

**Page 106 In school, students aren't separated according to ability:** OECD, *Lessons from PISA,* 137, 139, 146.

**Page 106 There is no "gifted" education:** Ibid., 142.

**Page 107 Contrary to the stereotype most of us probably hold:** Ibid., 147.

**Page 107 Accomplishment came from hard work:** Benjamin S. Bloom, *Developing Talent in Young People* (New York: Ballantine, 1985).

**Page 107 A body of recent research confirms:** Daniel Coyle, *The Talent Code: Greatness Isn't Born. It's Grown. Here's How* (New York: Bantam, 2009).

**Page 108 in a Japanese national survey:** Heine, "Is There a Universal Need for Positive Self-Regard?" 771–772.

**Page 111 But since our culture tends to downplay effort:** Dweck, *Mindset,* 41.

**Page 111 In one of Dweck's most well-known studies:** Mueller and Dweck, "Praise for Intelligence Can Undermine Children's Motivation and Performance," 33–52.

**Page 112 They didn't look at their effortful performance:** Dweck, *Mindset,* 72–73.

## Chapter 5. Hoverparenting: How Can We Foster Self-Control?

**Page 117 Research confirms that caring, involved parents:** Michigan Department of Education, "What Research Says About Parent Involvement in Children's Education in Relation to Academic Achievement," March 2002, http://www.michigan.gov/documents/Final_Parent_Involvement_Fact_Sheet_14732_7.pdf.

**Page 117 have fewer emotional problems:** Michael D. Resnick et al., "Protecting Adolescents from Harm: Findings from the National Longitudinal Study on Adolescent Health," *Journal of the American Medical Association* 278, no. 10 (1997), 823–832.

**Page 117 less prone to teen alcohol use:** Siobhan M. Ryan et al., "Parenting Strategies for Reducing Adolescent Alcohol Use: A Delphi Consensus Study," *BMC Public Health* 11, no. 13 (2011), http://www.biomedcentral.com/1471-2458/11/13/; and "Parents: Prevention Means Being Involved," *Substance Abuse and Mental Health Services Administration* 17, vol. 4 (July/August 2009), http://www.samhsa.gov/samhsanewsletter/Volume_17_Number_4/ParentInvolvement.aspx.

**Page 117 Their self-esteem is higher:** Michigan Department of Education, n.p.

**Page 118 Our over-involvement can also make it harder:** Alvin Rosenfeld, MD, and Nicole Wise, "Did You Know? The Overscheduled Child: Avoid the Hyper-Parenting Trap," Mandala Children's House Family Services Program, October 2005, http://www.mandalachildrens-house.com/DYK/Did_You_Know_Overscheduled_Child_.pdf; Madeline Levine, PhD, "What Price, Privilege? Has Our Overinvolved Parenting Style Created a Generation of Kids with an Impaired Sense of Self? If So, How Can We Work to Get It Back?" *San Francisco Chronicle*, June 25, 2006, http://www.sfgate.com/health/article/What-Price-Privilege-Has-our-overinvolved-2532643.php. Also, Madeline Levine, *The Price of Privilege: How Parental Pressure and Material Advantage Are Creating a Generation of Disconnected and Unhappy Kids* (New York: HarperCollins, 2006).

**Page 118 After all, experts tell us that babies need:** Lisa Baumwell, Catherine S. Tamis-LeMonda, and Marc H. Bornstein, "Maternal Verbal Sensitivity and Child Language Comprehension," *Infant Behavior and Development* 20, no. 2 (1997), 247–258, https://steinhardt.nyu.edu/scmsAdmin/uploads/006/931/Baumwell,%20L.,%20Bornstein,%20M.%20H.,%20%26%20Tamis-LeMonda,%20C.,%20Infant%20Behavior%20and%20Development,%201997.pdf.

**Page 118 What most American parents don't realize:** Pamela Paul, "Getting Sharp: Want a Brainier Baby?" *Time Magazine*, January 8, 2006, http://www.time.com/time/magazine/article/0,9171,1147180,00.html; and Kathleen Kiely Gouley, PhD, "Stimulation and Development During Infancy: Tuning in to Your Baby's Cues," NYU Child Study Center, n.d., http://www.aboutourkids.org/articles/stimulation_development_during_infancy_tuning_in_your_baby039s_cues.

**Page 121 homicide by gun is virtually unheard of:** Max Fisher, "A Land Without Guns: How Japan Has Virtually Eliminated Shooting Deaths," *The Atlantic*, July 23, 2012, http://www.theatlantic.com/international/archive/2012/07/a-land-without-guns-how-japan-has-virtually-eliminated-shooting-deaths/260189/.

**Page 122 Peak also quotes:** Lois Peak, *Learning to Go to School in Japan: The Transition from Home to Preschool Life* (Berkeley: University of California Press, 1991), 159–161.

**Page 123 Some researchers attribute:** Takashi Naito and Uwe P. Gielen, "The Changing Japanese Family: A Psychological Portrait," in *Families in Global Perspective*, ed. Jaipaul L. Roopnarine (Boston: Pearson, 2005), 63–84, quoted in David F. Lancy, *The Anthropology of Childhood: Cherubs, Chattel, Challenges* (New York: Cambridge University Press, 2008).

**Page 124 Another belief is that babies are born pure:** David W. Shwalb, Barbara J. Shwalb, and Junichi Shoji, "Japanese Mothers' Ideas about Infants and Temperament," in *Parents' Cultural Belief Systems: Their Origins, Expressions, and Consequences*, eds. Sara Harkness and Charles M. Super (New York: Guilford Press, 1996), 169–191.

**Page 124 A mischievous child was nothing:** Zahava Osterweil and Keiko Nagano-Nakamura, "Maternal Views on Aggression: Japan and Israel," *Aggressive Behavior* 18, no. 4 (1992), 263–270.

**Page 124 He found that when the children were asked:** George G. Bear, Maureen A. Manning, and Kunio Shiomi, "Children's Reasoning About Aggression: Differences between Japan and

NOTES · *287*

the United States and Implications for School Discipline," *School Psychology Review* 35, no. 1 (2006), 62–77.

**Page 125 In another study:** George G. Bear et al., "Shame, Guilt, Blaming, and Anger: Differences between Children in Japan and the US," *Motivation and Emotion* 33, no. 3 (2009), 229–238.

**Page 125 Research shows how people blame others:** Tugend, 84–85, discussing Nathanael J. Fast and Larissa Z. Tiedens, "Blame Contagion: The Automatic Transmission of Self-Serving Attributions," *Journal of Experimental Social Psychology* 46 (2010), 97–106.

**Page 125 Bear's studies are part of a body:** Bear et al., "Children's Reasoning," 66.

**Page 125 Japanese discipline is characterized by what one American author:** Catherine C. Lewis, *Educating Hearts and Minds: Reflections on Japanese Preschool and Elementary Education* (Cambridge, UK: Cambridge University Press, 1995), 125.

**Page 125 It is common in Japanese elementary schools:** Ibid., 125.

**Page 126 Although we sometimes feel driven to perfect:** Greg J. Duncan et al., "School Readiness and Later Achievement," *Developmental Psychology* 43, no. 6 (2007): 1428–1446, http://www.policyforchildren.org/pdf/School_Readiness_Study.pdf; summarized in Po Bronson, "In Defense of Children Behaving Badly," *Newsweek*, October 22, 2009, http://www.newsweek.com/blogs/nurture-shock/2009/10/22/in-defense-of-children-behaving-badly.html.

**Page 128 Experiencing and resolving conflicts:** Anthony D. Pellegrini and Catherine M. Bohn, "The Role of Recess in Children's Cognitive Performance and School Adjustment," *Educational Researcher* 34, no. 1 (January/February 2005), 13–9, http://evolution.binghamton.edu/evos/wp-content/uploads/2008/11/Pellegrini02.pdf.

**Page 128 It turns out even gun play has a purpose:** Tim Gill, *No Fear: Growing Up in a Risk Averse Society* (London: Calouste Gulbenkian Foundation, 2007), 42. Gill is discussing Penny Holland's work: see Penny Holland, *We Don't Play With Guns Here: War, Weapon, and Superhero Play in the Early Years* (Philadelphia: Open University Press, 2003). From Gill: "Holland argues that for younger children play fighting, gun play, and rough-and-tumble play are neither atavistic displays of animal aggression nor mindless re-enactments of yesterday's TV. Rather, they are outward signs of a sophisticated and largely unconscious learning process. According to psychologists, these forms of play allow children to perfect some important social skills in a context where real harm is not part of the game. . . . Researchers have known for years that most children quickly become skilled at reading the body language of play fighting—unlike adults" (42).

**Page 128 By allowing kids to practice:** Pellegrini and Bohn, "The Role of Recess," 14.

**Page 129 Research tells us that our personality:** See, for instance, Carol Dweck, "Can Personality Be Changed? The Role of Beliefs in Personality and Change," *Current Directions in Psychological Science* 17, no. 6 (December 2008), 391–394.

**Page 133 Kids get used to and learn how to manage:** See, for instance, Ellen Beate Sandseter, "Categorising Risky Play—How Can We Identify Risk-Taking in Children's Play?" *European Early Childhood Education Research Journal* 15, no. 2 (June 2007), 237–252.

**Page 133 Researchers worry more about:** Shirley Wyver et al., "Safe Outdoor Play for Young Children: Paradoxes and Consequences" (presentation, Australian Association for Research in Education International Education Research Conference, Melbourne, 2010), http://www.aare.edu.au/10pap/2071WyverBundyNaughtonTranterSandseterRagen.pdf.

**Page 133 There is growing evidence:** See Gill, *No Fear*, 29. Certain types of injuries have actually increased, like broken bones. Also see John Tierney, "Can a Playground Be Too Safe?" *The New York Times*, July 18, 2011, http://www.nytimes.com/2011/07/19/science/19tierney.html.

**Page 133 The greatest risk factor:** Ellen Beate Hansen Sandseter and Leif Edward Ottesen Kennair, "Children's Risky Play from an Evolutionary Perspective: The Anti-Phobic Effects of Thrilling Experiences," *Evolutionary Psychology* 9, no. 2 (2011), 259, http://www.epjournal.net/wp-content/uploads/EP092572842.pdf.

**Page 133 Another danger is that they will become complacent and unaware:** Gill, *No Fear*, 35, quoting Helle Nebelong, a designer of playgrounds in Copenhagen. She mentions that when a child is climbing on a standardized ladder, he doesn't have to pay attention to where he puts his feet, but this lack of awareness isn't a good thing. "Standardisation is dangerous because play becomes simplified and the child does not have to worry about his movements." Helle Nebelong, "Designs on Play," Free Play Network, n.d., http://www.freeplaynetwork.org.uk /design/nebelong.htm.

**Page 134 Norwegians believe in what one parenting expert:** See Wendy Mogel, *The Blessing of a Skinned Knee: Using Jewish Teachings to Raise Self-Reliant Children* (New York: Scribner, 2001).

**Page 134 What we don't realize:** Gill, *No Fear*, 16.

**Page 136 Gilda Morelli of Boston College:** G. A. Morelli and H. Verhoef, "Please Don't Interrupt Me, I'm Talking": Cultural Variation in Toddler's Attention-Seeking Efforts and Caregivers' Responses." (In preparation.)

## Chapter 6. Quality Time: The Value of Unstructured Play

**Page 143 Between 1981 (when I was thirteen):** William J. Doherty, PhD, "Overscheduled Kids, Underconnected Families: The Research Evidence," *Putting Family First*, n.d., http://www .puttingfamilyfirst.org/research.php.

**Page 143 One survey found that 79 percent:** Ann Duffett, Jean Johnson, and Steve Farkas, "All Work and No Play: Listening to What Kids and Parents Really Want from Out-of-School Time," Public Agenda, 2004, 9, http://www.publicagenda.org/files/pdf/all_work_no_play.pdf.

**Page 143 Today, the average American child:** "Health Benefits," National Wildlife Federation, n.d., http://www.nwf.org/Get-Outside/Be-Out-There/Why-Be-Out-There/Benefits.aspx.

**Page 144 A 2009 Kaiser Family Foundation study:** "Generation M: Media in the Lives of 8- to 18-Year-Olds," Henry J. Kaiser Family Foundation, January 2010, 2, http://www.kff.org /entmedia/upload/8010.pdf.

**Page 144 Pretend play is an especially crucial way:** Alison Gopnik, "Let the Children Play, It's Good for Them!" *Smithsonian Magazine* (July–August 2012), http://www.smithsonianmag .com/science-nature/Let-the-Children-Play-Its-Good-for-Them.html.

**Page 144 The more that kids play:** Susan Linn, *The Case for Make Believe: Saving Play in a Commercialized World* (New York: The New Press, 2008), 23.

**Page 144 Obesity has tripled:** "Adolescent and School Health: Childhood Obesity Facts," Centers for Disease Control and Prevention, last updated June 7, 2012, http://www.cdc.gov/healthy youth/obesity/facts.htm.

**Page 144 antidepressant use in American children is on the rise:** T. Delate et al., "Trends in the Use of Antidepressants in a National Sample of Commercially Insured Pediatric Patients, 1998 to 2002," *Psychiatric Services* 55, no. 4 (April 2004), 387–391, http://www.ncbi.nlm.nih .gov/pubmed/15067149.

**Page 144 the United States consumes 80 percent of the world's supply of Ritalin:** The U.S. consumed 80 percent of the world's supply of methylphenidate by 2005. Richard L. Myers, *The 100 Most Important Chemical Compounds: A Reference Guide* (Westport, CT: Greenwood Press, 2007), 179.

**Page 144 There is a growing vitamin D deficiency:** "Alarm Bells over Vitamin D Levels in Kids," CBSNews, August 3, 2009, http://www.cbsnews.com/2100-500165_162-5206429 .html.

**Page 144 poor distance vision:** Neville A. McBrien et al., "What's Hot in Myopia Research—The 12th International Myopia Conference, Australia, July 2008," *Optometry and Vision Science* 86, no. 1 (January 2009), 2–3, http://journals.lww.com/optvissci/Fulltext/2009/01000/What _s_Hot_in_Myopia_Research_The_12th.2.aspx.

**Page 144 hyperactivity than ever before:** Frances E. Kuo, PhD, and Andrea Faber Taylor, PhD, "A Potential Natural Treatment for Attention-Deficit/Hyperactivity Disorder: Evidence from a National Study," *American Journal of Public Health* 94, no. 9 (September 2004), 1580–1586, http://www.ncbi.nlm.nih.gov/pmc/articles/PMC1448497/.

**Page 144 The less children play, the more:** Gabrielle F. Principe, *Your Brain on Childhood: The Unexpected Side Effects of Classrooms, Ballparks, Family Rooms, and the Minivan* (Amherst, NY: Prometheus Books, 2011), 182.

**Page 145 As children repeat scenarios:** Laura E. Berk et al., "Make-Believe Play: Wellspring for Development of Self-Regulation," in *Play=Learning: How Play Motivates and Enhances Children's Cognitive and Social-Emotional Growth*, ed. Dorothy G. Singer et al. (New York: Oxford University Press, 2006), 79.

**Page 145 Kids love language-rich:** Ibid., 74–100.

**Page 146 The role of adults during:** Ibid., 110.

**Page 146 Besides, the study had been about:** Nikhil Swaminathan, "Fact or Fiction?: Babies Exposed to Classical Music End Up Smarter," *Scientific American*, September 13, 2007, http://www.scientificamerican.com/article.cfm?id=fact-or-fiction-babies-ex; Lori Cuthbert, "What's the Mozart Effect?" Curiosity.com, n.d., http://curiosity.discovery.com/question/what-is-the-mozart-effect.

**Page 146 kindergarten teachers are often constrained:** Edward Miller and Joan Almon, "Crisis in the Kindergarten: Why Children Need to Play in School," Alliance for Childhood, March 2009, 3, http://www.allianceforchildhood.org/sites/allianceforchildhood.org/files/file/kindergarten_report.pdf.

**Page 147 Invested parents are tempted:** Alina Tugend, "Family Happiness and the Overbooked Child," *The New York Times*, August 12, 2011, http://www.nytimes.com/2011/08/13/your-money/childrens-activities-no-guarantee-of-later-success.html.

**Page 147 Researchers found:** Principe, *Your Brain on Childhood*, 58. Principe is discussing the following study: NICHD Early Child Care Research Network, "The NICHD Study of Early Child Care: Contexts of Development and Developmental Outcomes over the First Seven Years of Life," in *Early Child Development in the 21st Century*, ed. Jeanne Brooks-Gunn, Allison Sidle Fuligni, and Lisa J. Berlin (New York: Teachers College Press, 2003), 181–201.

**Page 147 One well-known study:** Principe, *Your Brain on Childhood*, 58. Principe is discussing the following study: Frederick J. Zimmerman, Dimitri A. Christakis, and Andrew N. Meltzoff, "Associations Between Media Viewing and Language Development in Children Under Age Two Years," *Journal of Pediatrics* 151 (October 2007), 364–368.

**Page 147 Numerous studies have demonstrated:** See Principe, *Your Brain on Childhood*, 125–128 ("Kindercramming").

**Page 147 One cross-cultural study:** P. H. Seymour et al., "Foundation Literacy Acquisition in European Orthographies," *British Journal of Psychology* 94 (Part 2) (May 2003), 143–174.

**Page 147 This may be because the complex areas of the brain:** Principe, *Your Brain on Childhood*, 122.

**Page 148 "It's clear from our look at the brain's evolutionary history":** Ibid., 46.

**Page 152 He calls it the "flexibility hypothesis":** Ibid., 180. Principe discusses Mark Bekoff's work.

**Page 152 Similarly, the endless number of ways:** Ibid.

**Page 153 One study has shown that how well children play games:** Anthony D. Pellegrini and Robyn M. Holmes, "The Role of Recess in Primary School," in *Play=Learning*, ed. Dorothy G. Singer et al., 36–54.

**Page 153 Researchers believe that games:** David F. Lancy and M. Annette Grove, "Marbles and Machiavelli: The Role of Game Play in Children's Social Development," *American Journal of Play* 3, no. 4 (Spring 2011), 489–499, http://www.journalofplay.org/sites/www.journalofplay.org/files/pdf-articles/3-4-article-lancy-grove-marbles-and-machiavelli.pdf.

**Page 154 and it's not one all cultures share such an interest:** Sara Harkness et al., "Parental Ethnotheories of Children's Learning," in *The Anthropology of Learning in Childhood*, ed. David F Lancy, John C Bock, and Suzanne Gaskins (Walnut Creek, CA: AltaMira Press, 2010), 65–81.

**Page 156 In 1999 it was given in thirty-eight countries:** John J. Ratey, *Spark: The Revolutionary*

*Science of Exercise and the Brain* (New York: Little, Brown, 2008), 14; "Naperville's New P.E. Fitness Model Sparks Academic Success," Sparking Life, n.d., http://sparkinglife.org/page /naperville-central-high-school.

**Page 156 Researchers from Harvard:** Virginia R. Chomitz, PhD, "Is There a Relationship Between Physical Fitness and Academic Achievement? Positive Results from Public School Children in the Northeastern United States," *Journal of School Health* 79, no. 1 (January 2009), 30–37.

**Page 156 Active, playful breaks during the day:** Pellegrini and Holmes, "The Role of Recess in Primary School," 37–38.

**Page 156 Children who alternate:** Ibid., 43–44.

**Page 157 And a study published in *Pediatrics*:** Romina M. Barros et al., "School Recess and Group Classroom Behavior," *Pediatrics* 123, no. 2 (February 1, 2009), 431–436, http://pediatrics .aappublications.org/content/123/2/431.abstract.

**Page 157 They also help children avoid cognitive interference:** Pellegrini and Holmes, "The Role of Recess in Primary School," 38.

**Page 157 A recent Centers for Disease Control and Prevention:** Centers for Disease Control and Prevention, *The Association Between School-Based Physical Activity, Including Physical Education, and Academic Performance* (Atlanta: U.S. Department of Health and Human Services, 2010).

**Page 157 A 2013 policy statement by the American Academy of Pediatrics:** Robert Murray and Catherine Ramstetter, "The Crucial Role of Recess in School," *Pediatrics* 131, no. 1 (January 1, 2013), 183–188, http://pediatrics.aappublications.org/content/131/1/183.full.

**Page 157 Scandinavian nations:** *Creativity and Prosperity: The Global Creativity Index* (Toronto, ON: Martin Prosperity Index, January 2011), http://martinprosperity.org/media/GCI%20 Report%20Sep%202011.pdf.

**Page 157 Americans have been showing a decline:** Po Bronson and Ashley Merryman, "The Creativity Crisis," *Newsweek*, July 10, 2010, http://www.newsweek.com/2010/07/10/the -creativity-crisis.html.

**Page 158 Thirty percent of American children studied:** Barros et al., "School Recess and Group Classroom Behavior," 431–436.

**Page 158 Recess is often taken away as punishment:** Tara Parker-Pope, "The 3 R's? A Fourth Is Crucial, Too: Recess," *The New York Times*, February 23, 2009, http://www.nytimes .com/2009/02/24/health/24well.html.

**Page 158 Free play during recess is cognitively:** Barros et al., "School Recess and Group Classroom Behavior," 431–436.

**Page 158 Studies show that peers:** Kimiko Ryokai and Justine Cassell, "Computer Support for Children's Collaborative Fantasy Play and Storytelling." MIT Media Lab, January 1, 1997, http://pubs.media.mit.edu/pubs/papers/CSCL99.pdf.

**Page 160 As we drew closer:** "Educational Aspects in the United States and Germany," University of Michigan, n.d., http://sitemaker.umich.edu/schubert.356/kindergarten.

**Page 161 They were also less irritable:** "A History of Forest Schools," Forest Schools, n.d., http:// www.forestschools.com/history-of-forest-schools.php.

**Page 162 As a result, the German government:** Miller and Almon, "Crisis in the Kindergarten," 2.

## Chapter 7. High Pressure? What Asian Learning Looks Like

**Page 167 Including weekends, university-bound:** Chery Li, "Profile: A Recent Chinese High School Graduate from the City of Gaobeidian," *The Hopewell Journal*, July 23, 2012, http:// hopewelljournal.com/2012/07/profile-a-recent-chinese-high-school-graduate-from-the-city -of-gaobeidian/.

**Page 170 In one study, Chinese mothers regarded:** Ruth K. Chao, "Chinese and European American Mothers' Beliefs about the Role of Parenting in Children's School Successes," *Journal of Cross-Cultural Psychology* 27, no. 4 (July 1996), 403–423; Cecilia Sin-Sze Cheung and Eva M. Pomerantz, "Parents' Involvement in Children's Learning in the United States and China: Implications for Children's Academic and Emotional Adjustment," *Child Development* 82, no. 3 (May 2011), 932–950.

**Page 171 The cultural differences between China and the United States:** The terms "authoritarian," "authoritative," and "permissive" were conceptualized by Diana Baumrind in the 1960s. D. Baumrind, "Effects of Authoritative Parental Control on Child Behavior," *Child Development* 37, no. 4 (1966), 887–907.

**Page 171 Ruth Chao, a psychology professor at UC Riverside:** Ruth K. Chao, "Beyond Parental Control and Authoritarian Parenting Style: Understanding Chinese Parenting Through the Cultural Notion of Training," *Child Development* 65 (1994), 1111–1119, http://www.mfas.ucr .edu/publications/ChildDevelopment1994.pdf.

**Page 171 *Chiao shun* (training) and *guan* (love, govern, or care for):** Ibid., 1112.

**Page 172 In China, authoritarian parenting springs:** Ibid., 1113.

**Page 172 Taking care of and responding to your child:** Ruth K. Chao, "The Parenting of Immigrant Chinese and European American Mothers: Relations Between Parenting Styles, Socialization Goals, and Parental Practices," *Journal of Applied Developmental Psychology* 21, no. 2 (2000), 233–248, http://mfas.ucr.edu/publications/AppliedDevelopmentalPsychology2000 .pdf.

**Page 173 One of them even asked the researcher:** Sheena Iyengar, *The Art of Choosing* (New York: Twelve, 2010), 47–49.

**Page 173 They saw themselves as separate from their mothers:** Ibid.

**Page 174 In Chinese schools the smart kids:** Nicholas Kristof, "China's Winning Schools," *The New York Times*, January 15, 2011, http://www.nytimes.com/2011/01/16/opinion/16kristof .html.

**Page 176 The children who did better engaged:** Angela Lee Duckworth et al., "Deliberate Practice Spells Success: Why Grittier Competitors Triumph at the National Spelling Bee," *Social Psychological and Personality Science* 2 (2011), 174.

**Page 178 Yin, a former Beijing public schoolteacher:** Victoria Ruan, "Chinese Parenting Advice Undergoes a Small Revolution," *The Juggle* (blog), *The Wall Street Journal*, August 16, 2010, http://blogs.wsj.com/juggle/2010/08/16/chinese-parenting-advice-undergoes-a-small -revolution/.

**Page 178 Amy Chua's memoir hit a nerve:** Megan Gibson, "So What Does China Think of 'Tiger Mother' Amy Chua?" *Time NewsFeed*, January 27, 2011, http://newsfeed.time.com/2011/01/27 /so-what-does-china-think-of-tiger-mother-amy-chua/.

**Page 179 The Confucian mindset favoring:** Jin Li, "A Cultural Model of Learning: Chinese 'Heart and Mind for Wanting to Learn,'" *Journal of Cross-Cultural Psychology* 33, no. 3 (May 2002), 248–269. Li describes the "ideal learner" in China as being one who pursues learning for moral reasons as well as academic ones. The ideal learner holds personal beliefs about knowledge and learning that emphasize "moral purpose, that is, their need to perfect themselves." This is a Confucian idea—that individuals embark on a lifelong search for knowledge and self-improvement. The idea of constant self-improvement and cultivation, and the idea that learning is the ultimate pathway to this, permeate all cultural notions about education. Li also mentions that learning, rather than achievement, is emphasized, as opposed to in America, where achievement may be more likely to be much more central. Yet this orientation to "lifelong learning" instead of achievement may be part of what lies behind their high levels of achievement, due to the emphasis on constant effort.

**Page 179 In some ways this is a collective endeavor shared:** Large-scale reforms outlined in a government document in 2001 called for emphasizing attitudes and values over knowledge and skills, and moving away from rote learning toward the kind of experience-based learning that allows kids to construct their own knowledge. See Marc S. Tucker, *Surpassing Shanghai: An Agenda for American Education Built on the World's Leading Systems* (Cambridge: Harvard Education Press, 2011).

**Page 180 Korea has one of the highest:** "Education," Organisation for Economic Co-operation and Development, n.d., http://www.oecdbetterlifeindex.org/topics/education/; Organisation for Economic Co-operation and Development (OECD), *Education at a Glance 2011: OECD Indicators* (Paris: OECD Publishing, 2011), 14–15, http://www.oecd.org/edu/highereduca tionandadultlearning/48631582.pdf; Linda Darling-Hammond, *The Flat World and Education: How America's Commitment to Equity Will Determine Our Future* (New York: Teachers College Press, 2010), http://www.oecd.org/education/highereducationandadultlearning /48631582.pdf.

**Page 180 The South Korean government invests heavily in educating its children:** Fred Hiatt, "In South Korea, Too Many College Grads, Too Few Jobs," *The Washington Post*, October 24, 2011, http://www.washingtonpost.com/opinions/in-south-korea-too-many-college-grads -too-few-jobs/2011/10/21/gIQANu7eAM_story.html.

**Page 181 Many South Korean parents believe that a college education:** Ibid.

**Page 181 On the day of the nine-hour test:** Sungha Park, "On College-Entrance Exam Day, All of South Korea Is Put to the Test," *The Wall Street Journal*, November 12, 2008, http://online .wsj.com/article/SB122644964013219173.html.

**Page 181 Suicides from bullying are on the rise:** Paula Hancocks, "South Korea Teenagers Bullied to Death," CNN, July 26, 2012, http://edition.cnn.com/2012/07/25/world/asia/south -korea-school-bully/index.html.

**Page 181 The government has instituted:** Amanda Ripley, "Teacher, Leave Those Kids Alone," *Time*, September 25, 2011, http://www.time.com/time/magazine/article/0,9171,2094427,00 .html.

**Page 181 South Korea now has a glut:** Hiatt, "In South Korea, Too Many College Grads, Too Few Jobs."

**Page 181 Yet within South Korea itself:** Byong-man Ahn, "Education in the Republic of Korea: National Treasure or National Headache?" *Education Week*, January 12, 2012.

**Page 182 The birth rate in South Korea has dropped:** "Field Listing: Total Fertility Rate," Central Intelligence Agency, *The World Factbook*, n.d., https://www.cia.gov/library/publications /the-world-factbook/fields/2127.html.

**Page 182 One small but revealing finding:** Harkness, "Parental Ethnotheories," 73.

**Page 183 These days, around 18,000:** Alan Scher Zagier, "In South Korea, U.S. Education Means Split Families," Boston.com, April 1, 2012, http://www.boston.com/news/nation/articles /2012/04/01/in_south_korea_us_education_means_split_families/.

**Page 186 Parents may often go along with this:** Eva M. Pomerantz et al., "Changes in Early Adolescents' Sense of Responsibility to Their Parents in the United States and China: Implications for Their Academic Functioning," *Child Development* 82, no. 4 (July 2011), 1136–1151.

**Page 187 Research shows that feeling responsible:** Ibid.

**Page 187 Children in both countries:** Eva M. Pomerantz and Qian Wang, "The Role of Parental Control in Children's Development in Western and East Asian Countries," *Current Directions in Psychological Science* 18, no. 5 (October 2009), 285–289.

**Page 188 It may give them a feeling of purpose:** Cecilia Sin-Sze Cheung and Eva M. Pomerantz, "Why Does Parents' Involvement Enhance Children's Achievement? The Role of Parent-Oriented Motivation," *Journal of Educational Psychology* 104, no. 3 (August 2012), 820–832.

**Page 188 Our teens care about their parents':** "Adolescent Substance Use: America's #1 Public Health Problem," National Center on Addiction and Substance Abuse at Columbia University, June 2011, http://www.casacolumbia.org/upload/2011/20110629adolescentsubstanceuse .pdf, 8–9, 66-67.

**Page 190 For the vast majority of Chinese students at this point:** Yong Zhao, "Doublethink: The Creativity-Testing Conflict," *Education Week*, July 17, 2012, http://www.edweek.org/ew

/articles/2012/07/18/36zhao_ep.h31.html. Yong Zhao of the University of Oregon took a close look at the numbers while researching his book, *World Class Learners*, and discovered that the nations whose kids did so well on the PISA (the Program for International Student Assessment) did notably poorly on another test, the Global Entrepreneurship Monitor, or GEM, which assesses the entrepreneurial activities, aspirations, and attitudes of individuals in given nations. Zhao found that the nations (Japan, South Korea, Taiwan, and Singapore) who got among the best scores on the PISA had the lowest scores in their confidence in their ability to start a new business.

## Chapter 8. Every Child Counts: High Achieving, the Finnish Way

**Page 194 Children don't start academics:** Ellen Gamerman, "What Makes Finnish Kids So Smart?" *The Wall Street Journal*, February 29, 2008, http://online.wsj.com/article/SB12042535 5065601997.html.

**Page 194 Finnish children spend nearly three hundred fewer hours:** Jim Hull and Mandy Newport, "Time in School: How Does the U.S. Compare?" The Center for Public Education, December 2011, http://www.centerforpubliceducation.org/Main-Menu/Organizing-a-school /Time-in-school-How-does-the-US-compare.

**Page 194 While American children:** "PISA 2012 Participants," Organisation for Economic Co-operation and Development, 2012, http://www.oecd.org/pisa/participatingcountrieseconomies /pisa2012participants.htm.

**Page 195 In Finland, teachers teach between six hundred and seven hundred hours:** Organisation for Economic Co-operation and Development (OECD), *Education at a Glance 2011: OECD indicators* (Paris: OECD Publishing, 2011), 14–15, http://www.oecd.org/edu/higher educationandadultlearning/48631582.pdf, 425.

**Page 195 less time teaching:** Pasi Sahlberg, *Finnish Lessons: What Can the World Learn from Educational Change in Finland?* (New York: Teachers College Press, 2011), 64.

**Page 195 Today, over 99 percent of Finnish students:** Linda Darling-Hammond, "Steady Work: How Finland Is Building a Strong Teaching and Learning System," *Voices in Urban Education* 24 (Summer 2009), http://www.annenberginstitute.org/VUE/Summer09/Darling.php.

**Page 195 more than 90 percent graduate from upper secondary:** OECD, *Education at a Glance 2011*, 44.

**Page 195 Finland has steadily closed:** For instance, in 2006 there was only a 4.7 percent score difference between schools on the PISA science scale, while for the other nations, the difference averaged 33 percent. "How Does Student Performance Vary between and within Schools?" in Organisation for Economic Co-operation and Development (OECD), *Highlights from Education at a Glance 2008* (Paris: OECD Publishing, 2009), 90–91, http://dx.doi .org/10.1787/eag_highlights-2008-38-en.

**Page 196 A recent study shows that only 7 percent:** Ibid., 64.

**Page 196 Vocational education is not stigmatized:** Samuel E. Abrams, "The Children Must Play: What the United States Could Learn from Finland about Education Reform," *The New Republic*, January 28, 2011, http://www.tnr.com/article/politics/82329/education-reform -Finland-US.

**Page 196 Less pressure about getting:** Gamerman, "What Makes Finnish Kids So Smart?" *The Wall Street Journal*, February 29, 2008, http://online.wsj.com/article/SB120425355 065601997.html.

**Page 197 Starting in the 1970s:** Jenny Anderson, "From Finland, an Intriguing School-Reform Model," *The New York Times*, December 12, 2011, http://www.nytimes.com/2011/12/13/ education/from-finland-an-intriguing-school-reform-model.html.

**Page 197 To become a primary school teacher:** Sahlberg, *Finnish Lessons*, 73.

**Page 197 Finland stands out from other nations:** Ibid., 76.

**Page 197 They have more freedom:** Ibid., 71.

**Page 197 In Finland there is no concept:** Ibid., 92.

**Page 197 Instead, the Finnish government allocates the equivalent:** Ibid., 87.

**Page 198 In the United States, student or rookie teachers:** Kim Marshall, "It's Time to Rethink Teacher Supervision and Evaluation," *Phi Delta Kappan* 86, no. 10 (June 2005), 727–735, http://myboe.org/cognoti/content/file/resources/documents/80/807dc8a9/807dc8a925188551 db0ce0a6eb1c05f5f322fcf7/TeachersupervisionarticleKimMarshall.pdf.

**Page 200 While countries such as Finland:** Linda Darling-Hammond (professor of education, Stanford), in an interview with Dan Rather, "Finnish First," *Dan Rather Reports: Part Two*, video, 9 minutes 55 seconds, 2012, http://www.youtube.com/watch?v=RtYszdSU1Yg.

**Page 200 Its popularity peaked:** Torie Bosch, "Bring Back Home Ec!" *Slate*, June 5, 2012, http://www.slate.com/articles/health_and_science/future_tense/2012/06/home_ec_or_family _and_consumer_sciences_should_be_mandatory_for_students_.html.

**Page 201 All students have the right:** Sahlberg, *Finnish Lessons*, 60.

**Page 201 During lower secondary school:** Ibid., 26; Pasi Sahlberg, "Raising the Bar: How Finland Responds to the Twin Challenge of Secondary Education?" *Profesorado* 10, no. 1 (2006), http://www.pasisahlberg.com/downloads/Raising%20the%20Bar%202006.pdf.

**Page 201 In Finland, "school readiness":** Valerie Strauss, "A New Finnish Lesson: Why Gender Equality Matters in School Reform," *The Answer Sheet* (blog), September 6, 2012, http://www.washingtonpost.com/blogs/answer-sheet/post/a-new-finnish-lesson-why-gender -equality-matters-in-school-reform/2012/09/05/3703ad4c-f778-11e1-8253-3f495ae70650_ blog.html. From the article: "Another difference is that the primary purpose of early childhood education in Finland is not to enhance children's readiness for school. It is to support families in raising healthy and happy children. School readiness in Finland means that the school is ready to take children as they are and to be ready to serve different children as they are."

**Page 202 In Finland, children average seventy-five minutes:** Abrams, "The Children Must Play," n.p.

**Page 204 We should be able to apply:** Darling-Hammond, "Finnish First," n.p.

**Page 204 Pasi Sahlberg, director general:** Ibid., 69.

**Page 205 In the United States, 23.1 percent of children live in poverty:** UNICEF, *Innocenti Research Centre Report Card 10: Measuring Child Poverty: New League Tables of Child Poverty in the World's Rich Countries* (Florence, Italy: UNICEF Innocenti Research Centre, 2012), 2, http://www.unicef-irc.org/publications/pdf/rc10_eng.pdf.

**Page 205 "Education . . . is a process of living":** John Dewey, "My Pedagogic Creed," *School Journal* 54 (January 1897), 77–80, http://dewey.pragmatism.org/creed.htm.

## Chapter 9. Raising Kindness: Cultural Notions About Raising Kids Who Care

**Page 213 In 1970, the primary goal stated by most college freshmen:** Jim Holt, "You Are What You Expect," *The New York Times*, January 21, 2007, http://www.nytimes.com/2007/01/21 /magazine/21wwln_lede.t.html.

**Page 213 Empathy has declined over the past thirty years:** Jamil Zaki, "What, Me Care? Young Are Less Empathetic," *Scientific American*, January 19, 2011, http://www.scientificamerican .com/article.cfm?id=what-me-care.

**Page 213 more Americans than ever believe we have a "major civility problem":** Pam Jenkins, "Civility in America," Powell Tate, June 28, 2010, http://www.powelltate.com/insights /civility_in_america/.

**Page 213 Two-thirds of the students:** Richard Weissbourd, *The Parents We Mean to Be: How Well-intentioned Adults Undermine Children's Moral and Emotional Development* (Boston: Houghton Mifflin Harcourt, 2009). Also see Lisa Belkin, "Teaching Children to Do Good," *Motherlode: Adventures in Parenting* (blog), April 11, 2011, http://parenting.blogs.nytimes .com/2011/04/11/teaching-children-to-do-good/.

**Page 217 evidence that people who are compassionate to others experience lasting happiness:** See Sonja Lyubomirsky, *The How of Happiness: A New Approach to Getting the Life You Want* (New York: Penguin, 2008), particularly Chapter 5: "Investing in Social Connections." See also Emma M. Seppala, "The Best Kept Secret to Happiness," *Psychology Today*, November 5, 2012, http://www.psychologytoday.com/blog/feeling-it/201211/the-best-kept-secret-happiness.

**Page 217 UC Berkeley psychologist Alison Gopnik tells us:** Alison Gopnik, *The Philosophical Baby: What Children's Minds Tell Us about Truth, Love, and the Meaning of Life* (New York: Farrar, Straus & Giroux, 2009), 207–208.

**Page 218 Infants are born with:** Ibid.

**Page 218 The babies stared longer at the scene:** Stephanie Sloane, Renée Baillargeon, and David Premack, "Do Infants Have a Sense of Fairness?" *Psychological Science* 23, no. 2 (2012), 196, DOI: 10.1177/0956797611422072.

**Page 219 Even toddlers apparently feel a "warm glow":** Lara B. Aknin et al., "Giving Leads to Happiness in Young Children," *PLOS One* 7, no. 6 (June 14, 2012): e39211, http://www.plosone.org/article/info:doi/10.1371/journal.pone.0039211.

**Page 219 Other research has shown that rewards:** Felix Warneken and Michael Tomasello, "Extrinsic Rewards Undermine Altruistic Tendencies in 20-Month-Olds," *Developmental Psychology* 44, no. 6 (2008), 1785–1788, http://email.eva.mpg.de/~tomas/pdf/Warneken_Tomasello_DevPsy_2008.pdf. See also Richard A. Fabes et al., "Effects of Rewards on Children's Prosocial Motivation: A Socialization Study," *Developmental Psychology* 25, no. 4 (July 1989), 509–515.

**Page 221 there is a folk belief that:** Matthew Burdelski, "Socializing Politeness Routines: Action, Other-orientation, and Embodiment in a Japanese Preschool," *Journal of Pragmatics* 42, no. 6 (June 2010), 1606–1621.

**Page 223 One industry analysis showed:** Stephane Fitch, "Dillinger's Nightmare," Forbes.com, November 20, 2009, http://www.forbes.com/global/2009/1130/ideas-bank-robbery-crime-how-to-reduce-robberies.html. Based on an idea disseminated by FBI agent Lawrence Carr, the concept is that greetings deter potential robbers because they stamp out psychological "trigger points."

**Page 223 While American mothers often orient their babies:** See, for instance, E. Olcay Imamoglu and Selen Imamoglu, "Attachment Within a Cultural Perspective: Relationships With Exploration and Self-Orientations," in *Attachment: Expanding the Cultural Connections*, ed. Phyllis Erdman and Kok-Mun Ng (New York: Routledge, 2010), 46; and Marc H. Bornstein, Kazuo Miyake, and Catherine S. Tamis-LeMonda, "A Cross-National Study of Mother and Infant Activities and Interactions: Some Preliminary Comparisons between Japan and the United States," *Research and Clinical Center for Child Development* 9 (March 1987), 1–12.

**Page 223 This general difference continues:** Catherine S. Tamis-LeMonda et al., "Language and Play at One Year: A Comparison of Toddlers and Mothers in the United States and Japan," *International Journal of Behavioral Development* 15 (March 1992), 19–42.

**Page 223 Other research shows that while young American children:** Patricia M. Clancy, "The Acquisition of Communicative Style in Japanese," *Anthropology and Child Development: A Cross-Cultural Reader*, ed. Robert A. LeVine and Rebecca S. New (Oxford: Wiley-Blackwell, 2008), 165–181.

**Page 226 The more rituals and formulas are practiced:** Sennett, *Together: The Rituals, Pleasures and Politics of Co-operation* (New Haven, CT: Yale University Press, 2012), 91.

**Page 227 In France, interruptions in conversation:** Leo Hickey and Miranda Stewart, eds., *Politeness in Europe* (Tonawanda, NY: Multilingual Matters, 2005), 6.

**Page 229 Research shows that kids are motivated:** Paul D. Hastings et al., "The Socialization of Prosocial Development," in *Handbook of Socialization: Theory and Research*, ed. Joan E. Grusec and Paul D. Hastings (New York: Guilford Publications, 2007), 643.

**Page 230 Researchers tell us that three-month-olds:** Paul Bloom, "The Moral Life of Babies,"

*The New York Times Magazine*, May 5, 2010, http://www.nytimes.com/2010/05/09/magazine /09babies-t.html.

## Chapter 10. Raising Responsibility: Avoiding the Helplessness Trap

**Page 235 historians tell us that American children's chores:** Peter N. Stearns, *Anxious Parents: A History of Modern Childrearing in America* (New York: New York University Press, 2003), 125–162.

**Page 235 The amount of time spent on chores has declined 25 percent since 1981:** Sue Shellenbarger, "On the Virtues of Making Your Children Do the Dishes," *The Wall Street Journal*, August 27, 2008. http://online.wsj.com/article/SB121978677837474177.html.

**Page 235 This change is due mostly:** Viviana A. Zelizer, *Pricing the Priceless Child: The Changing Social Value of Children* (Princeton, NJ: Princeton University Press, 1994), 96.

**Page 235 Child-rearing experts continued to vigorously debate:** Stearns, *Anxious Parents*, 125–162.

**Page 235 In fact, there are practically no cultures where children don't help out:** David F. Lancy, *The Anthropology of Childhood: Cherubs, Chattel, Changelings* (New York: Cambridge University Press, 2008), 234.

**Page 236 Though we aren't used to thinking of kids:** Elinor Ochs and Carolina Izquierdo, "Responsibility in Childhood: Three Developmental Trajectories," *Ethos* 37, no. 4 (March 2009), 402.

**Page 236 begins by fifteen months:** M. Tomasello et al., "Understanding and Sharing Intentions: The Origins of Cultural Cognition," *Behavioral and Brain Sciences* 28, no. 5 (October 2005), 675–691.

**Page 236 their desire to start willingly pitching in:** Harriet L. Rheingold, "Little Children's Participation in the Work of Adults, a Nascent Prosocial Behavior," *Child Development* 53, no. 1 (February 1982), 114–125.

**Page 236 In many cultures parents begin to hone:** Thomas S. Weisner, "The 5 to 7 Transition as an Ecocultural Project," in *The Five to Seven Year Shift: The Age of Reason and Responsibility*, ed. Arnold J. Sameroff and Marshall M. Haith (Chicago: University of Chicago Press, 1996), 296, http://www.tweisner.com/yahoo_site_admin/assets/docs/Weisner_19962_The_5_to_7 _transition_project_F21.212162516.pdf.

**Page 236 Some cultures actually define intelligence:** Harkness, "Parental Ethnotheories," 67.

**Page 236 and adults cultivate this form of intelligence:** Thomas S. Weisner, "Cultural and Universal Aspects of Social Support for Children: Evidence from the Abaluyia of Kenya," in *Children's Social Networks and Social Supports*, ed. Deborah Belle (New York: Wiley, 1989), 70–90, http://www.tweisner.com/yahoo_site_admin/assets/docs/Weisner_19891_Social_support _for_Abaluyian_Kenyan_children_F14.231164743.pdf.

**Page 236 Carolina Izquierdo, a medical anthropologist at UCLA:** Ochs and Izquierdo, "Responsibility in Childhood," 394–395.

**Page 237 While American children do some chores:** Ibid., 398–400.

**Page 237 Today, chores aren't typically a way:** Stearns, *Anxious Parents*, 158.

**Page 238 Sometimes parents backtracked:** Ochs and Izquierdo, "Responsibility in Childhood," 399.

**Page 238 Parents didn't seem to think:** Ibid., 401–402.

**Page 238 The legendary and beloved pediatrician:** Ibid., 401.

**Page 238 It can be hard to wait:** Stearns, *Anxious Parents*, 151–152.

**Page 238 Parents and adults in other cultures:** Weisner, "Cultural and Universal Aspects of Social Support for Children," 70–90.

**Page 239 Not only are we ambivalent:** Ochs and Izquierdo, "Responsibility in Childhood," 406.

**Page 239 This is respectful, but it also:** Ibid., 399.

**Page 239 Doing household chores (particularly from a young age, around three to four):** "Involving Children in Household Tasks: Is It Worth the Effort?" College of Education and Human Development, University of Minnesota, September 2002, http://www.cehd.umn.edu /research/highlights/Rossmann/.

**Page 239 In other words, when children are:** Lancy, *Anthropology of Learning*, 131. Education consultants Marilou Hyson and Jackie L. Taylor tell us that our children can learn from being with children raised in cultures that prioritize responsibility. They write, "In many cultures, including most non-Western cultures, children are often expected to do real work that helps the family, care for brothers and sisters, share even their beloved possessions with younger children, and generally be more cooperative members of the community. . . . When a class includes children who are growing up within such cultures, other children may have a chance to learn more cooperative and caring ways of relating to their peers." Marilou Hyson and Jackie L. Taylor, "Research in Review. Caring about Caring: What Adults Can Do to Promote Young Children's Prosocial Skills," *Young Children* 66, no. 4 (July 2011), 74–83, http://www .naeyc.org/files/yc/file/201107/CaringAboutCaring_Hyson_OnlineJuly2011.pdf.

**Page 241 They grow more:** Anne Solberg, "Negotiating Childhood: Changing Constructions of Age for Norwegian Children," in *Constructing and Reconstructing Childhood: Contemporary Issues in the Sociological Study of Childhood*, ed. Allison James and Alan Prout (Bristol, PA: Falmer Press, 1997), 134–137.

**Page 241 "Anne regards this equality":** Ibid., 131.

**Page 241 Research on a group of more than three thousand adults:** Shellenbarger, "On the Virtues of Making Your Children Do the Dishes."

**Page 244 Cleaning isn't considered a menial task:** Adam Voiland, "Communing Through Cleaning," *U.S. News & World Report*, March 26, 2007, http://www.usnews.com/usnews/ news/articles/070318/26pitchin.htm.

**Page 244 Influenced as Japan is by Buddhist thinking:** Yutaka Okihara, "Pupil Participation in School Cleaning: A Comparative Survey," *Comparative Education* 14, no. 1 (1978), http:// www.tandfonline.com/doi/abs/10.1080/0305006780140104.

**Page 244 Anthropologists have noticed:** Harald Beyer Broch, *Growing Up Agreeably: Bonerate Childhood Observed* (Honolulu: University of Hawaii Press, 1990), 110. "Bonerate children have little need or desire to play with dolls or to play mother, father, and child because they are integrated into many daily household chores including looking after babies and toddlers."

**Page 244 It's common for five- to ten-year-old children:** Barbara Rogoff, *The Cultural Nature of Human Development* (New York: Oxford University Press, 2003), 122–123.

**Page 245 One study of Kenyan graduate students:** Ibid.

**Page 245 in a study of working-class Mexican families:** Ibid., 124.

**Page 246 In the Guatemalan Mayan community:** Christine E. Mosier and Barbara Rogoff, "Privileged Treatment of Toddlers: Cultural Aspects of Individual Choice and Responsibility," *Developmental Psychology* 36, no. 6 (2003), 1047–1060.

**Page 246 using what researchers call "power assertive" strategies:** "Are the 'Terrible Two's' a Cultural Phenomenon?" Kansas Association of Infant & Early Childhood Mental Health, n.d., http://www.kaimh.org/are-the-terrible-twos-a-cultural-phenomenon.

**Page 247 Sibling caregiving was common:** Howard P. Chudacoff, *How Old Are You? Age Consciousness in American Culture* (Princeton, NJ: Princeton University Press, 1989), 10–15.

**Page 248 Researchers have observed that children:** Beatrice Blyth Whiting and Carolyn Pope Edwards, *Children of Different Worlds: The Formation of Social Behavior* (Cambridge, MA: Harvard University Press, 1992), 16.

**Page 251 In Japan you almost never see:** However, they did use bikes to commute longer distances with kids in a bike seat.

**Page 252 When children are in the habit of being active:** Sandra Waite-Stupainsky and Marcia Findlay, "The Fourth R: Recess and Its Link to Learning," *Educational Forum* 66, no. 1 (Fall 2001), 16–25.

**Page 254 In Sweden teens of any age:** "Swedish Child Care," *Sweden.se: The Official Gateway to Sweden*, n.d., http://www.sweden.se/eng/Home/Society/Child-care/.

**Page 254 Japanese adolescents spend more time at home:** Fred Rothbaum et al., "The Development of Close Relationships in Japan and the United States: Part of Symbiotic Harmony and Generative Tension," *Child Development* 71, no. 5 (September–October 2000), 1131–1132, http://www.wjh.harvard.edu/~jweisz/pdfs/2000b.pdf.

**Page 254 their teenagers tend to see freedom:** Ibid., 1132.

**Page 254 A different response on our part:** See, for instance, Joseph Allen and Claudia Worrell Allen, *Escaping the Endless Adolescence: How We Can Help Our Teenagers Grow Up Before They Grow Old* (New York: Ballantine, 2009).

**Page 255 In a study of more than one thousand sixteen-year-olds:** Kari Trost, "Sweden," in *Adolescent Psychology Around the World*, ed. Jeffrey Jensen Arnett (New York: Psychology Press, 2012), 338.

**Page 257 Yet I've come to understand:** Ochs and Izquierdo, "Responsibilty in Childhood," 391–413.

**Page 257 Instead of merely talking to children:** Ibid.

**Page 257 The physical acts required to become competent:** Ibid., 391–413.

**Page 258 When parents themselves were involved:** Ibid., 406.

**Page 258 Marjorie Goodwin, a linguistic anthropologist:** Marjorie Harness Goodwin, "Participation, Affect, and Trajectory in Family Directive/Response Sequences," *Text & Talk* 26, no. 4–5 (2006), 513–541.

## Conclusion: It Takes a Village

**Page 262 In Finland the government ensures:** Lauri Vuorenkoski, "Finland: Health System Review," *Health Systems in Transition* 10, no. 4 (2008), 63, http://www.euro.who.int/__data/assets/pdf_file/0007/80692/E91937.pdf.

**Page 262 Child health clinic visits are free too:** Ibid.

**Page 262 There is generous paid parental leave:** "Families: Benefits for Families with Children," Kela, updated November 9, 2012, http://kela.fi/in/internet/english.nsf/NET/081101123937EH?OpenDocument.

**Page 262 all families get generously subsidized child-care:** *Early Childhood Education and Care in Finland* (Helsinki: Ministry of Social Affairs and Health, 2004), 3–5, http://pre20090115.stm.fi/cd1106216815326/passthru.pdf.

**Page 262 child benefits to help support single parents:** "Single-Parent Family," Kela, updated August 13, 2008, http://kela.fi/in/internet/english.nsf/NET/030812101514HL?OpenDocument.

**Page 262 adoptive parents:** "Adoption and Family Benefits," Kela, updated August 10, 2012, http://kela.fi/in/internet/english.nsf/NET/170403094205MH?OpenDocument.

**Page 262 parents who must temporarily:** "If Your Child Is Sick," Kela, updated October 8, 2012, http://kela.fi/in/internet/english.nsf/NET/180708140511HS?OpenDocument.

**Page 262 Every new family receives a free baby box:** "Maternity Package," Kela, updated October 5, 2012, http://kela.fi/in/internet/english.nsf/NET/180408150632HS?OpenDocument.

**Page 263 Immigrants who practice this custom:** Ruta Nonacs, MD, PhD, *A Deeper Shade of Blue: A Woman's Guide to Recognizing and Treating Depression in Her Childbearing Years* (New York: Simon & Schuster, 2006), 167–168.

**Page 263 In Japan, mothers typically travel:** Ibid., 168.

**Page 265 one of the world's most generous parental leave policies:** Rebecca Ray et al., *Parental Leave Policies in 21 Countries: Assessing Generosity and Gender Equality* (Washington, DC: Center for Economic and Policy Research, 2008), 7, http://www.paidfamilyleave.org/pdf/ParentalLeave21Countries.pdf.

**Page 265 does not allow children's television programs:** Radio and Television Act, SFS No.

2010:696 (2010), http://www.radioochtv.se/Documents/Styrdokument/Radio%20and%20 Television%20Act.pdf.

**Page 265 This child-centered, pro-parent approach:** UNICEF, "Child Poverty in Perspective: An Overview of Child Well-Being in Rich Countries," *Innocenti Report Card* 7 (2007), 2, http://www.unicef-irc.org/publications/pdf/rc7_eng.pdf.

**Page 266 A major report on the culture of the American family:** Carl Desportes Bowman et al., *Culture of American Families: Executive Report* (Charlottesville, VA: Institute for Advanced Studies in Culture, 2012), 6, http://iasc-culture.org/survey_archives/IASC_CAF _ExecReport.pdf.

**Page 266 The report states:** Ibid.

**Page 266 "Whatever American parenting is":** Lisa Belkin, "Are 'American' Parents Really That Bad?" *Huff Post Parents: The Blog*, February 16, 2012, http://www.huffingtonpost.com/lisa -belkin/american-parenting_b_1282253.html.

**Page 268 It's telling that first-generation immigrant children:** Richard Weissbourd, *The Parents We Mean to Be: How Well-Intentioned Adults Undermine Children's Moral and Emotional Development* (Boston: Houghton Mifflin Harcourt, 2009), 179–180; and Committee on the Health and Adjustment of Immigrant Children and Families, National Research Council and Institute of Medicine, *From Generation to Generation: Health and Well-Being of Children in Immigrant Families* (Washington, DC: National Academies Press, 1998), 6–7, http://www .nap.edu/books/0309065615/html/17.html.

**Page 268 a phenomenon known as the "immigrant paradox":** Claudia Kolker, *The Immigrant Advantage: What We Can Learn from Newcomers to America About Health, Happiness, and Hope* (New York: Free Press, 2011), 4.

**Page 268 Adults who work with immigrant children:** Weissbourd, *The Parents We Mean to Be*, 179.

# Index